Exchange
System
Administration

**New
Riders**

New Riders Professional Library

Exchange
System
Administration

201 West 103rd Street,
Indianapolis, Indiana 46290

Janice Rice Howd

Exchange System Administration

Janice Rice Howd

International Standard Book Number: 0-7357-0081-8

Library of Congress Catalog Card Number: 99-60970

Printed in the United States of America

First Printing: *April, 1999*

01   00   99   4   3   2

Trademarks

Warning and Disclaimer

Publisher
David Dwyer

Executive Editor
Al Valvano

Acquisitions Editor
Amy Michaels

Development Editor
Leah Williams

Managing Editor
Sarah Kearns

Project Editor
Clint McCarty

Copy Editor
Daryl Kessler

Indexer
Cheryl Jackson
Lisa Stumpf

Technical Reviewers
Lyle Curry
William C. Wade III

Proofreader
Debra Neel

Production
Louis Porter, Jr.

Contents

About the Author

Janice Rice Howd is the president of Hawk Technical Services, Inc., a Microsoft Solution Provider located in Merritt Island, Florida. She began training users on Microsoft products in 1992 and has been a practicing MCSE and MCT since 1995. As an independent trainer specializing in Microsoft Exchange, Janice has worked for CTECs throughout the United States, Canada, and the Caribbean Islands. When she isn't training, Janice provides consulting services ranging from initial architecture planning to post-installation troubleshooting nationwide. She earned a BSEE from Florida Institute of Technology and did graduate studies at RPI while working as an Advanced Technology Project Manager for the Department of Defense, Watervliet Arsenal installation. In her spare time, Janice can be found either in the Microsoft Newsgroups as an MVP answering Exchange Server administrative questions, or playing on the carpet with her husband Chris and their new baby daughter.

About the Reviewers

Lyle Curry is a program manager at Microsoft who specializes in Exchange courseware, and wrote several of the Microsoft Official Curriculum courses on Exchange. Lyle has been working with Exchange since before its initial release. Lyle frequently speaks at the Tech Ed and Exchange conferences, and has contributed to each of the Exchange Microsoft Certified Professional Exams. He is currently working on courseware for Windows 2000 Active Directory, as well as the next release of Exchange code named "Platinum."

William C. Wade III is a senior consultant specializing in Windows 2000 and Exchange design architectures and implementations. Bill has architected numerous large Exchange organizations, spoken at the Microsoft Exchange Conference, written several articles on Exchange, and was recently one of the authors of *Implementing Exchange Server*. Bill lives with his charming wife Julie in Issaquah, Washington, and can be reached at wadeware@halcyon.com.

I'd like to dedicate this book to my husband Chris. He is my love and my life, and I couldn't have done this without him.

Acknowledgments

There are so many people without whose help I would not have been able to write this book. I'd like to thank all of my family and friends who I pretty much ignored for the last several months, and who forgive me and love me anyway. Most importantly, I'd like to thank my husband Chris, whose love, support, and understanding are very much appreciated. Also, thank you to my daughter Walker Sage, who helped me stop working and start playing each night while this book was in progress.

I'd also like to thank Bill Wade and Lyle Curry for spending so much valuable time and effort improving this book. Their contributions were indispensable. And I certainly don't want to forget Leah Williams and Al Valvano. Their confidence in me helped me through some pretty tough areas.

And finally, thanks to Bill Wade, Marywynne Leon, and Doug Hauger (authors of *Implementing Exchange Server*) for allowing me to include some of their figures illustrating backup and restore procedures for Chapter 6.

Tell Us What You Think

As the reader of this book, *you* are our most important critic and commentator. We value your opinion and want to know what we're doing right, what we could do better, what areas you'd like to see us publish in, and any other words of wisdom you're willing to pass our way.

As the executive editor for the Networking team at New Riders Publishing, I welcome your comments. You can fax, email, or write me directly to let me know what you did or didn't like about this book—as well as what we can do to make our books stronger.

Please note that I cannot help you with technical problems related to the topic of this book, and that due to the high volume of mail I receive, I might not be able to reply to every message. When you write, please be sure to include this book's title and author, as well as your name and phone or fax number. I will carefully review your comments and share them with the author and editors who worked on the book.

Fax: 317-581-4663
Email: newriders@mcp.com
Mail: Al Valvano
          Executive Editor
          New Riders Publishing
          201 West 103rd Street
          Indianapolis, IN 46290 USA

Introduction

Although there are other administration books available to help you administer your Exchange Server, this one is different in that it is just loaded with real-world experience and examples to help you apply scenarios to your own environment.

Additionally, this book is focused on administering Exchange Server versions 4.0, 5.0, and 5.5, with the most attention being given to version 5.5. If you don't have version 5.5 now, you should consider upgrading to it soon; there are a number of improvements to it that make it a worthwhile purchase. These improvements include the following:

- The Enterprise version has unlimited message storage size. The BackOffice version is still limited to 16GB per database.

- Exchange core services can run on a Microsoft Cluster.

- The MADMAN SNMP Management Information Base is now supported.

- Offline address books allow users to download only those items that have changed since the last download, resulting in much better download performance.

- A "soft delete" option can be implemented to allow clients to recover messages that have been deleted and purged from their deleted items folders.

- S/MIME and X.509 v3 certificates are supported for message encryption.

- IMAP4 protocol support has been added for message retrieval.

- LDAP v2 (and some version 3) support is now built into the Exchange X.500 directory so that directory objects can be changed using an LDAP client.

- Directories can be synchronized between Exchange and other LDAP servers.

- Exchange can refer client LDAP requests to other LDAP servers.

- Virtual organizations can be created on a single Exchange server, which is perfect for Internet Service Providers who want to host their client mailboxes on Exchange Server.

- Internet Mail Service has been improved to include support for SSL, SASL, and ETRN.

- Connectors for Lotus Notes, PROFS, and SNADS now ship with Microsoft Exchange Server Enterprise.

- Support for server-side scripting has been included to facilitate the creation of public folder applications and workflow.

- IRC Chat Service can be hosted on Microsoft Exchange.

- Outlook client for both Windows 3.x and Macintosh operating systems is now available.

- Scheduling functionality has been added to the Outlook Web Access component of Exchange.

- Exchange automatically checks for inconsistencies in the databases, looks for synchronization problems with directory updates and public folder replication, and cleans out old and expired objects from the directory and public information store.

- The backup and restore API is improved with the release of Exchange 5.5 so that more data can be backed up in an evening. Data throughput is now around 15GB per hour—limited, of course, by your hardware.

Who This Book Is For

This book was written for Exchange administrators working for companies of all types and sizes that have all manner of Exchange implementations. It is intended to help those administrators who are already maintaining an Exchange server but feel that perhaps their procedures are not quite right. It gives step-by-step guidelines on what needs to be done every day as well as what needs to be done periodically. It also gives some guidelines on identifying and solving problems that you might encounter with your Exchange server.

This book does not teach you how to deploy Exchange in your company. It does not teach you how to use NT, or prepare you for the Exchange certification exam. If you are looking for a concise guide to help you administer your Exchange server without a lot of extraneous fluff, then this is the book for you.

How This Book Is Organized

This book is organized into four parts:

- **Daily Administration.** The first part of this book walks you through the tasks that need to be performed every day in most companies. This includes information on how to get around in the Exchange Administrator Program, steps to take to administer different Exchange recipients, how to administer public folders and public folder replication (including newsgroups and system folders), things to look for in your various messaging queues, tips for managing your disk resources, procedures for backing up your Exchange server, and tasks you can perform that will help prevent problems with your Exchange server.

- **Periodic Administration.** The second part of this book helps you identify tasks that need to be done once in a while. It tells you when to do them, why to do them, and how to do them. Tasks you need to perform periodically include upgrading and optimizing your server, managing your intersite connectors and Directory Replication, generating reports, and performing various tasks intended to minimize the likelihood of problems with your Exchange server.

- **Troubleshooting and Disaster Recovery.** The third part of this book is intended to help you prepare yourself for the inevitable problems and disasters. Although Exchange tries to be self-optimizing and self-recovering, there will be times at which you need to intervene. Therefore, use Part III to create your disaster recovery plan, identify the problems and disasters you are experiencing, and subsequently repair them.

- **Appendices.** This last part of this book is actually my favorite. There are a ton of useful tidbits in here, including a maintenance schedule that summarizes the tasks covered throughout this book, a great section on the Registry with lots of useful tips for tuning your Exchange server, a section on Raw Mode that provides helpful information on getting more functionality out of your server—as well as troubleshooting problems you may be experiencing—a short update on what is changing in the next release of Exchange (code named Platinum), and a section on using the Import/Export features of Exchange, including several sample header files.

Conventions Used

In this book, certain typographical conventions have been applied. Command-line commands, directory names, filenames, GUI parameters, Registry settings, and objects are all highlighted in monospaced font; menus and buttons selected by the reader are boldfaced; and errors are signified by the use of quotes.

I

Daily Administration

1

Understanding the Exchange Administrator Console

BEFORE YOU CAN ADMINISTER EXCHANGE, you need to understand how to interpret information found in the Console, and how to best optimize the features it offers. You must know how to run the administrator executable to administer both local and remote servers and how the various command switches can help make your job easier. Once you understand these aspects of the Console, you must assign administrative permissions appropriately and utilize the different objects in the Configuration container. This chapter will help you complete these tasks so you can begin administering users.

Running the Administrator Executable

To run the Exchange Administrator program, select the **Microsoft Exchange Administrator** icon from the Microsoft Exchange folder that was created during installation. This icon is a shortcut to the application that is located, by default, at `c:\exchsrvr\bin\admin.exe`. (Obviously, if you installed to a different drive or changed the directory name, the location will change accordingly for you.) You will initially be prompted to enter the name of the Exchange Server you want to administer. Type in the computer name of the server that is running Exchange. As long as you have been granted permission to administer the Exchange site, you will be able to open the Exchange Administrator tool.

If you have just completed the installation of Exchange, you must first log on using the Windows NT account used during installation. In other words, if you were logged in as Bjamison when you installed Exchange, you must be logged in as Bjamison in order to initially administer Exchange. After you are logged in, you can easily reconfigure the permissions as you see fit. We will be discussing permissions later in this chapter.

Command Line Switches

Using the shortcut to ADMIN.EXE created at installation is the obvious way to administer Exchange. The ADMIN.EXE program also has several switches that you should become familiar with, which you can use to do various useful things, such as access the raw directory or start Server and Link Monitors from a batch file. You should note that the Administrator Console is launched when you perform any of these tasks. The following tasks can be launched using command line switches:

- Raw mode
- Help
- Server
- Start monitor
- Suspend monitor
- Import
- Export

Raw Mode

Use the command `admin.exe /r` to access the Exchange X.500 directory in raw mode. When the Administrator window pops up, it will appear to be exactly the same as a regular execution of ADMIN.EXE. However, if you check under the File menu, you will find a Raw Properties option, and under View will be a Raw Directory option. Typically, it is not a good idea to go mucking around in here. Editing the directory in raw mode is like editing the NT Registry—you must be careful or you can cause undesired results. However, this is a useful switch to know for troubleshooting or for getting a look at the inner workings of Exchange. Raw mode will be discussed in more detail in Appendix C, "Raw Mode."

Help

With the `admin.exe /h` command, you can get a description of the command line switches. You may need to remember one and not have this book handy! If you memorize just one switch you can get the list of supported switches.

Server

Use the command `admin.exe /s servername` to administer a given server immediately. For example, if the last time you used the Administrator tool you were at a remote site working on their local CHICAGO server and today you are in New York and want to administer the NYC server, type **admin.exe /s NYC** to connect to NYC directly. If you don't do this, you will have to wait either for the Admin program to establish a session with CHICAGO before you can connect to NYC, or you will have to wait for the time-out to expire.

Start Monitor

To start a Server or Link Monitor from the command line or from a batch file, use `admin.exe /m site¦monitorname¦servername`. Insert the directory name of the site in which the monitor is defined, the directory name of the monitor you want to start, and the name of the server on which you want to run the monitor (this is the server that will actually run the monitoring process, not the server to be monitored). For example, if you want to run a monitor called Link to London from the Paris server but the monitor was created in the United States site, type **admin.exe /m United States¦Link to London¦Paris**. This command is handy for starting monitors at scheduled times. You can use AT or WinAT utilities to run the batch file containing the monitor startup parameters.

Suspend Monitor

Use the command `admin.exe /t option` on any server that you will be voluntarily bringing down for maintenance in order to prevent that server from causing monitor alerts. Options that are supported include the following:

- **n** Suspends repairs
- **n** Suspends notifications
- **nr** Suspends both repairs and notifications

For example, if you know that there is a Server Monitor or Link Monitor monitoring the functionality of the CHICAGO server and you need to take the CHICAGO server off line, use `admin.exe /t nr` to prevent actions from being taken to repair the server and to prevent notifications from being generated due to the server being down. When CHICAGO is brought back up, run `admin /t` to reset the server to normal monitoring. This will prevent notifications from being generated to administrators who normally respond to service failures.

Using SRVANY.EXE to Start Your Monitors

SRVANY.EXE is a tool available in the NT Resource Kit that can be used to create an NT service that will start your monitors. You won't have a window to look at to view status, but you will receive the notifications defined in your monitor properties. See the NT Resource Kit for details.

Keep in mind that repairs and notifications won't be suspended until one polling cycle has occurred, so you should verify that each monitor receives a maintenance mode notification before you actually bring the server down for maintenance.

Import

Use the command `admin.exe /i importfile` to do directory imports from text files in which `importfile` is the name of the text file to be imported. You can also specify the name of the server into which you want to import (`/d servername`), whether or not a progress bar should be displayed during import (`/n`), and the name of an import options file defining how you want your import to run (`/o optionfilename`).

For example, if you want to import a file called `import.txt` into the CHICAGO server using specific import options defined in IMPOPT.TXT but don't want the status bar displayed, use `admin.exe /i import.txt /d CHICAGO /n /o impopt`. This is a great utility to use if you need to import data into the Exchange directory from some foreign system for directory synchronization or user property updates. For example, suppose your human resources department maintains an up-to-date database of your employee phone numbers and addresses that can be exported to a comma-separated value (*.CSV) file. You can write a program to manipulate the fields in the file to correspond with Exchange directory names and use the `import` command to automatically import any changes every night! Schedule this to run at night using either AT or WinAT. See Appendix E, "Importing and Exporting," for sample import files.

Export

Use the command `admin.exe /e exportfile` to do directory exports to text files. You can also specify the following:

- Which server you want to export data from (`/d servername`)
- Whether or not you want a progress bar to be displayed (`/n`)
- The name of an export options file that allows you to specify how the export will be performed (`/o optionfilename`)

For example, if you want to export data from the ORLANDO server to a file called ORLANDO.TXT using options defined in the file `expopt.txt` and don't want the status bar to be displayed, type **`admin.exe /e orlando.txt /d orlando /n /o expopt.txt`**. Exporting data from Exchange may be necessary if you are using Exchange data to update a different database. For example, if you have another database that supports *.CSV file imports, you could have Exchange export data to that format every night and then import to the other system. Like the other commands, this can easily be scheduled using either AT or WinAT.

Interpreting the Console

Now that you know all of those switches, let's just go back to the shortcut to launch the ADMIN.EXE program all by itself. You are probably wondering what exactly it is that you are looking at, given that the Administrator Program has so many options to configure. In this section, we will discuss the difference between an object and a container, how to tell what server you are administering and why it matters, and how to configure the administrator console to your personal preferences.

Objects Versus Containers

The first concept to understand in interpreting the Console is the difference between an object and a container. An *object* is simply an item that has properties. Objects appear only on the right side of the Administrator Program. If you see an object on both the left and right sides, it is a container. If it exists only on the right, it is an object. For example, DS Site Configuration is an object in the Configuration container (see Figure 1.1).

A *container* is essentially an object with added capabilities. Like an object, it has properties you can configure directly. Unlike standard objects, however, it also functions as a holding area for other objects.

Containers are always found on the left side of the Administrator Program. If you select one, you will see the objects it contains on the right side of the Console. Take a look at Figure 1.1 to see how containers are presented within Exchange. For example, the Configuration object is also a container.

You can correlate the difference between objects and containers nicely with the concept of folders and files and how they are displayed in Windows Explorer. Containers behave and are displayed similarly to folders, and objects behave and are displayed similarly to files.

Distinguishing Which Server Is Being Administered

It is not enough to simply understand the difference between objects and containers if you are administering Exchange. You also need to know to which server the objects and containers you are editing belong. In other words, you should always know which server you are administering at a given time. It is really easy to get mixed up because Exchange allows you to seamlessly administer any server in a site.

When the Administrator program is launched, you are either prompted to select a server to administer, or the program connects to the server it was connected to the last time you closed it[1]. Each time you open it, you should either use the /s switch to identify the specific server you want to work on, or double-check the Administrator interface to verify what server is currently selected. The Microsoft Exchange Administrator title bar explicitly states what server is currently selected, as shown in Figure 1.1.

---

1. You will be prompted for a server only if you have not selected the Set as default check box when entering a server name and you were only connected to one server the last time you closed the Administrator Program window.

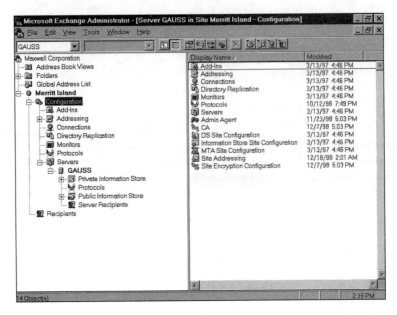

Figure 1.1   The Microsoft Exchange Administrator's Console is where you will perform most of your administrative duties.

The Administrator program also highlights the current site and server in boldface so that it is easier to discern which server is being administered. You should always know which server you are connected to because changes you make during your session are made to the databases managed by the server you are connected to, even if you select the name of a different server.

In other words, suppose you have two servers in your site: ORLANDO and TAMPA. You are currently connected to the ORLANDO server but you want to change a property on the TAMPA Private Information Store. You select TAMPA and Private Information Store and make your change. It is easy to believe that because you selected TAMPA, the change you made is effective immediately, but the truth is that you made the change to the directory on ORLANDO. ORLANDO needs to update the directory on TAMPA in order for TAMPA to be made aware of the change immediately. If you edit the wrong directory, the update will take at least five minutes. If you want to administer TAMPA, you simply need to access the Administrator program's File menu and select **Connect to server**. Either type or select **TAMPA** from the list. Now that you have connected to TAMPA, you will notice that you essentially have two Administrator windows. Be sure to select the correct one for the administrative tasks you wish to perform.

Configuring the Console to Preference

There are also lots of things you can do to make the Administrator console look and act the way you need it to. I personally really like to be able to configure the toolbar at my customer sites because it can help you do repetitive tasks more easily. Things you can configure fall into two categories: view options and tools options.

View Options

Under the View menu you can select to view just mailboxes, distribution lists, custom recipients, public folders or hidden recipients when you have a recipients container selected. You can also choose to sort by name or modification dates, or you can hide the toolbar and status bar. Almost any place that columns are defined you can rearrange them or add different data to them under the View, Columns menu option. This option is handy, for example, if you use Custom Attributes to contain employee ID numbers and want to view your user employee ID numbers in the Administrator console's Global Address List (GAL).

Tools Options

Some of the features you can customize using the Tools menu are as follows:

- Configuring the display and alias generators for your site
- Indicating whether you want a permissions page to show up on all the objects' property sheets
- Specifying whether you want to display the rights that are associated with permission roles
- Defining how text files will be created and what character set will be used in them
- Customizing your toolbar

You can find the Display name generator and Alias name generator options for new mailboxes you create under Tools, Options. You should configure the display and alias generators for your site at each Administrator Console that is used to create mailboxes because the settings are local to the machine running the Console. The display name and alias should be created based on a predetermined formula that is documented in your company's standard operating procedures so that your GAL appears uniform in format.

Creating Users on the Wrong Server

It is really easy to accidentally create users on the wrong server if you are not paying attention to which server you are administering. This can make your network traffic less than optimized if not corrected.

Using the Global Address List

I like to use the Sort by Last Modified Date when I've been off-site for a few days. It lets me see quickly what may have changed while I was away.

Use the Permissions tab under Tools, Options to indicate whether you want a permissions page to show up on all the objects' property sheets and whether you want to display the rights that are associated with permission roles, such as Permissions Administrator (I always set this property as soon as the Administrator Program is installed). You can also configure Exchange to delete the NT account when a mailbox is deleted, but I wouldn't recommend it; you can never recover that account SID without restoring from a backup.

You can use the File Format tab to define how text files will be created and what character set will be used in them. These settings can be overridden in the import/export option files or from the interface. Also under the Tools menu option, you can elect to customize your toolbar by adding buttons that do things you need to do regularly, such as moving mailboxes or doing directory exports.

Administrative Permissions and Permissions Inheritance

Along with becoming familiar with the Administrator Console comes the task of determining who else will be an administrator. One of the most important administrative decisions is who will have what levels of access and responsibility within Exchange. In this section we will look at who should be an administrator and how to configure permissions appropriately. Table 1.1 gives a list of the permissions available within the Exchange Administrator Program.

Assigning Permissions

Who should be an administrator and at what level? That is a question that warrants considerable contemplation. To answer it, you need to plan what administrative tasks will be performed by what users and then assign the most restrictive permissions that still allow the user to do the job. I find that the best approach is to create a list of what job needs to be done and correlate the job with a user or group of users. This list can then be used to assign the appropriate level of permissions.

Table 1.1 **Rights Assigned to Users with Specified Roles**

	Add Child	Modify User Attribute	Modify Admin Attribute	Delete	Logon	Modify Permission	Replication	Mailbox Owner	Send As	Search
Service Account Admin	X	X	X	X	X	X	X	X	X	
Permissions Admin	X	X	X	X	X	X				
Admin	X	X	X	X	X					
View Only Admin					X					
User		X						X	X	
Send As									X	
Search										X

There are a myriad of combinations that can be applied to administrator roles in your organization. I find that most environments with multiple sites divide their administrative responsibilities into two groups. I refer to these groups as Global Administrators and Local Administrators. Global Administrators are assigned the Permissions Admin role at each site's Configuration container in order to perform high-level configuration and troubleshooting. Local Administrators are assigned the Admin role at the local site's recipients container in order to add, modify, and remove accounts. The Local Administrators also need to have View Only at the Organization level to allow them to logon.

Keep in mind after you've assigned permissions that you must train your administrators how to use those permissions properly. This includes teaching them not only what to do and how to do it, but also what not to do. Generally, the types of things you should teach administrators *not* to do fall into two categories: destructive and invasive.

- *Destructive* things include anything that will cause your Exchange system to fail to perform adequately. This could be something minor, such as forgetting to change the service account password in the correct locations, or it could be something significant, like messing up the routing table or deleting a recipients container or server from the admin interface.

- *Invasive* things include such mistakes as regenerating routing tables or forcing directory updates during business hours when it should have been done in off hours, or invading user privacy by reading users' mail.

Adequate training of your administrative personnel will go a long way toward minimizing both destructive and invasive mistakes.

In determining who should be assigned what permissions, let's start with the least restrictive role: Permissions Admin. Typically, it is a good idea to limit the people who have Permissions Admin rights to the Configuration container to a very small, select group. These are probably the same people who will know the Exchange Service Account's password. Generally, these are Tier 3 support personnel.

Exchange Administrator Platform

Exchange Administrator still cannot run on Windows 95 or Windows 98 because of their inability to establish the same sort of trust relationship with the domain that NT clients can.

Permissions Admin Role

A user with Permissions Admin rights on the Configuration and Site containers can administer any object within the site. The user with Permissions Admin can also create and delete any object in the site. This includes changing existing permissions on objects. It is important to control who has this right so that you don't have rogue administrators giving themselves permission to open users' mailboxes. This level of privilege should be given out with extreme caution; both Permissions Admin rights and the Service Account password are basically keys to the whole store (and directory).

Container-Specific Permissions

You should also identify who will have other levels of control. For example, think about who will be creating and modifying recipients—which requires Admin on the site's recipients container—and who will modify mailbox permissions—which requires Permissions Admin on the Site's recipients container. Again, Permissions Admin rights give an administrator the ability to assign himself all levels of access. This permission at the Site level allows the administrator to give himself access to user mailboxes.

Distribution List Management Permissions

Another level of administration can be assigned to Distribution List (DL) management to allow an existing DL to be managed from the client. This is done by assigning ownership to a user on the DL's General tab. In addition to the DL owner, anyone with Admin rights on the DL or on the DL's recipients container will be able to change distribution list membership from the client.

Configuring Permissions

In order to view or change the permissions on most objects, you will need to configure the Permissions tab under Tools, Options to **Show Permissions page for all objects**. You may also want to go ahead and select **Display rights for roles on Permissions page**. I personally always configure this as soon as I have the Administrator Program installed. I find it useful for troubleshooting and to quickly view access rights and roles.

Permissions assigned at the Organization level apply only to the Organization container. There is no inheritance by child objects from this level. Permissions assigned at the Site level apply only to the Site container and the site's recipients containers. They do not propagate down through the configuration objects. Only permissions assigned at the site's Configuration container are passed down to the actual configuration objects. This gives you considerable control over who will be able to do certain tasks.

For example, an administrator who needs to be able to add and modify mailboxes does not need permissions on the Configuration container. Additionally, you can assign permissions within the Configuration container objects individually if that is the structure of your IS department.

Administering Remote Servers

One of the types of administrators we discussed in the last section was the Global Administrator. If your responsibilities fall in this category, it is likely you will need to administer Exchange from a remote location. As in the rest of NT administration, it is generally recommended that you do your administration from a client workstation rather than from the actual server. In this section we will look at communication requirements between the workstation you want to administer from and the server you want to administer, and how to set yourself up to do remote administration.

The Limits of Admin Rights

Although you can create and modify recipients if you have Admin rights on the recipient, you cannot configure Send on Behalf of permissions or Alternate Recipient permissions. To configure these properties, you must have explicit or inherited Permissions Admin rights on the individual recipient object.

Management Roles Versus Required Permissions

I have been to companies where the administrative functionality is broken out such that within a single site there are many levels of control. Some of these levels broke out as follows:

- **User Management.** Admin rights on their own site's recipients containers.

- **Connector Management.** View-Only rights on the Organization, Site, and Configuration containers. Admin rights on the Connectors container.

- **Public Folder Management.** View-Only rights on the Organization, Site, and Configuration containers. Admin rights on public folders and on the Public Information Store.

- **Global Management.** Permissions Admin on the Organization, Site, and Configuration containers.

Obviously, the levels you should identify in your model should reflect your IS department's responsibilities. Although this type of administration distribution exists, it is rare. I don't prefer this model because it becomes difficult to find the correct administrator to perform a task.

Communication Requirements

Exchange Server communicates using Remote Procedure Calls (RPCs). This means that although a client workstation is generating a request for information on the server, the actual procedure is carried out on the remote server. Both the Exchange Administrator console and the Outlook/Exchange clients use RPCs to communicate with the Exchange Server. As a result, your network and clients must support RPCs.

Remote Administration Options

The Exchange Administrator program can be run from any NT Workstation that can establish an RPC session with the Exchange Server (including dial-up connections). Due to the centralized, single-seat administration feature of Exchange, it is a simple matter to select **File, Connect to server** to administer another server in your site, in another site, or in a different organization. You simply must have permission to administer the server you are attempting to access.

To install the Exchange Administrator program on the workstation that you want to work from, simply run the Exchange setup utility, choose **Complete/Custom**, and select *only* the Exchange Administrator option. This will prevent a new Exchange server from being installed, but all of the necessary admin files will be copied to the local workstation.

Contents of the Site Configuration Container

As an Exchange administrator, you need to become familiar with everything that can be configured within Exchange. We discussed earlier in this chapter what objects and containers *are*. Now we are going to talk about what each object and container *does*. All of the configuration objects are contained in the—you guessed it—Configuration container.

Service Account Passwords Failing to Replicate

Occasionally, changes made to the service account password on the Configuration container fail to replicate to other servers in the site and/or to other sites. This can happen if you have a network problem between the server on which the change is made and the server that is to receive the update. To correct for this, you should verify the change by checking your connector functionality after the services are restarted on the bridgeheads in the remote site and on other servers in the local site. If you have a mail delivery problem or services fail to start, change the property on the Configuration container for servers in the same site and on the Site Connector property pages for servers in remote sites. This will also update the service startup properties defined in Control Panel, Services.

The Configuration container not only holds all of the objects and containers that are used to administer a site, but it also has its own properties. If you ever need to change the Service Account password, that change needs to be reflected on this page. The procedure is as follows:

1. Change the password in User Manager for Domains or on your non-NT server. Synchronize the change to all NT Domain Controllers.

2. Change the password on the Configuration container's Service Account Password tab.

Changing the password in these two places is important. I have been to numerous customer sites where either the password was recently changed in User Manager but not updated in Exchange, or the password was changed on a foreign user account manager and synchronized with the PDC but not updated within Exchange. This results in the services failing to start when the server reboots. What generally happens is that the account password is changed but then several days pass before the server needs to reboot or one of the services requires a restart. Obviously, if the services don't start, your users do not have access to their email. Changing the password on this tab is supposed to change it for all of the following:

- Servers within the site (because they all use the same service account)

- Site Connector bridgehead servers that use the Override tab to connect to the site where the change was made

- Service startup property pages in the Control Panel for servers in the same site

Add-Ins Container

Within the Configuration container are several containers and objects. The first one in the list is the Add-Ins container. This container is pretty much non-configurable. In it you will find the extension dynamic link library information for your foreign connectors' administration files. These files are necessary for you to be able to change the properties of the associated connector. They should not be modified or renamed. If they are, you will need to recover them from either another Exchange server or from the installation CD-ROM.

Addressing Container

There are some pretty cool things you can do in the Addressing container. You'll notice upon opening it that there are three additional containers: Details Templates, E-Mail Addresses, and One-Off Addresses. In the Details and One-Off Addresses containers, you'll find another container for each language that you have installed support for. Inside those containers, you'll find templates that define how information is displayed to the clients when they enter such things as addresses or access mailbox properties. There isn't really any administration to be done in here, but if you ever wanted to reconfigure how a search dialog box (or another dialog box found in the Details Templates) looks to your users, you can edit it in the appropriate property pages.

Connections Container

You will find the configuration pages for existing cc:Mail Connectors, MS Mail Connectors, Internet Mail Service, various site connectors, and newsfeeds in this container. The container itself has no administrative properties. We will be looking at administering connectors in Chapters 4, "Queue Management," and 9, "Managing Intersite Communication and Replication."

Directory Replication Container

This container holds the Directory Replication Connectors that have been configured to other sites in your organization. The container itself has no administrative properties, and administration of the replication connector is addressed in Chapter 9.

Monitors Container

Any Server Monitors or Link Monitors that have been defined for this site will be found in the Monitors container. (Notice that there aren't any unless someone intentionally configures one.) We will be discussing server and link monitoring in Chapter 7, "Daily Proactive Troubleshooting."

Protocols Container

You will find a Protocols container both at the Site and Server levels of the Exchange directory. The properties that you can configure are identical at each level, with the only difference being that the Server level properties override any settings that are different at the Site level. Periodically you may need to add MIME types if your users complain that incoming attachments are not decoded properly, or if people to whom your users send mail cannot decode the attachments originating in your site. You can easily add a new type by accessing the MIME Types property page on the Protocols object and clicking **New**. You may also need to periodically add to the list of hosts that either are or are not allowed to access your Exchange server via one of the supported protocols. This is done from the Connections tab by clicking **New** and entering in the IP address and subnet mask that you wish to block or allow.

DS Site Configuration Object

The only administration property for this object is the Offline Address Book tab. This is where you configure Exchange to generate a list of email addresses that will be downloaded to your remote users. This list is stored in the Offline Address Book system folder. That folder is in a subfolder named after the corresponding site's X.500

distinguished name. The actual data for the folder is stored in the Public Information Store of the first Exchange Server installed in a site.

You may need to periodically go in to this property page and regenerate the address book, particularly if you make a number of changes that you want to be downloadable to your users immediately. If you don't regenerate manually, the address book won't be automatically regenerated until the scheduled time, which is every day at 4:00 am by default. Bear in mind that regenerating the address book does utilize system resources even if you haven't made any changes. You should take this into account before you decide to manually regenerate since it will affect server performance when the regeneration process is running.

Information Store Site Configuration Object

In the property pages of the Information Store Site Configuration object, you will find options for both the Private and Public Information Stores (PRIV.EDB and PUB.EDB) on all servers in the site. Important things to be aware of in here for general administration are message tracking for messages processed by the Information Store service and Storage Warnings generated and sent to mailbox and folder owners. We will be discussing these topics later in Chapters 2, "Administering Users," and 3, "Administering Public Folders," respectively.

MTA Site Configuration Object

The MTA Site Configuration object is used to configure properties that apply to all Message Transfer Agent services in the site. The only administrative function to be aware of here is message tracking, which we will talk about in Chapter 4. The information on the Messaging Defaults tab is used to control the connection parameters between MTAs in the same site as well as between MTAs transferring data between sites via the Site Connector. We will discuss some of these properties in Chapter 13, "Troubleshooting Your Exchange Server."

Site Addressing Object

You will find the routing table used by the MTA on the Routing tab of the Site Addressing object. You can also configure the schedule at which the routing table is recalculated on the Site Addressing object's Routing Calculation Schedule tab. Other information defined on this object includes what server is responsible for building the routing table and what algorithms are for generating Exchange user proxy addresses. None of these properties are likely to require regular reconfiguration or maintenance and subsequently will not be covered in any depth in this book. For more information, see the *Exchange Server Resource Guide*.

Site Encryption Object

If your organization uses Microsoft Key Manager to enable users to encrypt or digitally sign messages, you will need to configure this object. Information that you should enter includes what server maintains the Key Manager database and what encryption algorithms will be used. Generally, Key Manager needs to be configured only once, so the properties found in here are not used for regular administration. Although we will not be discussing this object further in this book, you can find more information in the *Exchange Server Resource Guide*.

Server Container

These individual server containers have property pages that function as pretty much a catch all for the stuff that Microsoft didn't have a better place for. Inside the server's container you will find another container representing each server installed in the site. If you get the properties of one of the servers, you will notice that there are several configuration options available. This is where you can install support for foreign languages, select the default services to be monitored in a Server Monitor, and change the location of the system databases. The remaining property pages relate to general administration issues and will be discussed in Chapter 12. There are also a number of additional objects and containers stored within each server. Their descriptions are discussed in the following sections.

Private Information Store Container

The Private Information Store container has several areas of configuration that can help you with administration. Not only can you obtain a quick view of who is currently logged on to their mailboxes, but you can also easily see how much space each user is taking up on the server. The columns for both of these objects can be rearranged and reconfigured by accessing the View, Columns menu option. When you obtain the properties of the Private Information Store, you will see tabs that hold the same logon and mailbox resource information as you saw from the main admin window and a couple other useful pages. We will be discussing soft deletes and storage limits in Chapter 2, and covering diagnostics logging in Chapter 13.

Protocols Container

This is the same as the Site level Protocols container—please see the "Protocols Container" section earlier in this chapter for a description.

Public Information Store Container

Any time a user places a document in a public folder, that data is actually stored in the PUB.EDB file of the Public Information Store identified on the Private Information Store property page for the server that holds the user's mailbox. Technically, System Folders are also Public Folders, and newsgroups that are brought into your organization via a newsfeed are actually added as Public Folders. There are many administrative tasks associated with managing public folders which will be covered in depth in Chapter 3. This object is used to set the default configuration options for all public folders created or stored on the selected server.

Server Recipients Container

This container simply holds all the recipient objects that have been defined on the selected server. There is no administration to be done with the actual container. Recipient administration is covered in Chapter 2.

Directory Service Object

The Director Service object allows you to configure settings for the directory on the selected server. You can force an in-site directory update where the selected server pulls changes from the other servers in the site, and you can check knowledge consistency where the selected server searches the other servers in the site for new servers that may have been added and parses any replication messages from other sites to find mention of downstream sites. Neither of these two tasks is something that you should need to do regularly, but they do relate to troubleshooting so they will be covered in Chapter 13 along with diagnostics logging.

Directory Synchronization Object

Use the Directory Synchronization object to define incoming and outgoing templates to map properties between MS Mail and Exchange Server. If your Directory Synchronization is not functioning properly, you can enable diagnostics logging here. Diagnostics logging for MS Mail and DirSync will be covered in Chapter 13.

Message Transfer Agent Object

The MTA object at the Server level is where you will find queues for the following objects:

- Private Information Store
- Public Information Store
- MS Mail Connector
- Connections between sites
- X.400 connections

Chapter 4 focuses on queue management, and diagnostics logging will be addressed in Chapter 13.

System Attendant Object

Because it is the System Attendant's job to maintain any message tracking logs that you enable, the control for how long to keep the tracking logs on your server is located on this object's General tab. The default is seven days, after which the log files will be purged. Message tracking will be discussed further in Chapter 13.

Summary

This chapter focused on the process of accessing the Exchange Administrator's console and the different switches that can be used to perform a few administrative tasks from a command line. We also discussed how to interpret the data found in the GUI, how permissions are assigned, and the requirements for administering remote Exchange servers. We concluded with a brief summary of the objects and containers found within the Administrator console. Now that you know what you are looking at and how to use the Administrator Program, we are going to talk about what to do with that knowledge in terms of administering users in Chapter 2.

2

Administering Users

NOW THAT YOU ARE FAMILIAR with how to interpret the Exchange Administrator's console and with the different objects you find there, it is time to start talking about daily administration duties. We will begin with how, when, and why you need to add, remove, and modify user mailboxes and manage remote users. We will then be moving on to distribution lists management, resource accounts, and storage limits. User administration is one of the things you will be doing the most of in your job, so it is important to have a good understanding of the methods available to you and when to apply them.

Managing Mailboxes

Most large companies will have to perform mailbox management tasks every day, whereas small to mid-sized companies may be able to get away with weekly management. The goal, as always, is to prevent these tasks from building up to the point at which they become unmanageable. Ideally, mailbox administration should be scheduled during off hours.

Adding Mailboxes

Any time you hire a new employee, bring in a temporary contractor, or obtain a messaging customer, it is likely you will need to add a mailbox for him. In this section, we will address how to add mailboxes in addition to template use and creation, which can make your administrative life a lot easier. Mailboxes can be added to your site in a number of ways. These include the following:

- Individually using the Exchange Administrator console
- Individually using User Manager for Domains (if the extension .dll is installed)
- In bulk using the Import tool

Using the Exchange Administrator Program

Regardless of the size of your Exchange organization, you will need to add users in dribs and drabs. Every company I have worked with added new hires one at a time using either the Exchange Administrator Program or User Manager for Domains. The ones that used the Exchange Administrator Program typically did so because of their administration structure. Generally, I've found that when network and messaging administrative functions are divided into different administration groups, users were added using the Exchange Administrator Program.

To create a mailbox from the Exchange Administrator, select **File**, **New Mailbox** or click the **New Mailbox** button on the toolbar. The screen that allows you to configure the mailbox is shown in Figure 2.1. The only required fields are Display, Alias, and Primary Windows NT Account. As you type in the user's first name, last name, and middle initial, Exchange will automatically generate a display name and alias for you based on the formula entered into the Auto Name dialog box. Modify the formula to your company's standard operating procedures to simplify your mailbox creation duties.

Using User Manager for Domains

In addition to using the Exchange Administrator Program, you can also create users one at a time from within User Manager for Domains. I find this to be handy in companies in which the same group of people is responsible for both network and messaging administration. The drawback to this method is that you can't take advantage of templates that you may have created to simplify the assignment of distribution list membership. When you create a user from within User Manager for Domains, you can use NT account templates, but not Exchange mailbox templates. For this reason, you may find that it is better to always use the Exchange Administrator Program to create your user mailboxes.

Figure 2.1   Configure user mailboxes using the Mailbox properties.

After the Exchange Administrator is installed on a Windows NT Workstation or Server, you will notice that there is a new menu option available in User Manager for Domains called Exchange. You can access Exchange mailbox properties for the mailbox associated with a selected NT account from here, as well as reconfigure your preferences with respect to how User Manager for Domains operates with Exchange.

To create a new mailbox from within User Manager for Domains, you must create a new NT account. After the NT account configuration is complete and you click the **Add** button, you will be prompted for the Exchange server on which you want this new user's mailbox to be created. Of course, if you have already identified a specific server on the Exchange menu Options tab, this step will be skipped. Select the appropriate Exchange server and you will see the same mailbox properties that are displayed in Figure 2.1. You should note that the Alias field is already filled in with the NT username, the Display field is filled in with the NT full name, and the Notes field on the Phone/Notes tab is filled in with the NT description. User Manager for Domains does not use the formula you entered in the Auto Naming tab to generate user information.

Using the Import Tool

In many cases, you can use the Import tool to populate the directory with user account information. It can save you a lot of time that otherwise would have been spent adding users one at a time. To create a mailbox from an import file, create a comma-separated value file where the first row contains at least the following information:

- Obj-Class
- Delivery-Mechanism
- Directory Name
- Alias Name
- Display Name
- Primary Windows NT Account
- Home-Server

You can use the BackOffice Resource Kit HEADER.EXE tool to create the file header. After it is created, open the file and add the appropriate mailbox information into the columns. See Appendix E, "Importing and Exporting," for some sample import header files and ways to use them.

Using Templates

In many cases you will want to use an existing mailbox as a template for creating new accounts. I highly recommend this because it can save you a lot of time by preconfiguring any property found on the mailbox property pages. Commonly configured properties are distribution list memberships, job titles, office addresses, and office departments. It is important to realize that any filled-in property that isn't name related or the Primary Windows NT account can be defined in the template mailbox. A template can be used with the Migration Wizard, with the Import tool, and when you are creating single mailboxes manually from within the Exchange Administrator. Unfortunately, the mailbox template is not available if you are creating the mailbox from within User Manager for Domains.

Using Migration Wizard

If you are migrating to Exchange or need to add several new mailboxes at once, you can use either the Migration Wizard or the Import tool; both are included with Exchange Server.

In addition to populating the directory with user account information, the Migration Wizard also brings in most of the user and shared data that existed on the previous messaging system. If the Migration Wizard doesn't migrate the data from your current messaging system, take a look at www.microsoft.com/exchange or www.slipstick.com. Creative companies are always adding new migration utilities for Exchange Server.

Creating NT Accounts from Within Exchange

Although Exchange can create an NT account at the same time the mailbox is being created, you will not be able to apply NT templates to the new NT account.

Removing Mailboxes

You will probably want to remove mailboxes that belonged to former full-time or temporary employees, or to customers who have stopped subscribing to the messaging service. Mailbox removal should be done only after you are certain that the user will not be returning, and that no additional incoming messages are likely to be addressed to that user. I find that 90 days is plenty of time to wait before removing a mailbox.

Before determining to remove a mailbox, however, you will want to disable it for a period of time. To disable a mailbox, disable the primary NT account. You are probably going to do that anyway because it is bad practice to simply delete NT accounts without a grace period. Keep in mind it is likely there will still be new mail coming in after you disable the mailbox, so it is better to either give another user permission to access the old mailbox, or to move the old messages out of the mailbox and assign the new user as an Alternate Recipient from the Exchange Administrator.

The first step to take before removing a disabled mailbox after the grace period is to move all your user's mail to another location. There is nothing quite like the feeling of having deleted a mailbox only to learn the next day there was important data in there that the replacement employee needs to do their job. Single mailbox recovery from backup is difficult to say the least (see Chapter 14, "Disaster Recovery"). You will also need to decide what to do with the user's old NT account.

You can move the mailbox data in a number of ways. One way is to use a personal folder store, or a .PST file. Simply log into the user's mailbox from the Outlook client; add a personal folder to the user profile under Tools, Services; and move all the messages in the Inbox and subfolders into the personal folder. You can then give this .PST file to the person who replaced the former mailbox owner. Alternatively, you could move all the data to a public folder and give a group of users permissions on the folder.

Personally, I prefer the public folder alternative because it is the easiest to implement and easiest to teach users how to use. The least desirable option is to simply back up the Private Information Store with the intent of restoring the user's data from backup should it become necessary. It's a well known fact that if all you have is a backup of the Private Information Store, you will inevitably be required to restore messages from the user's old mailbox from the backup. This is a corollary to the rule that states that if you simply use a .PST you will never be required to recover data from the mailbox.

After you have all the data moved or properly backed up, feel free to delete the mailbox. There is no Undo for this option.

The defaults for what happens to a user's Windows NT account when the corresponding mailbox is deleted are defined in the Exchange Administrator console under Tools, Options. The Permissions tab has an option called Delete primary Windows NT account when deleting a mailbox, which is not selected by default. If you do decide to select it, be forewarned that the account is gone forever and can only be recovered from a backup of your security account database.

Modifying Mailboxes

Although you will only need to add or delete a given mailbox once, you will probably need to modify it several times. There are many reasons why you might need to modify a mailbox. See Table 2.1 for a list of scenarios and ways you can respond to them.

If you are modifying just one mailbox, it is best to select it in the Exchange Administrator program and access its property pages. Unfortunately, you can't get properties of multiple mailboxes from the GUI, so if you need to edit more than 10 mailboxes, it is easier to use the Import/Export features of Exchange. To do this, export the user information to a file, change it, and import it back into the Exchange directory. I like to use the HEADER.EXE tool from the BackOffice Resource Kit because it really simplifies the creation of the header file, which is necessary to get the right properties out of the Exchange directory. If you do a mailbox Export from the Tools menu in Exchange without first creating a header file, you won't get all the properties. Default Export provides only the data in Table 2.2.

Table 2.1   **Modifying a Mailbox**

Situation	Your Response
A user wants her name changed in Exchange	Edit the Last, Display, and Alias name fields on the General tab, as well as the foreign email addresses defined on the E-Mail Addresses tab.
A user is transferred	Edit the job title and location information on the General tab.
Company reorganizes	Edit the Organization tab for several employees to reflect new management and new subordinate employees.
Area code changes	Edit the Phone/Notes tab for several employees.
A user requires a delegate	Define delegate Send On Behalf Of or Send As permissions.
A user leaves the company	Set up an alternate recipient for the former employee's mailbox.
A user is being harassed	Configure delivery options to block mail from being delivered.
A user requires special rights	Override properties such as storage limits, deleted item retention parameters, and the right to access the server using various Internet protocols.

Table 2.2 **Mailbox Properties You Can Export**

Property Name	Description
Obj-Class	Mailbox
First Name	User's given name
Last Name	User's surname
Display Name	The way the user's name is displayed in the global address list
Alias Name	User's mailbox alias
Directory Name	Unique directory identifier (analogous to an NT security ID)
Primary Windows NT Account	The NT mailbox owner
Home-Server	The Exchange server on which the mailbox resides
Email Addresses	Foreign proxy addresses for foreign connectors
Members	Distribution list members
Obj-Container	Recipient container that holds the mailbox
Hide from AB	Whether or not the account is hidden from the address book

If you compare the list of default properties with the list of things you might need to change, you'll see it falls very short. You can use the HEADER.EXE tool to export other information, such as phone numbers, manager name, and storage limits…in other words, everything else.

Managing Remote Users

In addition to managing mailboxes, you will also need to take special precautions if some of your users are accessing their mailboxes from remote locations. A remote user is a user that uses a dial-up connection to access your network. After the user is validated by your NT domain controller, he will have access to any domain resources that have been shared with him, including Exchange resources. Remote users can access email and public folders as if they were running local to the network.

There are a few things to keep in mind if you have remote Outlook users. These include the storage location for user messages, synchronization of the Offline Address Book, and roaming profiles.

Running the Administrator Program Remotely

You can run the Exchange Administrator across a dial-up connection as long as there is sufficient bandwidth to support RPCs. If there isn't, you're likely to wind up with time-out problems. Keep in mind that you need to have the appropriate permissions in the site you are trying to administer, so you may need to change your domain authentication settings to allow you into the new domain.

Storage Location for Messages

The first problem to address is the storage location for your users' messages. Your remote users need to be able to see their messages even when they are not connected to the Exchange server. For example, a technical sales representative will need access to the product information files stored in public folders on the server while in the field. Because the sales rep is not connected to the server, action must be taken to allow the sales rep to view the data while off line. Therefore, you should configure them with either an offline storage file (.OST) or a personal folder store (.PST) to store email messages.

OST

In terms of remote users, it is far better to use an offline storage file (OST) file than a PST file. The OST is a file stored on the users' local hard drives that allows the users to synchronize private and public folders to it for offline use. Messages synchronized to the OST are copies—all ..ata remains on the server. When the users work offline, they make changes to the local OST that are uploaded to the Exchange server after the users reconnect. This means that data stored in an OST is backed up as part of your regular Private Information Store backup. Your users don't have to worry about local backups of their OST files. An OST can be enabled from within Outlook by accessing the Services item in the Tools menu:

1. Select the Microsoft Exchange Server service.

2. Choose **Properties**.

3. Select the **Advanced tab**.

4. Click the button labeled **Offline Folder File Settings** to configure the location of the OST file and encryption settings or to compact or disable the OST file.

PST

You could alternatively use a *personal folder store (PST)* to store user mail for offline use. Although there are a lot of good reasons to use PSTs, remote access is not one of them. Problems such as having to do your own local backups and issues with folder sharing and Calendar sharing far outweigh the advantages.

For example, I have seen lot of problems with users who have a local PST file defined as the primary location for incoming messages. This setting causes a new Calendar folder to be created in the PST file. Appointments stored in the PST Calendar folder are not visible to other Exchange users because the data is not stored on the server. This also causes problems when you want to assign delegate access. I've even seen users accidentally delete large PST files, realize their mistake, and attempt to recover from the Recycle Bin, only to learn that the Recycle Bin did not have enough room for the PST file and thus was permanently deleted. The bottom line is that you should only use PST files when you have a compelling reason to do so.

I have been to companies where some of the employees travel infrequently and although they need access to some of the data in their mailbox while on the trip, they don't want to synchronize an entire 50MB mailbox to their local hard drive. PSTs worked great for them for the trip; they were able to right-click and drag to copy messages to the PST. This left a copy on the server that would continue to be backed up. If you do decide to use a PST, add it as a service to the user's profile.

The local PST should be defined as the primary location for incoming messages if you want to make it available for offline use; otherwise, the user must remember to move things into it. This leads to the problems discussed earlier because PST files can't be shared in the same way as Exchange folders. Also, it requires a little more training because the PST is visible as an additional component in the Outlook GUI, as opposed to the OST, which is transparent to the user. And keep in mind that if a user forgets her PST password, Microsoft provides no way for that lost password to be recovered. However, there are some third-party tools available to recover lost PST passwords. The OST is a much better solution for offline storage.

Synchronizing Offline Address Books

After you have decided how to solve the offline message access problem, you should think about offline address books (OABs). If your users need access to company email addresses offline (and they almost certainly will) you need to configure the OAB. The first thing to decide is what recipients you want to make available to your users. If you run Outlook 8.03 or later and Exchange 5.5, offline address book synchronization isn't as big a deal as it was in previous versions of Outlook. Outlook 8.03 and Exchange 5.5 support downloading only changed items in the OAB.

If you use versions of Outlook prior to Outlook 8.03, however, then electing to download the OAB in the client results in the *entire* OAB being downloaded from the server to the client. This can be a problem if you are hoping to provide the entire Global Address List (GAL) to your users and your GAL is large. If you are in this boat, you should consider upgrading your clients and servers to the most recent releases. Another solution is to limit the OAB to a specific recipients container(s). It is likely that your users email people in their own office most of the time, so limiting the OAB to the user's own recipients container may work for you.

PST File Usage

PST files are necessary for migrating data from MS Mail MMF files to Exchange, or if you are using the Outlook client without the Exchange server component. They are also great for testing folder applications before releasing them to the public.

After you determine how much data the OAB will contain, configure it for each site in your Exchange Organization on the DS Site Configuration object. The Offline Address Book tab allows you to identify the containers to be made available and the server in each site that generates the OAB. To download the OAB to the client, your users will select **Tools, Synchronize** from the Outlook menu bar and choose **Download Address Book**. A window will pop up asking whether all changes since the last synchronization should be downloaded and whether details should be downloaded.

If you are running older clients, you should check the Microsoft Exchange 4.0 and 5.0 compatibility box so that the address book is stored in a format the client can understand. You should also change the OAB server if the server selected is experiencing performance problems. The default value for this field is the first server installed in a site. If you need your changes to be effective before the next scheduled time (found on the Offline Address Book Schedule tab), click the **Generate All** button. The default schedule is every day at 4:00 AM. If this corresponds with your normal work day, you should consider configuring this to be done during off hours.

Managing Roaming Profiles

The last thing to think about when it comes to remote users is roaming profiles. Most of your user configuration data is stored in the HKEY_CURRENT_USER section of the Registry. Therefore, if you have roaming profiles configured, many of your user Outlook settings will follow the users around to different computers on the network.

You should consider implementing a system policy to enable the Slow Net option. This option causes the client workstation to detect the speed of the link so that when it is operating across a slow network connection, the user is prompted to log on using the locally cached profile. Otherwise, when the user logs in, his profile is downloaded from the profile directory and his previous user Registry settings are applied to whatever workstation he is working on at that time. This can be a problem for remote users because downloading all that data across a slow modem connection can take what seems like forever. Keep in mind that the OST file is stored in the user's profile and will therefore synchronize across whatever connection is available for bringing down the profile. This can be a real performance issue if you don't plan for it.

Managing Distribution Lists

In addition to managing mailbox recipients, you will also need to administer distribution list recipients. Distribution list (DL) management can be troublesome if you have not optimized the levels of administration in your organization. Let's take a look at configuring a DL administrator and how to add, remove, and modify DLs. We will also discuss administration of DLs from remote sites, the effects of large distribution lists on Exchange, and printing and backing up your DLs.

Configuring a DL Administrator

One of the many nice features of Exchange distribution lists is that after the list is created, the administrator can assign an Exchange user to manage the DL membership from the client. This user then becomes the *list administrator*, also known as the *list owner*. This is the only directory object in Exchange that can be administered from the client. To identify a DL administrator, access the DL property pages and select the **General** tab. Specifying a user in the Owner field allows that user to add and remove members from their Outlook client (see Figure 2.2).

Adding Distribution Lists

The process of adding a DL is very similar to adding a mailbox. From the Exchange Administrator, click the **New Distribution List** button on the tool bar to configure the DL property pages. Assign to the list a descriptive name and owner, and identify the membership on the General tab. To get the best performance out of your distribution list expansion server, you should use nested DLs whenever possible and keep the membership of any one DL under 3,000. You may also want to define the following:

- Distribution lists of which this new list will be a member on the Distribution Lists tab.
- Users that are or are not allowed to send mail to this distribution list.
- Custom attributes you define for your site.
- Advanced options.

Figure 2.2 Configure distribution list settings by using the DL property pages.

Advanced options are found on the Advanced tab. They include a simple display name (used if you are directory synchronizing with systems that can't read as many characters as are in your display name), trust level (used if you want to prevent this DL from synchronizing with MS Mail or cc:Mail), and message size limits. They also include whether Exchange should report delivery problems to the list owner and/or message originator, allow out-of-office messages to the originator (not enabled by default), and whether the list itself or the list's membership should be hidden from the address book.

Removing Distribution Lists

Removing a distribution list is as easy as clicking the big, black **X** in the Exchange Administrator tool bar. You can also delete a list by pressing the Delete key on your keyboard or clicking **Edit, Delete** from the Administrator console. Deleting a DL does not delete any of the members' mailboxes.

Modifying Distribution Lists

You can modify DLs either in the Exchange Administrator console or from the Outlook client if you are the DL's owner or have Administrator permissions on the DL.

To add or remove members by using the Exchange Administrator console, select the DL in the address list and get its properties. Click the **Modify** button to add or remove members from the list. Other properties you may want to modify include the parent DLs that this DL is a member of. You can add the current DL to other DLs by clicking the **Distribution Lists** tab and clicking **Modify**.

You also may want to configure Delivery Restrictions. Delivery Restrictions allow you to control who is allowed to send messages to the currently selected DL. This is a handy feature for your really big lists (such as Everyone) or for lists that deliver messages to all top-level management. The Advanced tab also has some useful options that let the Exchange server report delivery problems to the list owner and/or message originator, allow out-of-office messages to the originator (not enabled by default), and indicate whether the list itself or the list's membership should be hidden from the address book. See Table 2.3 for the DL options available to you.

Table 2.3 **Using the DL Options to Customize the Performance of Individual DLs**

Property Page	Modification	Purpose
Delivery Restrictions	Accept messages from	Only allow explicitly listed users/DLs to send messages to the DL.
	Reject messages from	Allow everyone to send to the DL except explicitly listed users/DLs.

Property Page	Modification	Purpose
Advanced	Message size	Prevent users from sending large messages/attachments to members of the DL.
	Report to distribution list owner	Send NDRs to the DL owner to allow expired mailboxes to be removed from the membership.
	Report to message originator	Send NDRs to the message sender to allow the sender to communicate information using an alternative method.
	Allow out-of-office messages to originator	Allow automatically generated replies to be sent to the originator. Disabled by default.
	Hide from address book	DL is hidden from GAL. Users must type in full address to send to it.
	Hide membership from address book	Membership is hidden from DL properties obtained from the client. Must not be selected for client-side administration to be possible.

To add or remove members from within Outlook, the owner would log in to her account using Outlook and get properties of the appropriate DL from the address book. The owner can then click the **Modify Members** button in the properties page to add or remove members from the list.

Administering DLs from Other Sites

This is easy—you can't. The distribution list information that is displayed in other sites is read-only. There is no workaround for remote-site administration other than exporting the distribution list to a file and importing it into the site from which you want to administer it.

Microsoft's Bedlam DL

A good example of the usefulness of DL restrictions actually happened at Microsoft. A DL with upward of 50,000 users was used for a mass mailing within Microsoft. Several of the recipients did a reply to the list, rather than a reply to the message originator. Needless to say, there were considerable resource and network problems as a result that could have been prevented by restricting the users allowed to send to the DL.

A user in Site A can administer a DL created in Site B from the Administrator Program if the user first connects to a server in Site B. Administration from the remote site cannot be accomplished from the client. This actually amounts to administering a DL from the site in which the DL is defined. As a result, you need to ensure that the owner(s) you identify for the DL have mailboxes in the same site in which the DL is being created.

If you are desperate, you can create a mailbox in the same site as the DL for the explicit purpose of administering the DL. The new mailbox would be identified as the DL owner, and the primary Windows NT account identified on that new mailbox would be the real user you wanted to use to administer the account. In my opinion, this is a really messy way to work around the cross-site administration issue, and you should only do it if you have no alternative. I've seen this solution work in companies in which all the DLs are defined in a hub site that exists primarily to route mail between remote user sites. This is a nice configuration performance-wise because you can have the hub site's servers do the DL expansion. The problem is that because no user mailboxes are defined in the hub site, you can't pick a DL owner to do the client-side administration.

A better way to take advantage of your hub site is to use nested lists whenever possible. The nested lists should be defined in the same site as the DL owner in order for them to be easily administered. However, the parent list should be defined in the hub site. With this configuration, a user sends a message to the parent list and causes the whole list, including the nested lists, to be resolved in the hub site. Do yourself a favor and just use administrators that are in the same site as your DLs if you have any choice at all in the matter.

Managing DL Expansion

Large distribution list expansion can consume considerable server resources. By default, the Exchange server on which the message originates is used to expand the DL membership. In other words, suppose Fred is on the CHICAGO server and is sending a message to a DL defined on the ORLANDO server. The list will be expanded on CHICAGO by default. This may not be what you want, especially for large DLs.

If you have sites with multiple servers defined within a single geographical location within the site, it is better to identify a dedicated server to do all your DL expansion, or at least offload the expansion of your really large lists to a lightly utilized server. Unfortunately, if your messaging topology has a single server in each site, you can't really benefit from this option. Each site in which a DL is defined must have at least one expansion server.

Use the Expansion Server property on the General tab of your DL to configure an expansion server. You can further optimize this by using nested lists when possible and configuring a few Registry settings. If you have a large organization of more than

20,000 users, find the key HKEY_LOCAL_MACHINE\SYSTEM\CurrentControlSet\Services\ MSExchangeMTA\Parameters. Optimize the key DL Member Cache Size from the default value of 15,000 to a larger value. This key is what defines how many names will be cached in memory. Increasing the value will allow the expansion server to cache more names in memory and therefore improve performance. You may also increase the values for Dispatcher threads and Transfer threads to optimize the processing of messages sitting in the expansion server's queues.

Printing the Membership List of DLs

There is no built-in ability to print out the membership of a DL. However, you can manually accomplish this by opening the DL properties in the Exchange Administrator console and clicking the **Modify** button on the **General** tab. Select all the users listed in the **Distribution list members** dialog box and press **Ctrl+C** on your keyboard. This copies the members to the Clipboard. You can then paste this list into a text editor to print. Alternatively, you can use the export utility to export DL information to a text file. You can then edit the file to find the Members column of information. You'll need to clean it up a bit, but all the information will be there.

There is also a utility called ONDL available in the Resource Kit. This is a command-line utility that allows you to get a screen display of DL membership. I prefer ONDL to the cut-and-paste method because there is a lot of extra information that can be gleaned from this tool. We will be discussing this tool further in Chapter 13, "Troubleshooting Your Exchange Server."

Expanding Remote Distribution Lists

In situations where you have multiple single-server sites, you should consider creating your distribution lists in a site where you can take advantage of a dedicated expansion server. The MTA General tab of each server's MTA properties allows you to force distribution lists created in remote sites to be expanded in the remote sites.

For example, suppose William has a mailbox on the INDIANA server, which is the only server in the MID-WEST site. Every time William sends to any DL defined anywhere in his organization, the DL will be expanded on INDIANA by default. By deselecting the Expand remote distribution lists locally option on the MTA General tab of the INDIANA server, you can force the INDIANA server to forward messages sent to DLs defined in other sites to be first routed to the other site for expansion. If the remote site has SEATTLE identified as the DL expansion server for the DL named Engineers, every time William sends a message to Engineers it will be expanded on SEATTLE. You can see how this option can give you considerable control over DL expansion.

Backing Up DLs

Distribution lists are objects in the directory and are therefore backed up with the directory. However, you may want to have additional backups available in the event that a DL is accidentally deleted or modified in a way from which it is difficult to recover. I've seen situations in which the primary administrator is out of the office for a few days and leaves someone else in charge of the Exchange server and returns to find several email messages indicating membership problems with the DL. Rather than spend valuable time trying to troubleshoot the problem to prevent having to restore from backup, this administrator was able to use the Import utility to recover the DL. This worked only because the administrator wisely used the Export utility to export her DLs to a text file.

Managing User Resource Mailboxes

Like mailboxes and DLs, a resource mailbox is also a recipient that requires your attention and consideration. A *resource mailbox* is an Exchange mailbox set up strictly for resource scheduling purposes. Such resources as conference rooms, shared notebook computers, and overhead projectors can be "invited" to meetings as if they were other users in your company. After the resource mailbox is created, you can set it up to automatically accept all incoming scheduling requests or you can assign a user to act as the delegate for the account. Generally, it is a good idea to assign a delegate to handle your resource mailboxes. The delegate will be responsible for mediating any scheduling conflicts.

There are five steps to setting up a resource account with a delegate to manage it:

1. **Create the delegate account.** You can elect to create a dedicated account to manage your resources, or you can use an existing mailbox. Creation of a delegate account is exactly the same as creating a regular mailbox. See the "Adding Mailboxes" section earlier in this chapter for more information about adding new users.

2. **Configure the delegate account.** You may want the delegate account to automatically process all incoming meeting requests. The configuration options are found in the client under **Tools, Options**. Select the **Calendar Options** button on the **Preferences** tab, and then click the **Resource Scheduling** button to see your account configuration options (see Figure 2.3).

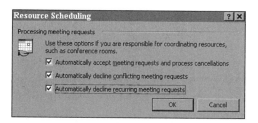

Figure 2.3 Configure the delegate and resource accounts to process appointments automatically.

3. **Create the resource account.** Create the resource account the same way you would create an ordinary mailbox. The account should be named descriptively so that it is obvious to your users that it is a resource account. You may also want to create a separate recipients container for your resource accounts to make it easier for your users to find them in the GAL. Alternatively, you could configure a custom attribute for the resource account, identifying the account as one for a resource. You can subsequently create Address Book views to display the accounts logically to your users.

4. **Configure the resource account.** Log in to the resource account's mailbox and access the **Tools, Options** menu item. We walked through how to force the account to automatically process meeting requests and cancellations in step 2. You should configure the appropriate options for the resource account. After this is complete, you need to assign permissions to the delegate account identified in step 1. To do this, click the **Delegates** tab and add the delegate account defined in step 1. Select the delegate's name and click **Permissions**. Give the user Editor permissions in the **Calendar** drop-down list, and select **Delegate receives copies of meeting-related messages sent to me**. Also choose **Send meeting requests and responses only to my delegate, not to me** and click **OK**.

5. **Configure automatic processing of meeting requests.** The last step is to configure the delegate account to automatically process incoming messages for the resource account as soon as they are received. To do this, access the **Tools, Options** menu from the delegate account. On the **Preferences** tab click the **E-Mail Options** button. Select **Advanced E-Mail Options** and select **Process requests and responses on arrival**.

After the account is set up, meeting requests sent to the resource account will be automatically forwarded to the delegate, where they will be automatically processed if the delegate account is logged on. Depending on your configuration, the delegate can also take care of scheduling conflicts with the resource. If you elect not to use a delegate, the resource account must be logged in to process incoming meeting requests.

Directory Update Issues

In many companies, you will find yourself adding, removing and modifying mailboxes at least weekly—if not daily. The time of day that you actually perform this type of administration can affect your server and network performance.

Managing Replication Within a Site

You should be aware that mailbox additions, modifications, and deletions all change the directory, and that any change to the directory will force your Exchange server to announce to all other servers in the site that there has been a new change. The other servers in the site will request the changed directory information, and your server will transmit the requested directory update to the other servers. Although the traffic associated with this update may not be large (only items changed in the last five minutes are sent in an update), it is traffic that you can control.

If possible, you should do all mailbox additions, modifications, and deletions during off-hours or when you know your network and Exchange servers are not as heavily utilized. You can even create scripts during regular working hours using the Import/Export features in Exchange that cause accounts to be added, deleted, or modified after hours. This can be facilitated by creating a standard operating procedure that notifies your user community that all routine mailbox maintenance, including the addition or removal of mailboxes, will be done after 5:00 PM. They should also be advised that they can help you do this efficiently by providing the proper, correctly filled-out work orders to you in a timely manner.

Managing Replication Between Sites

Directory updates between sites are not as much of a problem because you as the administrator define at what times you want a given site to request updates from a remote site. This schedule is independent of the actual changes that occur in the remote site, and the remote site will not notify your site if there has been a change. At the scheduled time, the Directory Replication Bridgehead server in your site will send an email request to the Directory Service running on the Directory Replication Bridgehead server in the destination site. The destination server will process the email request by creating a new message to your server that includes all items that have changed since the last update. To optimize this, you should schedule directory replication between sites to be at least once every day and it should happen during off hours. We will discuss troubleshooting the Directory Service in Chapter 13.

Managing Mailbox Storage Limits

Another important consideration when administering users is the amount of space you will allow each mailbox to use. This includes both message storage and storage dedicated to deleted items. I am continually surprised by the number of companies that do not implement or enforce mailbox storage limits. It is my belief that storage limits are critical to your ability to plan server resource usage and prepare for future resource shortages. The amount of space you allow your users will have a huge impact on the storage solutions you purchase for your company, not to mention your backup and restore procedures. There is no reason that users need to save every single email message they have ever received, and yet this exact scenario is a reality in almost every company I have worked with. If you do not already have storage limits configured, now is the time to do it.

Setting Limits

The first step to managing mailbox storage usage is to set limits. Setting storage limits is easy. There are only a few steps to take. First, define the amount of disk space the majority of your users will require and how often you want them to be warned of an excess. Second, configure PST files for your users that can be used to clean their server-based mailboxes (review the limitations of PSTs in the "Storage Location for Messages" section earlier in this chapter). Third, publish a standard operating procedure defining the new storage limit program and how to move data to a PST. Finally, configure the limits on the Private Information Store objects on your servers.

Defining Disk Space

Define the amount of disk space that most of your users will require. You should take a look at the existing mailbox sizes on your server to get a feel for this. Most users should not require more than 50MB of disk space for their email. Depending on your environment, you may allow them as much as 100MB or as little as 30MB.

I have been to a few companies that are migrating to Exchange and NT from a POP3 server servicing UNIX clients. In this scenario, the UNIX clients were accustomed to downloading all data to be stored locally. These companies decided not to allow the users any storage space at all on the server, and the clients are configured to download all incoming messages to a local PST file. This may be a bit drastic, since in many companies this requires users to back up their own hard drives—a task difficult to get users to actually perform if they have never experienced a hard disk crash. However, this is an excellent solution if you are an ISP running Exchange.

You should also decide how often you want storage warning messages to be generated to your users. By default, storage warning messages are automatically created and sent out at 8:00 PM every day. This is probably good enough for most companies as long as it doesn't conflict with the normal working hours.

Configuring PST Files

The next task to complete is configuring PST files for your users. This is necessary so that when a user exceeds his allotted disk space limit he has a place to put mail that he doesn't want to delete. There are a few limitations to PSTs. They cannot exceed

16,384 folders, and each folder can contain no more than 16,384 items. A PST also cannot be larger than 2GB in total size. Your users should be taught to password-protect their PST files to prevent unauthorized use because anyone that can connect to your PST file can add it to their local profile. Also point out that if they forget their passwords, passwords cannot be recovered for them and they will lose anything stored in the PST file (although there are third-party utilities that allow password recovery). In addition, PSTs cannot be shared as a normal Exchange personal folder. There is no concept of delegates for PSTs, so anyone who needs access to the PST must add it to his profile as a service. These limitations should be communicated to your users so there are no future unpleasant surprises.

Creating a Standard Operating Procedure (SOP)

A new standard operating procedure (SOP) should be created and distributed to reflect the new limited storage policy. It should define the limits you have identified, the storage warning schedule, how to reduce the size of a mailbox, including use and limitations of PST files, and what will happen to users who refuse to comply with the storage limitation policy (perhaps suspending sending and/or receiving privileges).

After the SOP is approved and distributed, you must actually enable storage limits on the servers in your site. This is done from the General tab on the Private Information Store property pages accessed in each server container.

Enforcing Limits

It isn't enough to simply distribute a SOP defining your storage limit policy—you also need to enforce it. Fortunately, Exchange can do that for you if you configure the punishments you want to dole out to the offending users. On the General property page of the Private Information Store object where this configuration is performed, you have the following three options:

- **Issue warning (K).** Check the corresponding box and enter a number in the field corresponding with the storage limit on the mailbox in KB (1MB = 1000KB). When this limit is exceeded, the user will receive a warning message from the system at the time defined on the Storage Warnings tab on the Information Store Site Configuration object.

- **Prohibit send (K).** Check the corresponding box and enter a number in the field corresponding with the storage limit on the mailbox in KB (1MB = 1000KB) at which you want to prevent the user from sending new messages. When this limit is exceeded, the user will receive a warning message from the system at the time defined on the Storage Warnings tab on the Information Store Site Configuration object, and will no longer be able to send messages.

- **Prohibit send and receive (K).** Check the corresponding box and enter a number in the field corresponding with the storage limit on the mailbox in KB (1MB = 1000KB) at which you want to both prevent the user from sending new messages *and* prevent their ability to receive new messages. When this limit is exceeded, the user will receive a warning message from the system at the time defined on the Storage Warnings tab on the Information Store Site Configuration object, and will no longer be able to send or receive mail using this mailbox.

There are always a few users who require exceptions to storage limits. For example, you can't expect the president of your company to comply with this policy, and you certainly can't expect to keep your job if you prohibit the president from sending or receiving mail. The good news is that although you definitely want to define your storage limits at the broader, Information Store level so that all user mailboxes created in that information store are subject to the limits defined on it, Exchange allows you to override these settings on an individual mailbox level. Each mailbox will automatically be configured to have the **Use information store defaults** box checked. You can uncheck this box and either leave the limit options blank so that there are effectively no limits on this mailbox, or you can enter in the appropriate limits for this particular user. Unfortunately, you cannot configure limits for a group of users from the GUI. You can, however, use the Import tool to configure several users at once. The Import tool was discussed in the "Managing Mailboxes" section earlier in this chapter.

Soft Deletes

Disk space will be used for both the messages your users decide to keep as well as the messages they decide to delete, if you decide to configure this option. This is because Microsoft Exchange 5.5 includes a new feature called Deleted Item Retention, which is more commonly referred to as a *soft delete*. This feature allows you to retain items that your users have deleted and purged from their deleted items folder for a period of time.

The purpose of deleted item retention is to allow users to easily recover accidentally deleted messages without having to restore from backup. This property is configured for the masses at the server Private Information Store properties and can be overridden for individual users at the mailbox level.

Soft deletes are not enabled by default, but if you decide to implement them you have a few options. You can elect to simply enter a number corresponding to the number of days for which you want a message to be recoverable. As long as it hasn't been more than the designated number of days since the user purged the message, she can recover it from the client by selecting the **Deleted Items** folder and choosing **Tools, Recover Deleted Items** option. Additionally, you can check the box **Don't permanently delete items until the store has been backed up**. This will prevent Exchange from removing deleted items until the private information store has been backed up, even if the number of days since the item was deleted has been exceeded.

I would personally use both options if I were going to bother at all. I admit that I am fatalistic in that I believe that if you don't want a message to be removed from your system, don't delete it. Most users will learn this lesson fairly quickly if you don't recover their deleted items for them. In any event, only the Outlook 98 client allows users to recover deleted items within the retention time.

Summary

In this chapter, we studied how to administer several types of recipients. We looked at how to add, remove, and modify mailboxes and distribution lists; the effects of directory changes on your network; how to configure and manage resource accounts; and managing mailbox storage limits. Public folders are the only other type of recipient that you will need to administer, so let's move on to Chapter 3 to discuss public and system folders and newsgroups.

3

Administering Public Folders

Now that you know how to administer user mailboxes and distribution lists, let's discuss the administration of Exchange folders. There are three areas to be covered: public folders, system folders, and newsgroups. We will start with public folders.

Public Folder Issues

The public folders (PFs) that we will be looking at in this section are user created. First, we are going to talk about permissions for public folders. Next, we will discuss how to add, configure, and remove them. We will then be looking at determining the location of the data stored in them and how to manage folder size. Replication configuration and management, and conflict resolution will be addressed at the end of the section, while resolving some of the major problems will be addressed in Chapter 14, "Disaster Recovery."

Folder Permissions

In order to create a folder, you must have permission to create it. Permissions are assigned in two places: Client permissions from the client and the Administrator Program, and Top Level Folder Creation permissions from the Administrator Program.

Client Permissions

You can access *Client permissions* either from the Outlook client by opening the properties of a particular public folder, or you can access them from the Administrator console by getting folder properties and clicking the **Client Permissions** button on the **General** tab. The Create subfolders permission must be assigned to a user before that user will be allowed to create a subfolder in the selected parent folder. If this permission is not assigned, the create subfolder options will be grayed out in the client. Generally, Client permissions and the right to create subfolders are administered by the folder owner, not by the Exchange administrator.

Client permissions will be inherited from the parent folder such that if Bill has a folder called WADEWARE that has author permissions assigned as the default permission, then any subfolders created under WADEWARE will also provide default author permissions. If Bill wants to change this, he will have to manually access the client permissions of the new subfolder and change them explicitly. If WADEWARE has subfolders and Bill changes the client permissions on the WADEWARE folder, he can elect to propagate the change to WADEWARE's subfolders.

Top Level Folder Creation Permissions

As an Exchange administrator, you need to keep a close reign on the *Top Level Folder permissions*. This property is defined site-wide on the Information Store Site Configuration object's Top Level Folder Creation property page. The default is that everyone can create top level folders! This is terrible and will cause anarchy in your public folder hierarchy if you don't change it immediately. You should reconfigure this as soon as you install Exchange because it allows any user who has a mailbox to be able to right-click the words **All Public Folders** in the client and create a folder that will show up in the folder listing of every other user in the organization.

Many users don't understand the significance of a public folder, and won't realize that the existence of the folder they just created will be evident on everyone else's client. You need to determine one of the two following things:

- Who will be responsible for the creation and management of the top level folders?
- What top level folders do you want to create and manage?

My feeling is that in most companies it is better for the Exchange administrator to be responsible for all folder creation and management. The most successful public folder implementations I have seen were completely designed by the Exchange administrator, with input provided by various department heads or geographic locations. I like to see a top level folder design in one of two scenarios:

- Each geographic location has a single top level folder that is visible only to users in the same geographic location.
- Each department has a single top level folder that is visible only to users in the same department.

Both of these scenarios work wonderfully and, if necessary, you can allow a user in each location or department to be in charge of the hierarchy within the parent folder. The beauty of this arrangement is that you control who can actually view each public folder in your organization.

After you have determined who will be responsible for the folders, access the aforementioned property page and select the **List** option button under Allowed to create top level folders. Identify the user with permission. The good news is that once you identify an account in this box, the right to create top level folders will be denied to anyone not explicitly listed.

Adding, Configuring, and Removing Public Folders

Now that permissions are assigned, let's discuss how to add, configure, and remove public folders. Some tasks must be performed from the client, while others are performed from the Administrator Program. We'll look at what you can do from the Outlook client, in addition to tasks that can be performed from the Exchange Administrator console.

Adding Public Folders

Public folders cannot be added manually from the Exchange Administrator console. You must be logged in to the Outlook client as a user with the correct permissions in order to perform this task. To add a public folder, access the Exchange server using your Outlook client and open your folder list. Expanding the Public Folders item and then expanding the item All Public Folders brings up a list of all public folders (PFs) that the currently logged on user has the right to see. Public folders are created and displayed in a hierarchical fashion. Expanding All Pubic Folders displays the top level PFs that are available in your organization and visible to your account.

I generally right-click the location at which I would like to add the folder and choose **New Folder**, although in many cases I find using the **Copy** folder feature useful. The Copy feature allows you to copy all existing properties of an existing folder to the new folder.

If the New Folder option is grayed out or not available, you do not have permission to create a folder at the level you have chosen.

Configuring Public Folders

After you have created the folder, there are a number of configuration options you can set up. Get the folder's properties from the client by right-clicking the folder and selecting Properties. Briefly summarized, some of these options are as follows:

- From the client, you can configure folder assistants to process incoming messages according to rules you create.

- You can set a folder up as a moderated folder. All messages sent to moderated folders are first forwarded to a holding location to be reviewed for their content and appropriateness for a given topic area.

- You can create and set up custom views to display your data in a certain format when users first access the folder.

- You can create forms that are installed to the folder in a way that makes them easily accessible to the end user.

Client access permissions are also configured from the folder's properties. Whether or not a folder that the administrator has defined in the Newsgroup Hierarchies portion of the Administrator console will be available to NNTP clients is also configured here.

As an administrator, there are several configuration options that you must perform from the Administrator console. In addition to being able to reconfigure the client access permissions, you can also do the following:

- Configure and administer folder replication

- Identify distribution lists of which a given folder will be a member

- Control age limits

- Unhide the email address from the global address list

Removing Public Folders

Public folders can be removed from a given server from the Administrator console or they can be deleted from all servers from the client. You may want to delete a particular instance of a folder if usage monitoring indicates that it is no longer being accessed, or you may want to delete all instances of folders that were dedicated to a particular project that has since been completed. In any case, before a folder is removed, be sure you won't need it any longer. It is difficult to restore a folder from backup.

To remove an individual copy of a folder from a given server, access the Exchange Administrator console. You can remove copies of public folders stored on any server that you have administrative rights to, but you can't remove a folder using the Administrator Program if there is only one copy of it. In other words, the Administrator Program can only be used to remove replicas of a folder. It cannot be used to remove a folder entirely from the organization. The actual removal can be performed at either the folder level or the server level of administration.

To remove a folder from the server level, access the Public Information Store properties of the server that you want to remove the folder from. The Instances tab gives a list called Folders on this Information Store. This lists all public folders, newsgroup folders, and system folders that this server's information store actually manages. All data for the listed folders is stored in the selected server's PUB.EDB file. To remove a folder from this Information Store, select the folder on the right and click **Remove**.

To remove a PF from the folder level, select the appropriate folder in the Administrator console and get its properties. The Replicas tab displays two lists. On the left is a list of servers in the selected site, and on the right is a list called Replicate folders to. This is a list of all servers on which the folder currently exists. Select the server from which you want to remove the PF on the right and click **Remove**. See Figure 3.1 for an example of the options for folder removal.

Generally, I prefer to use the Folder level when removing public folders because I can see at a glance exactly where other replicas of the folder reside. Unfortunately, you will only be able to remove replicas from the Folder object if you are currently connected to the site in which the folder resides. If you are in a remote site and wish to remove a folder from a server in that site, you will need to remove the replica from the Server object.

Note that public folders can be deleted only by the folder's owner while logged into the client. Select the folder and click the black **X** on the Outlook toolbar.

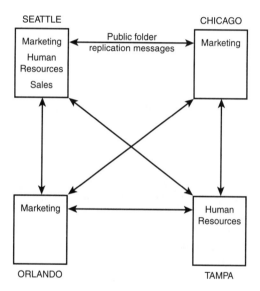

Figure 3.1   Use the Administrator Program to remove one of the Marketing or Human Resources public folder replicas. You must use the client to remove the Sales folder because there is only one instance of it in the organization.

Location of Public Folder Data

Public folders have three components: content, hierarchy, and directory data, which are described in Table 3.1.

Table 3.1 **Public Folder Data**

Component	Description
Content	The actual data in a public folder is stored in the PUB.EDB file of all servers configured to maintain a replica of the public folder. The content data is accessed by the client via the Information Store service on the server that hosts the public folder content.
Hierarchy	When a client expands the list of All Public Folders, the hierarchy data displayed is actually obtained from that user's Public Information Store (PUB.EDB), not the Directory. To find out which server is providing the hierarchy to your users, access the Private Information Store properties for the users' home server. The field called **Public Folder Server** identifies the server that will be queried for hierarchy data by all users with a mailbox on this server. The default setting is the users' home server.
Directory	When a client browses for the public folder's email address in the global address list, the client is querying the Directory (DIR.EDB). The information in the Directory needs to correlate with that stored in the public information store, but the bottom line is that two separate databases contain the information being requested, and two separate services respond to the client's queries.

When a user creates a new public folder, the location of the contents to be stored within the public folder is determined by the location of the parent folder. If a user is creating a subfolder underneath MANUFACTURING, and MANUFACTURING is stored on the CHICAGO server, then the subfolder will also be stored on the CHICAGO server. This is true no matter where the user's home server is or where the user's public information store is. If the user is creating a top level folder, it is stored on the server identified as the user's public folder server.

Managing Public Folder Size

Now that you know where the actual data is stored, it is important to control the amount of space that data will be allowed to consume on your hard disk. Depending on the folder in question, there are a few options for controlling your public folders. These include storage limits and item expirations.

Public Folders and the GAL

Public folder email addresses are hidden from the global address list (GAL) by default.

Storage Limits

Storage limits for public folders are analogous to storage limits for mailboxes. They are configured generally at the Public Information Store level on a given server and can be overridden at the folder level. For example, if a server is configured to allow folders up to 100MB in size, then the owner of any folder on this Information Store that exceeds 100MB in size will receive a warning message at the next scheduled time. This time is configured on the Information Store Site Configuration Storage Warnings property page.

It has been my experience that folder storage limits are extremely difficult to identify as a Standard Operating Procedure because folders contain such different types of information. As a general rule, I like to assign folder storage limits equal to my user mailbox storage limits for any folders that are managed by individual users. Corporate folders probably should not have storage limits simply due to the nature of the data they must contain.

Remember that, unlike mailboxes, public folders cannot be prevented from sending or receiving mail when the storage limit is exceeded. This is because the prevention of sending and receiving mail will interfere with any replication settings you may have configured. If you simply cannot enable public folder storage limits, consider configuring age limits on items stored within public folders.

You will probably have occasion to allow select folders more space on a given information store than is defined by the general Public Information Store settings. To override the general settings, access the properties of the folder that you want to configure from the Administrator console.

Item Expirations

You will find yourself in situations in which you can't limit the size of a folder, but you can limit the age of items stored in it. This is another way to manage public folder size. Age limits can be set globally per server on the Public Information Store Age Limits tab. Alternatively, you can elect to configure age limits on a given folder replica or on all replicas of a given folder. Age limits for all replicas of a specific folder can also be configured at the folder level by accessing the Limits tab. The purpose of age limits is to expire data from public folders when it has become too old to be of use. This can help you keep your folders at a manageable size by preventing them from maintaining a copy of messages that relate to topics that aren't current.

Age Limits and Replicas

Although age limits can be set for only certain replicas of a public folder, this is a bad practice. It is possible that a given user may access data stored in different replicas of the same folder, and if the age limits vary, the user will not be able to depend on a given level of service. Always configure age limits to be the same for all replicas of a folder.

Suppose James is the owner of the Classifieds public folder that contains postings from users selling things from washing machines to Girl Scout cookies. There is no reason to keep these postings for very long, since it is expected that these items will sell within a reasonable period of time. The administrator of James's Public Information Store configures an age limit of 14 days for items stored in the Classifieds folder. Therefore, if an item hasn't sold within 14 days of posting the sale information, the seller can simply repost to the folder. Obviously, some folders lend themselves to limits, while others do not. I would not implement an age limit policy on a public folder that contains, for example, Standard Operating Procedures or instructional manuals, since I would not expect that data to be obsolete very soon.

The Combined Approach

I recommend using a combination of both storage limits and expirations if possible. The reason for this is that although Exchange performs what Microsoft likes to refer to as online defragmentation, this procedure does not actually reduce the size of the information store. As a result, you will find that your PUB.EDB file grows continuously over time and does not reduce in size when users delete even large amounts of data.

Suppose Mark is the administrator of his company's Exchange organization. He has implemented storage warnings, but not expirations, for his public folders. Andy is the owner of a public folder in the organization that is heavily utilized. Like most folder owners, he doesn't clean it out regularly. Andy receives a storage warning message, so he goes through the folder and deletes all the old and useless messages. This totals 60MB of data. After he is finished, Mark looks at the resource usage for this folder and finds that it has been reduced by 60MB. He then looks at the size of PUB.EDB and finds that it has not been reduced at all. The reason this happens is that Exchange's online defragmentation only frees up space for Exchange to use, not for other applications to use. PUB.EDB now has 60MB of unused space in it that Exchange will utilize. The reason for this is performance. Because Exchange does not have to compact the EDB file when data is deleted and then expand it again when data is added, the database become more efficient. This is a somewhat common database practice, but if your goal is to optimize your server disk usage, this may not be an acceptable scenario.

If Mark had implemented expirations on this public folder, small amounts of data would have been deleted daily, rather than building up to 60MB over time. This would have resulted in significantly less free space available within PUB.EDB, since PUB.EDB would not have grown as quickly. If you find yourself in a situation in which PUB.EDB is very large but you know your users have deleted a considerable amount of data, the utility ESEUTIL can be used to do an offline defragmentation of your information store. ESEUTIL will be discussed further in Chapter 11, "Periodic Proactive Troubleshooting."

Offline Defragmentation
Use EDBUTIL for Exchange versions 4.0 and 5.0.

Public Folder Replication Administration

Now that we know how to manage the size of public folders, let's look at managing replication. There are three main situations that warrant the configuration of public folder replication. These include the following:

- Users need to access public folder data across sites, and you either don't have a permanent connection between sites or don't want to allow dynamic RPC connections across the connection.

- User access of a public folder is causing bottlenecks and performance problems at the folder server.

- Data stored in a public folder is critical to your users' ability to do their jobs. Downtime is not an option.

In each of these situations, it is necessary for you to be able to administer and verify the successful replication of your folders. This includes keeping track of folder and server replication status and public folder resources.

Configuring Replication

A folder can be configured for replication two ways. The first method is to push it onto another server using the folder's Replicas tab. Access the **Replicas** tab from the Exchange Administrator program by opening the public folder's properties. You'll find public folders listed in the public folder hierarchy in the Administrator Program. Alternately, you can pull it onto your server via the Public Information Store Instances tab. After replication is initiated, the Information Store service on the folder's home server will propagate the data stored in the selected folder as email messages addressed to the information store of the replica servers.

The first step you need to take after configuring replication is to verify whether it has taken place at all. The easiest way to do this is to check the public folder resources listing on the replica servers. This list is available by expanding the Public Information Store on the replica server and selecting the phrase **Public Folder Resources**. On the right side of the Administrator console, you will see a list of the display names associated with all public and system folders currently stored on this server. If you do not see the folder that you recently configured to replicate, it has not yet replicated. Unfortunately, there is no way to force replication.

After replication is complete, the folder's display name will show up in the list, along with such information as how much space the folder takes up and how many items are in it. The columns and information displayed can be configured according to your preferences by accessing the **View**, **Columns** menu. While this same information can be viewed by accessing the properties of the Public Information Store and selecting the **Public Folder Resources** tab, I find it easier to use the snapshot view provided in the Administrator Program. Also, there are a number of replication-related counters available in the Performance Monitor. We will be looking at these in Chapter 13, "Troubleshooting Your Exchange Server."

Monitoring Folder Replication

Now that you know replication is configured correctly (because you can see that it happened once) you must monitor it to be sure it continues to happen as scheduled. The easiest way to get a quick view of this is to use the Administrator console. There are two places where you can verify replication:

- At the server
- At the folder

To verify replication of all folders that are managed by a given server, expand the Public Information Store of that server. From here, you can get a view of both Folder Replication Status and Server Replication Status. The Folder Replication Status view can be configured to tell you a number of useful things, such as the last time an update was received and whether the local copy has been modified. If the local copy of the folder has been modified but the update has not been replicated yet, the Status column will reflect the term Local Modified; otherwise, it will read In Sync. The Server Replication Status view will allow you to compare the status of all servers that maintain folder replicas. Information that you will find in this view includes the following:

- The name of each server that maintains a Public Information Store
- The replication status
- The last time an update was received by the local server from the highlighted server
- The average amount of time it takes to send updates from the local server to the highlighted server
- The amount of time it took to transmit the last update sent from the local server to the highlighted server

You might also elect to check replication of specific folders by viewing the properties of the folder in question. The Folder Replication Status property page gives a list of all servers that maintain replicas of this specific folder, along with the replication status and last and average transmission times.

I find that it is preferable to administer replication from the server level because you can get a quick view of whether the entire Public Information Store is replicating correctly. If it appears that replication of your local store is not working, take a look at the Folder Replication Status view of your server. From this view, you can tell which folder may be having a problem. The last place to look is the actual folder's replication status pages.

Refresh the Data Displayed in the Administrator Program

Because the Administrator Program will have a short delay in the display of recent updates to your replication schedule, you should access the Public Information Store's Replication Status tabs to refresh the view.

In addition to verifying replication on an ad-hoc basis, you can also configure diagnostics logging to log events to the Event Viewer, where you can then use Crystal Reports to compile and display the data. Two of the most useful counters allow you to log non-delivery reports and miscellaneous replication errors. We will be looking at diagnostics logging in more detail in Chapter 13.

The Backfill Process

If there is a problem when you are replicating, Exchange has a fail-safe mechanism called *backfill* that it uses to correct the out-of-sync public folders. This is necessary because replication messages are generated and sent out without the prior knowledge of the receiving server. In other words, one public information store does not know if or when an update will be sent from another information store because updates are generated and sent only when a change has been made. To compensate for this, Exchange uses status messages to keep up to date. Every server that maintains public folder replicas sends a status message to every other server in your organization that maintains replicas of the same public folders. The status message is generated every 24 hours.

Status messages are designed and implemented to help you keep your folders synchronized. In an organization that maintains four public information stores that replicate the same folders, status messages are generated, as shown in Figure 3.2. You can see that all information stores are sending status messages to all other information stores.

Status Message Hell

In certain cases, status messages can cause serious problems. I remember one customer I worked with had been advised by a previous consultant to install Exchange into a single site in which the servers in the site were all across very slow, non-permanent links (i.e., RAS connection) to a hub server. (Obviously, this was a terrible design, but they didn't plan to change their environment.) They were experiencing message delivery problems as a result of status messages. Every server in their site maintained a copy of a series of public folders, but changes were allowed only at the hub server. Because changes were allowed only at the hub server, status messages between all servers were not necessary. However, status messages *were* being sent between all servers.

This site had 20 servers maintaining public folders. Each of these 20 servers was generating a status message to the remaining 19 servers. Therefore, every night 380 status messages were being sent across these slow links, effectively causing the user messages to be blocked and resulting in a lot of angry customers. The solution to this problem was to edit the Registry. See Appendix B, "Exchange Registry Tuning," for more information about Exchange Registry edits.

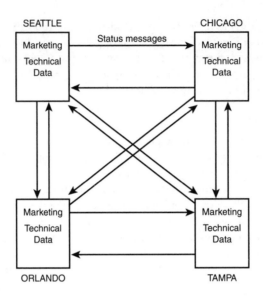

Figure 3.2 Status messages can quickly overwhelm an already busy network.

Suppose CHICAGO has not received any public folder updates during the last 24 hours due to a network problem. CHICAGO has no way to know that it didn't receive the update because it did not request the update. CHICAGO will receive a status message from SEATTLE, ORLANDO, and TAMPA indicating their current information store change numbers. CHICAGO will compare those change numbers with its locally stored change number information and determine that it missed some data. CHICAGO will request the changed information from whichever information store transferred the data quickest during the last successful update.

Conflict Management

A conflict is when the same message on two different message stores is changed during a single replication cycle. Hence, there are two different copies of the same message. You can expect that any replicated folder that allows users to change its contents or properties will occasionally experience conflicts. There are two types of conflicts to be aware of: content conflicts and administrative conflicts.

Content Conflicts

The public folder strategy implemented in Exchange is termed "multi-master". What this means is that, unlike the security account database in NT, data can be created, removed, or changed from any server maintaining the public folder, and that the change actually occurs in the local `PUB.EDB` file. Because each folder ultimately is supposed to contain the exact same data (as an exact replica), *content conflicts* can occur if users with edit permissions access public folder data stored on different servers. Content conflicts happen only in scenarios such as the following:

1. The Publishing folder is maintained on servers ORLANDO and CHICAGO.

2. Amy is a user on the ORLANDO server with edit permissions on the Publishing folder.

3. Leah is a user on the CHICAGO server with edit permissions on the Publishing folder.

4. Both Amy and Leah make a change to the same document during the same replication cycle.

Because Amy edits documents on the ORLANDO server and Leah edits documents on the CHICAGO server, the document each of them edited is in conflict. This is true only because replication did not have a chance to take place. Part of your implementation of public folders should include a stage at which you evaluate both the necessity of replication and the times at which it is appropriate to replicate public folders. The idea is to optimize the schedule so that conflicts rarely happen. In any event, conflicts most certainly will happen anyway, so you need to know how to deal with them.

Fortunately, Exchange will notice the conflict during the next scheduled replication cycle. A conflict message will be generated and sent to the users that created the conflict and to anyone with Folder contact permissions on the folder (usually the folder's owner). The conflict can be resolved by manually combining the information from the conflicting messages into a single message and choosing the **Keep This Item** button, or by keeping all conflicting messages as separate documents by choosing **Keep All**. Exchange cannot merge the documents together for you.

Same Server "Conflicts"

Two users editing the same document on the same server are not technically generating a conflict. When this happens, the user that saves their change last will overwrite any changes the first user made to the document.

Effects of Age Limits on Replication

Items that are expired out of one server but not out of another (due to asynchronous age limits) are not considered changed items for purposes of replication. It is for this reason that replicas of the same public folder can conceivably have different amounts of data in them.

Folder Design Conflicts

A *folder design conflict* happens whenever two or more people change the properties or
design of the same public folder before the changes have a chance to replicate to the
other public information stores. This change could be an edit to the permissions list,
folder assistant, or any other property that is managed from the client. Exchange will
make note of the design conflict and send an email message to anyone with Folder
contact permissions on the folder. Unfortunately, the notification just alerts the contacts to the fact that there was a design conflict—not to what the conflict was.
Although Exchange will automatically resolve the conflict by incorporating the last
saved changes, it really is up to the folder contacts to determine a solution to the
design conflict and to implement the solution manually. In other words, Exchange will
not merge the designs together, so if the folder contacts want all changes to be effective, they will have to resolve the conflict manually.

System Folder Issues

System folders are public folders that are created and used by the system. In this section, we will discuss issues surrounding the Free and Busy folder, the Events folder,
and the Organizational Forms folder. Specifically, we will look at what these folders
are for, where they are stored, and how to optimize them.

Free and Busy Folder

Calendar data is stored in a system folder assigned the X.500 name of your site.
Properties of this folder are accessed from the Administrator console by expanding
System Folders and then expanding SCHEDULE+ FREE BUSY. You will see one
Free and Busy folder for each site in your organization. The default for Exchange is
for all users to store three months of free and busy information in this shared system
folder so that their schedule can be used for meeting arrangements.

When you access the properties of the Free and Busy folder for your site, you will
notice at the bottom of the page which server is acting as the home server for this
folder. The default is the first server in your site, but you may need to change this. A
symptom of a poorly designed Free/Busy scenario is poor server performance first
thing in the morning when everyone is bringing up the Outlook client. Outlook creates a session with this system folder as part of its startup sequence.

You will notice that most people access their calendars when they first get to work
in the morning. This traffic can have a considerable detrimental effect on the server
that maintains the Free/Busy data, particularly if the server in question also houses
user mailboxes. Your users will notice this performance problem and complain about
it. You can correct it by moving the Free/Busy folder to a server that is less heavily

utilized. Better yet, move this folder to a dedicated public folder server. Moving a system folder is as simple as moving a public folder. Simply replicate the folder to the new server, verify that it replicated, and remove it from the original server.

Free and Busy Folder Optimization

Your clients will always connect to folders in a given sequence: Public Folder Server, Home Server, Random Site Servers, Servers in other sites via affinity. As a result, you can improve client performance by placing folders where your clients will access them first. The default server for a client's Public Folder Server is his Home Server. By replicating the Free and Busy folder to other servers in your site, clients will connect to the folder that is closest to them first. For example, Lyle's mailbox is on the SEATTLE server. The SEATTLE server is also Lyle's Public Folder Server. The first server in Lyle's site is actually the REDMOND server, accessible via a T1 connection.

By default, when Lyle opens his Outlook client, he accesses the Free and Busy data on the REDMOND server. Because everyone on the SEATTLE server is accessing their schedules the same way, performance is slow. The administrator of this environment could achieve considerable performance improvements by replicating the Free and Busy folder to the SEATTLE server. The drawbacks include a delay for schedules being updated on the replicas and bandwidth consumption due to replication, but the benefit of better connection speed is probably worth the drawbacks.

Client Version Issues

In addition to the calendar folder's location, you may find yourself having problems if you don't have a standard client implemented in your environment. For example, if you are coexisting with MS Mail clients using Schedule+ version 1.0, your users will be able to invite each other to meetings. However, Schedule+ 1.0 users will not be able to interpret fields such as meeting locations or be able to see that the meeting will be recurring on a regular basis. Other data that does not map correctly includes Outlook's ability to identify meetings as tentative and to block out of office times. Schedule+ 1.0 users will view tentatively scheduled times as free, and will view out of office times as busy.

You will also find that although Schedule+ 1.0 users can open each other's calendars, they cannot open the calendars of your Outlook users. Schedule+ 95 Windows clients can download an additional driver from Microsoft to allow them to open Outlook calendars (Macintosh clients are not supported for this feature). Outlook users are able to open both Schedule+ 1.0 and Schedule+ 95 calendars without problems.

For example, suppose Chris uses Outlook, Barb and Frank both use Schedule+ 1.0, and Peter uses Schedule+ 95 with the updated driver. Chris can see everybody's calendars. Barb and Frank can see only each other's calendars, and Peter can see Chris' calendar.

For more information about interoperability, see the Microsoft white paper entitled "MS Outlook 97 and 98 Interoperability with: MS Exchange Client, MS Mail 3.x, MS Schedule+ 95, MS Schedule+ 1.0."

Events Folder

Like the Free and Busy folder, the Events folder is maintained by the system. The difference is that it is used to store scripts. Visual Basic scripts can be created from the Outlook client and stored in the appropriate Events Root folder. They can be run when certain events occur in public folders and mailboxes. The Events Root folder is located within the System Folders container. It displays an object for every server in your organization that has the Exchange Event Service installed. These objects will be named `EventConfig_servername,` in which `servername` is the name of the corresponding server. The catch is that the script must be available to the mailbox or folder in which it is supposed to run.

For example, a script installed on a server in the North America site that is configured to run when an event occurs in the Human Resources folder will not run on a replica of the folder on a server in the South America site . This is because the Events folder contents are not available across site connections by default. To enable the event across sites, replicate the folder to a server in the site where you want the script to run, or configure an affinity between the sites. The same is true for mailboxes. If you create a script to run against certain mailboxes, performance is best if the script is installed on the server on which the mailboxes are homed.

You may have trouble with scripts if you don't implement them in a manner consistent with Microsoft recommendations. By this, I mean that scripts are intended to perform duties triggered by public folder and mailbox events periodically—not constantly. They are not a substitute for the Inbox Assistant feature in Outlook. If you attempt to create and run a script that is supposed to process every incoming message, you will find that the script misses a few. This is because the Event Service simply is not designed to handle a large load of incoming messages. Exchange is multithreaded such that messages can be incoming on more than one thread. When this happens, the Event Service may miss messages being delivered by the additional threads.

Organizational Forms Folder

In addition to Free and Busy and Events folders, another system folder you may need to administer is the Organizational Forms folder. You will not have an Organizational Forms folder unless you manually created one—this folder is not created by default. You can use this folder to hold forms that you want to make available to users in your organization. The default location for this folder is on the first server installed in the site. To verify this, expand System Folders and expand EFORMS REGISTRY. The Organizational Forms folder will be listed in this container. To change the location of the Organizational Forms folder, replicate the folder to the appropriate server, verify that it replicated, and remove it from the original server.

Event Script Security

Scripts use the Exchange service account security context during run time. Because the service account has permission to perform virtually any task on your Exchange server, you should carefully consider who will be allowed to create the scripts that will be stored in the Events folder.

Although this folder is intended to contain forms with organization-wide availability, it will not be available across site boundaries by default. To allow users to access the forms contained in it regardless of what site they are in, I recommend replicating the folder to each site. You could allow access to it via Public Folder affinity as well, but you can't limit access across sites to specific folders or users using Public Folder affinity. You will also gain a performance improvement by replicating this folder; data will be available on a user's local area network as opposed to across a WAN link. Typically, content in this folder is not dynamic (forms are not being constantly tweaked), so replication overhead should be minimal.

Newsgroup Issues

In addition to public folders your users create and those your system uses, you may need to administer public folders created as a result of newsgroup configuration. Any time you configure a newsfeed to bring newsgroups into your Exchange Organization, Exchange creates a public folder to correspond with each newsgroup. In this section, we will discuss administration of push and pull feeds, management of the folders containing newsgroup messages, and how to deal with newsfeed control messages.

Push Versus Pull Feeds

A *push feed* is initiated by your ISP, whereas a *pull feed* is initiated by your Exchange server. It is my experience that push feeds are far more common than pull feeds because generally the ISP administrator needs to retain control over this type of traffic and resource usage.

Because the ISP is initiating the connection for a push feed, the Internet News Service (INS) does not play a significant role. The primary job of the INS in push feeds is to send out any changes to the newsgroups that originated within the Exchange organization.

Organizational Forms Library Permissions

The default permission on the Organizational Forms library is simply Reviewer. This means that, initially, no one will be able to store forms in the library. Change the client permissions on this folder to Owner for users who will be responsible for creating the forms that will be used organization-wide, but leave the default permission as Reviewer so that users can download forms.

Publishing Forms

Forms are created and published from within the client. In Outlook98, access the **Tools, Forms, Design a Form** menu option to create a form from scratch. After you've finished the design, use the **Tools, Forms, Publish Form** option from within the Form Designer window to publish the form in the Organizational Forms library.

Pull feeds are managed solely by the Exchange INS. The INS connects to the news server and downloads all data that has changed since the last download. Exchange maintains the news server's system time locally for comparison during subsequent downloads.

Newsgroup Management

Newsgroup management is not really any different from public folder management. The only real difference is that data in newsgroups always expires. The default age limit for a newsgroup is seven days, although this is easily changed on the age limits properties for any newsgroup public folder. Age limits were discussed earlier in this chapter.

In addition to general public folder administration duties and managing control messages (discussed in the next section), there is one other administrative duty you are likely to have. This is backfilling newsfeeds, a procedure that you should not need to do very often. *Backfilling* a newsfeed allows you to download messages that are older than the last time you connected to the news server. You may need to do this if you have had trouble with your newsfeed and were forced to use the Mark All As Delivered button on the newsfeed's Advanced property page. You can use the utility INSTIMES to reset the time stored on the local Exchange server to a time corresponding with when you want messages to be downloaded from.

Newsfeed Control Messages

Whenever a group is added or removed from a newsfeed, or a user deletes a previously posted message from a newsgroup, the news server generates a control message. These messages accumulate in the NNTP Site properties object on the Control Messages property page. It is up to you to go in there and either accept or delete these messages. Exchange can only process the acceptance of control messages generated as a result of a user deleting a previously posted document (Cancel). Acceptance of add group (NEWGROUP) or remove group (RMGROUP) control messages does not cause Exchange to add or remove public folders or reconfigure the newsfeed.

If you really want to add or remove a group from your newsfeed, you need to work with your service provider. Additionally, Exchange does not generate NEWGROUP or RMGROUP control messages, although it does generate Cancel messages. This means that any folders that you have set up to export or import to a newsfeed as newsgroups must be added to or removed from the newsfeed using the newsfeed's properties in cooperation with your ISP.

Summary

This concludes our discussion of public folder administration. You should now be familiar with the types of daily tasks necessary to maintain public folders in your organization. The next chapter will focus on managing Exchange's native and foreign messaging queues.

4

Queue Management

NOW THAT WE KNOW HOW TO manage recipients such as mailboxes, distribution lists, and public folders, it is time to look at some of the administration required "behind the scenes." This chapter will address the tasks necessary to maintain message transport in your organization by delving into the different messaging queues Exchange uses as mail holding points. These queues include MTA queues, IMS queues, MS Mail queues and queues created by third-party connector installations. We'll also take a look at performance monitoring and message tracking because these areas are so helpful when managing queues.

MTA Queues

The Exchange Message Transfer Agent (MTA) service is installed on every Exchange server in your organization during Exchange setup. This service is responsible for all message transfer between Exchange servers within the organization, as well as transfer to foreign X.400 connectors and MS Mail connectors. The MTA is X.400 compliant, which means that it natively supports connections to foreign X.400 systems in addition to supporting internal connections and connections to remote sites via Site Connectors.

All queues managed by a given MTA are found on the MTA object in the Administrator console. To locate this object, perform the following steps:

1. Expand the site container in which the server is defined.

2. Expand the configuration container for that site.

3. Expand the servers container.

4. Select the name of the server that manages the queue you want to check.

On the right side of the console you will find the Message Transfer Agent object for the selected server. When you go into the Properties dialog box, a series of tabs are displayed. The Queues tab, shown in Figure 4.1, displays all queues that are current for this MTA.

From the Queues tab you can view the status of messages being held by the MTA for the Private and Public Information Stores, X.400 connectors, and MS Mail connectors. You can also view server objects in the same site or in other sites accessible via site connectors, as well as delete items from the queue or reprioritize them.

Although Exchange takes measures to prevent corrupted messages from stopping up your queue, you should take a look at your queues regularly to be sure there isn't something stuck in there. I have been to sites where the local administrators don't bother to check the queues regularly and found all sorts of undelivered messages there. The point of checking the queue is to identify corrupt messages as well as identify the cause of the message corruption. Most companies I've worked for did not need to look at them more often than once or twice a day, as long as their networks were not experiencing any problems. The best thing to do, in my opinion, is to configure Performance Monitor logging and then set up alerts to notify you when certain parameters are exceeded. You will most likely find that after your alerts are configured correctly, your Exchange Administrator will know of a WAN outage before your network administrator does. Through troubleshooting steps it is relatively easy to determine what the problem is. Troubleshooting and performance monitoring will be covered in more detail in Chapter 13, "Troubleshooting Your Exchange Server".

Performance Monitor Counters for Site and X.400 Queues

The NT Performance Monitor is a great tool to use to keep track of your queue status. Microsoft also created several handy real-time Performance Monitor charts to use to keep track of your Exchange server. Use the Server Queues chart located in the Microsoft Exchange program group to get a quick, real-time view of your MTA queues. The *Server Queues chart* is a histogram chart that gives the current status of your server's queues. You will see the Work Queue Length for the MTA as a whole, in addition to the Send and Receive Queue Size for the Public and Private Information Stores. Additionally, the Performance Monitor objects MSExchangeMTA and MSExchangeMTA Connections both have a number of useful counters if you are interested in generating your own custom charts from your server data. These objects allow you to track MTA performance for all your site connectors, X.400 connectors, and queues the MTA maintains for in-site communication. We will be looking at Performance Monitor counters and pre-configured charts in Chapter 13.

My recommendation is to use real-time charting only when necessary. As a rule, it is better to create log files of your data and display the data off-line rather than leave a chart running all the time. You can optimize your logging by setting an update interval of no less than 120 seconds (no need to overwhelm your system with a bunch of useless logging or oversized log files). Increase the frequency of logging only when you are troubleshooting a specific problem. By doing this, you save yourself the overhead of drawing the chart on your system, and you also get a log file of more data counters than you think you need. Oftentimes, it is the data that you didn't even think you needed that hold the key to problems you may be experiencing.

I also recommend using Performance Monitor's Alert capability. After you decide what is an acceptable level of performance for your server, create alerts that fire off when your expectations are not being met. Hopefully, you will be able to head off a problem before it becomes a catastrophe as a result of your system's quick notification to you that something has gone awry.

Configuring Message Tracking

In addition to tracking system performance, most companies will find it a good idea to configure message tracking. This way, when a message appears to be lost, you can figure out where it got stuck. By default, Exchange will not do any message tracking at all.

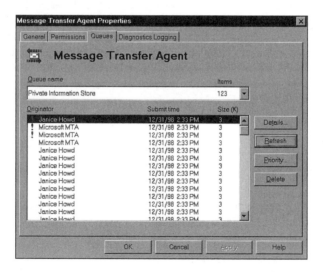

Figure 4.1 Use the MTA Queues tab to determine whether there are messages stuck in the queues.

Message tracking for all messages generated, transferred, or received by Exchange needs to be configured in at least two places. The first is on the Information Store Site Configuration object and the second is on the MTA Site Configuration object. In both of these locations, you will find a check box on the lower left portion of the General tab labeled Enable message tracking. Select this box to start tracking.

Enabling tracking at the Information Store level causes Exchange to track every message generated or received by any native Exchange user within that site, even if the message is destined for another user on the same home server. Additionally, enabling tracking at the MTA level causes Exchange to track all messages passed between servers. Both levels are necessary for full tracking to be enabled within a site, and you don't have to stop and restart either the MTA or Information Store services to get tracking to start. For full tracking in your organization, you may need to track at connector levels as well. Connector tracking will be discussed in the "Configuring SMTP Message Tracking" and "Configuring MS Mail Message Tracking" sections later in this chapter.

Message tracking logs are created and maintained by the System Attendant service of the server handling the message. As a result, you will find evidence of a message being transferred distributed across multiple servers in your environment. For example, a message generated on the CHICAGO server that is sent to a recipient on the ORLANDO server will be logged to the tracking logs on both CHICAGO and ORLANDO. These logs are stored by default in the \EXCHSRVR\TRACKING.LOG directory on the local hard drive of the appropriate server. A log file for each day that an event triggers an entry to be written to the log is created. This log file contains every event generated by every tracked service, not just MTA related events. The filename for log files is MMDDYYYY.LOG, such that a file created on October 28, 1998 is named 10281998.LOG. We will be looking at how to track a message in Chapter 13.

Disabling Message Tracking on Individual Servers

IS message tracking can be disabled on individual servers in an Exchange site by adding a Registry key of

```
Value: X.400 Service Event Log
Data Type: REG_DWORD
String: 0
```

to

```
HKEY_LOCAL_MACHINE\SYSTEM\CurrentControlSet\Services
\MSExchangeIS\Parameters\Private
```

To disable MTA message tracking for individual servers, add the key

```
Value: X.400 Service Event Log
Data Type:  REG_DWORD
String: 0
```

to

```
HKEY_LOCAL_MACHINE\SYSTEM\CurrentControlSet\Services
\MSExchangeMTA\Parameters
```

IMS Queues

In addition to keeping track of your native Exchange queues, you will probably need to deal with at least one additional connector queue. Because the Internet Mail Service (IMS) is necessary to facilitate the transfer of messages between your Exchange users and foreign SMTP users (in addition to potentially backboning two sites together across the Internet), the IMS queue is the connector queue you will most likely need to manage. The Exchange IMS queue is created during installation of the Internet Mail Service using the wizard found in the Exchange Administrator console.

Unlike the MTA queues, you will find that all connector queues are defined at the site level in the Administrator console. Expand the site that holds the IMS you want to view, expand the configuration container, and select the connections container. On the right side of the screen you will see one object for each Internet Mail Service defined in your site. In parentheses at the end of the display name, you will see the name of the server that is actually responsible for the IMS connector. This will help you determine on which server you should configure monitoring or diagnostics logging, as well as on which server your SMTP message tracking logs are being maintained. To locate the IMS queues, perform the following steps:

1. Expand the site container in which the IMS is defined.

2. Expand the configuration container for that site.

3. Expand the connections container.

4. Select the name of the IMS that you want to check.

The Queues tab allows you to view one of four queues:

- Outbound messages awaiting delivery

- Outbound messages awaiting conversion

- Inbound messages awaiting delivery

- Inbound messages awaiting conversion

Unfortunately, this queue tab is a little different from the MTA queue tab in that a total for the number of messages stuck in each queue is not displayed along with the queue name. This makes it a little inconvenient because you need to actually select each queue in order to find out what is currently in it, as opposed to the MTA queue, which summarizes for you in the queue drop-down list. After you have selected a queue from the IMS queues list, you can cancel the delivery of a given message or force the IMS to retry delivery immediately. Messages stuck in various queues indicate different potential problems with your Exchange server, as you can see in Table 4.1.

Tracking.Log Share Permissions

Due to the way message tracking is performed within Exchange, it is important to not alter the share permissions on the `tracking.log` directory on your Exchange servers. If the share permissions are altered, you may inadvertently prevent message tracking queries from being processed correctly.

Table 4.1 **Identifying Queue Problems**

Symptom	Possible Cause
Inbound messages awaiting delivery	MTA problem. The Exchange MTA needs to route messages from the IMS to the correct home server. If the MTA is stopped, mail will queue up until you restart the MTA service. This queue is actually MTS-IN and is located in the Information Store.
Outbound messages awaiting delivery	SMTP problem such as a failed connection to the Internet or difficulty resolving an IP address. Since this queue is actually part of the file system in `EXCHSRVR\IMCDATA\OUT` and not really managed by Exchange, messages stuck in this queue generally remain stuck until the time-out period has expired. After the time-out period, the messages are returned to the sender.
Inbound messages awaiting conversion	Information Store corruption or service problem, or IMAIL process problem. This queue is actually part of the file system and can be seen in `EXCHSRVR\IMCDATA\IN`.
Outbound messages awaiting conversion	Information Store corruption or service problem, or IMAIL process problem. This queue is actually MTS-OUT and is located in the Information Store.

Messages coming into your organization from the Internet are first received in the `EXCHSRVR\IMCDATA\IN` directory as part of your file system. The IMAIL process runs and converts the message content to MDBEF format, and the message is then moved to the MTS-IN queue in the Information Store. From MTS-IN, the Exchange MTA picks up the message, evaluates routing, and delivers the message appropriately. Similarly, messages leaving your organization destined for an Internet SMTP recipient are routed by the Exchange MTA to the MTS-OUT queue of the Information Store on the server that runs the IMS. IMAIL runs to convert the content to SMTP format and the message is moved to the `EXCHSRVR\IMCDATA\OUT` directory as part of your file system. Because problems can occur in so many different areas, you should consider using Performance Monitor to help you head them off. Let's take a look now at using the Performance Monitor and message tracking to manage your IMS.

The IMAIL Process

The IMAIL process, which runs in your Information Store, converts message content and encrypts attachments. If this process fails, message content can't be converted and the messages won't move to the delivery queues.

Performance Monitor Counters

In addition to checking the queues from the Administrator program, you may wish to keep track of your IMS using the Performance Monitor. The IMS has a separate set of objects that are used for this function, in addition to a set of preconfigured charts. Take a look in the Microsoft Exchange program group and open the IMS Queues chart. This chart displays four useful bits of information:

- The number of messages currently queued inbound to be processed for users in your Exchange organization
- The number of messages to be delivered to users on the local server inbound from the IMS
- The number of messages queued to be converted to Internet Mail format by the IMAIL process
- The number of messages that are in the queue awaiting delivery to Internet users

The information you collect using the Performance Monitor should be used to identify performance thresholds so that you can plan for growth when those thresholds are exceeded. Growth with the IMS generally entails the creation of a dedicated connector server to run the IMS.

Performance Thresholds

You need to determine what acceptable performance thresholds for these counters are. I have seen high security environments decide that a slow IMS is acceptable in exchange for certain ESMTP functionality, such as recipient verification or "anti-spam" processing. In general, if it appears that the number of messages queued inbound is increasing rather than decreasing or staying the same, you probably need to offload some of the IMS processing to another Exchange server. My recommendation in this area is that you run Performance Monitor to create a baseline during your highest traffic time period during the day for several days. Use the information gleaned from this baseline log to determine what your environment's thresholds should be.

Adding a Dedicated Connector Server

If you find that the local users are receiving more email than predicted, you may decide to add a dedicated connector server so that user messaging performance is not being affected by SMTP processing. This is also a good solution if the IMAIL process is lagging.

A nice bonus to dedicating a server to connector processing is that your users' regular messaging functionality will not be interrupted by problems with the connector server. Additionally, you can monitor the number of messages incoming and outgoing to determine the growth requirements of your network and approximate when it will be appropriate to scale your messaging system by adding a connector server. For example, suppose you notice that your incoming and outgoing message transfers regularly exceed your baseline values at the same time that your users complain of slow access to the server. You might consider adding a connector server. There are several counters on the `MSExchangeIMC` object that we will be exploring further in Chapter 13. We will be discussing the IMS-specific preconfigured charts at that time. If you do decide to reconfigure a server to be dedicated to IMS, don't forget to run the Performance Optimizer to allow Exchange to reallocate your server's resources correctly. Performance Optimizer will be discussed further in Chapter 8, "Managing Server Resources."

Configuring SMTP Message Tracking

In addition to watching the actual performance of your IMS, you will probably need to track the successful processing of messages your users send to Internet recipients. This can be helpful when troubleshooting because message tracking can lead you to find the point at which the transmission is failing. Exchange can allow you to track the creation and transmission of SMTP messages up to and including the point at which the message exits or enters your Exchange organization. In other words, Exchange can't track a message after it leaves or before it enters your organization. Enabling message tracking on the IMS allows Exchange to determine whether a message has been successfully handed off to the IMS, successfully processed, and successfully transferred into or out of your organization.

Message tracking for the IMS is not enabled by default. To enable it, get the properties of each IMS you want to configure for message tracking. On the Internet Mail tab, you will see a check box on the bottom left corner of the page that reads Enable message tracking. Check this box and then stop and restart the IMS to begin tracking messages processed by the IMS. Message tracking will be logged to the same tracking log files discussed earlier in this chapter. We will look at how to track a message that has been logged in Chapter 13.

MS Mail Queues

In addition to keeping track of your IMS queues, you also may need to keep track of MS Mail queues if you are coexisting with an MS Mail environment. This involves not only keeping an eye on a number of queues, but also using the Performance Monitor and Message Tracking to be kept abreast of message transfer problems. The Exchange Microsoft Mail Connector (MSMC) is installed during setup if you select the Complete/Custom option and choose to install it. It is necessary only if you have a need to coexist with an existing Microsoft Mail installation. The MSMC was the first connector created to connect an Exchange server to a foreign system, and as such was not created using the Exchange Development Kit (the EDK wasn't available at the time). As a result, the MSMC's architecture is different from that of any other connector, and the queues that it uses are different from any other connector queues.

The MSMC works as follows:

- Messages sent from MS Mail users to Exchange users are routed to the MS Mail MTA (frequently called PC MTA). The MS Mail MTA hands them off to the Exchange shadow post office, where the Microsoft Mail Connector Interchange picks them up and hands them to the Exchange MTA. The Exchange MTA then routes them to the correct location within the Exchange organization:

    ```
    Exchange MTA <-> MSCI <->Shadow PO <-> PCMTA
    ```

- Messages sent from Exchange users to MS Mail users are routed to the shadow post office by the Exchange MTA. From the shadow post office, the PC MTA picks them up and forwards them to the correct MS Mail post office.

As a result of this process, there are several places that a message could get stuck. These include Exchange's MTA queue, Exchange's MSMC queue, and MS Mail queues.

Exchange Queues

The native Exchange queues to be concerned with are the MSMC queue and the MTA queue we discussed earlier in this chapter. The MSMC queue lists messages that are awaiting routing from the shadow post office defined on the Exchange server that manages the connector.

The MSMC queue is accessible from the MSMC object in your site's configuration container. You will find a tab named Connections that identifies all MS Mail post offices that your Exchange organization communicates with. Select one of the listed post offices and choose the **Queue** button to view messages awaiting delivery to the selected post office. You can also delete or return messages to the originator from the queue window in the event a user mistakenly sends a message that they subsequently wish to recall. Optionally, you can elect to use the MS Mail Administrator to view the queue of your Exchange server's shadow post office, because the Exchange shadow post office is actually an MS Mail post office. I personally would not administer the shadow post office using the MS Mail Administrator because it really is not necessary and requires additional actions on your part.

Best Queue Monitoring Practices

For best functionality and performance, use Performance Monitor logging rather than chart mode to configure and start log files. Also, take advantage of Performance Monitor's alert features to monitor your queues.

Using the MS Mail MTA with Exchange

The MS Mail MTA is used to route messages between two or more MS Mail post offices. One of the first things this MTA does when connecting to a remote post office is check for a unique post office ID number. Because all Exchange shadow post offices have the same post office ID number, the MS Mail MTA cannot be used to connect to more than a single Exchange shadow post office.

You may also find messages destined for your MSMC stuck in your native Exchange MTA queue. This can happen if there is a routing problem to the server that manages the MSMC. Only you can decide what is an acceptable delay for messages to be routed between your Exchange and MS Mail networks, since this is largely dependent on the type of network defined. The best thing to do is monitor this over time to create a baseline value. Significant deviations from this baseline could indicate a problem. Use Performance Monitor to monitor the status of your MSMC functionality in addition to your internal MTA functionality.

PC MTA Queues

When configuring the MSMC, you can elect to either use Exchange's PC MTA service (configured from within the MSMC) or continue to use the MS Mail MTA that has been routing mail for your existing MS Mail network. Both of these MTAs have the same functionality, although the older MS Mail MTA is not supported by Microsoft because it was not fully lab-tested as the routing component between Exchange and MS Mail. The job of both MTAs is to poll the appropriate MS Mail post offices for mail that is being sent to other post offices. If the PC MTA is not configured correctly, you will find that messages remain in the queues on your MS Mail post offices or in your shadow post office.

There is no single location to find messages stuck in PC MTA queues. Depending on how your MS Mail network is set up to route mail, you may need to check the queues of multiple MS Mail post offices to locate a stuck message. To open an MS Mail queue, use the MS Mail Administrator that you normally use to administer your MS Mail network. The Exchange Administrator program cannot be used to view a queue on a foreign system.

Performance Monitor Counters

Monitoring of both Exchange and PC MTA queues for the MSMC is advisable, as is monitoring of your other connectors. You will notice in the Performance Monitor that there are loads of MS Mail Connector-specific counters. There are two objects in addition to the Exchange MTA object to be aware of: MSExchangeMSMI and MSExchangePCMTA. You will also notice that there are no MSMC-specific preconfigured charts, so I will give you a few guidelines on what to monitor.

PC MTA vs. MS Mail MTA

Exchange ships with an updated version of the MS Mail MTA, frequently referred to as the PC MTA. This updated version is more reliable, more efficient, and can handle more traffic than the MS Mail MTA. In fact, the benefits are so significant that it is worth considering including Exchange as the MS Mail hub post office even in environments where you will not be migrating to Exchange.

Definitely monitor the Messages Received counter on the `MSExchangeMSMI` object (selected by default when you open this object). This counter will tell you the number of messages received by the MSMC from MS Mail since the MSMC service was started. You probably have a problem if you notice that the number is not growing, which would indicate that no mail is being transferred in.

Also consider monitoring the `MSExchangePCMTA` file contentions/hour and LAN/WAN messages moved/hour. A high number of file contentions indicates you may have a file locking problem or an overloaded post office. Use the LAN/WAN messages moved/hour to keep track of the average traffic passed between Exchange and MS Mail users. My experience is that this number should be fairly consistent. If the number of messages being moved per hour drops significantly from the norm, you probably have a network problem preventing mail from routing correctly.

Configuring MSMail Message Tracking

Monitoring connector performance with the Performance Monitor tool is useful for identifying network problems and performance bottlenecks, but it cannot be used to track problems with individual messages. As with other foreign connectors, you will probably occasionally need to track the successful processing and transfer of messages your users send to MS Mail recipients. As with the IMS, Exchange can allow you to track the creation and transmission of messages sent to and received from MS Mail recipients up to and including the point at which the message either exits or enters your Exchange organization. Exchange has no authority or ability to track a message after it leaves your organization or before it enters your organization. Enabling message tracking on the MSMC allows Exchange to determine several factors, including the following:

- Whether a message has been successfully transferred to or from the MSMC.
- Whether a message has been processed correctly.
- Whether a message has been successfully transferred into or out of your organization.

Again, message tracking for the MSMC is not enabled by default. To enable it, get the properties of each MSMC you want to configure for message tracking. On the Interchange tab you will see a check box near the bottom left portion of the page that reads Enable message tracking. Check this box and then stop and restart the MSMC to begin tracking messages processed by the MSMC.

Third-Party Connector Queues

You will need to manage queues for any third-party connectors you have installed in your Exchange Organization. Third-party connectors can be installed in a number of ways. The cc:Mail connector is installed during Exchange setup if you choose to do a Complete/Custom installation and select it. Other connectors that ship with

Exchange are the Lotus Notes connector, OV/VM connector, and SNADS connector. These are installed by running a separate setup utility off the Exchange installation CD. Custom connectors can also be created using the Exchange Development Kit.

Any third-party connector you purchase, develop, or install from the Exchange installation CD will have been created using the Exchange Development Kit. As a result, the architecture for their communication with the Exchange server will be consistent with that of the IMS. This means that messages to be sent to the foreign system will be stored in a queue maintained by the Information Store of the server on which the connector is configured. The Information Store maintains two queues for each foreign connector, which are called MTS-IN and MTS-OUT. MTS-IN contains data inbound to Exchange from the foreign host and MTS-OUT contains data outbound to the foreign host from Exchange. You can view both of these queues from within the Exchange Administrator console.

To view the queues for these connectors, access the connector's properties from within the Exchange Configuration container (the same place you found IMS and MSMC objects). The Queues tab will display the data in the MTS-IN and MTS-OUT folders for the selected connector. If you have message transport problems outside of Exchange—that is, if messages are getting stuck in queues managed by the foreign system—you will have to use whatever tools that system provides for you to find the message in the queue.

Summary

Queue management is something that you will need to do every day. I recommend using the Performance Monitor to create log files of your connector performance that can be viewed at a later time, in addition to creating Performance Monitor Alerts. In order to best serve your clients, you need to determine what are acceptable thresholds for your Exchange server's performance based on actual current message transport data. Use these thresholds to define your Alerts and to plan for future scaling of your organization. With properly defined thresholds and Alerts, you will be better positioned to address both valid and invalid user concerns. You will also be able to preventatively administer your messaging system.

In addition to managing your server's queues, you will also need to keep track of your hard disk resources. In Chapter 5, we'll take a look at what kinds of data use up your disk space and how you can best optimize the placement and generation of this data.

## 5

Managing Disk Resources

ONE OF THE MOST IMPORTANT AREAS of administration is managing your disk resources. Unless you have Exchange version 5.5 Enterprise, you are dealing with a 16GB limitation on the total size to which each of your databases can grow. Even in version 5.5, you will face issues such as the amount of time it takes to back up and restore a database that will probably cause you to enforce your own guidelines on total database size. The decisions you make in terms of what data to keep and where to keep it can have a significant impact on your server's functionality, not to mention your ability to recover fully and quickly from a disaster. We will be discussing disaster planning and recovery in Part III, "Troubleshooting and Disaster Recovery." Let's take a look now at the administrative part of resource management. This includes a variety of methods you can use to control the amount of data in your drives. The data that we're concerned about will be found in databases, transaction logs, archives, and tracking logs. In addition, we'll discuss journaling, a feature added in the release of Exchange 5.5 Service Pack 1.

Databases

Microsoft Exchange utilizes three main JET32 databases, although you may need to administer additional databases in some scenarios. This section focuses on controlling the amount of data stored in the Private Information Store, Public Information Store, and Directory Databases. Your environment may also include a Directory Synchronization database if you coexist with a Microsoft Mail network, or you may have a Key Manager database to provide digital signature and encryption functionality to your messaging system. Because the Directory Synchronization and Key Manager databases aren't core to the server's functionality, we will only touch upon them briefly.

Optimizing Your Private Information Store

The term *Private Information Store* refers to data stored in the database file PRIV.EDB. This file is by default located in the \exchsrvr\mdbdata directory on the disk you identified during installation, or on the disk that the Performance Optimizer decided was the fastest for random access calls. The Private Information Store contains all private user data. This includes users' email messages, in addition to any documents stored in your users' mailbox or private folders. Additionally, PRIV.EDB stores rules that your users create from their client. These rules include how to manipulate incoming messages and views or filters your clients create to customize the display of their personal data.

To optimize your users' access to their mailboxes, you need to strike a difficult balance between financial resources and user satisfaction. By financial resources, I don't mean just the cost of new disks—I mean the cost of adding additional servers as well as the cost of upkeep, such as backup and restore procedures. Options to consider include the following:

- Adding additional hard disks to the RAID5 array that your database is stored on
- Enforcing mailbox storage limits
- Enacting a "clean mailbox" policy

Adding Additional Hard Disks

If you are using RAID5—which you most certainly should be if not already—you can elect to add disks to your array when you begin to run low on disk space. This is not the solution I would recommend in most cases because, in my opinion, it is putting a bandage on a bigger problem. The problem is invariably user abuse of server disk storage. Adding drives only encourages your users to continue with their bad practices. This solution can become very expensive, very quickly; the only scenario in which you can simply add drives is if there are empty slots in your array. If you have maxed out your array's capacity, you will need to upgrade to a larger capacity array. Admittedly, I have seen companies in which this is the solution of choice. Their feeling was that if the money was available, it was easier to upgrade than to retrain and restrain the users.

Enforcing Mailbox Storage Limits

A better solution to disk management than adding disks to your array is to implement and enforce storage limits. We talked about storage limits in detail in Chapter 2, "Administering Users," including how to enable and enforce those limits automatically in Exchange. It is important for you to stay on top of storage limits even though your Exchange server will do a lot of the work for you. Your options for storage limits, as discussed earlier, include the following:

- Issuing warnings
- Preventing your users from sending mail
- Preventing your users from sending *and* receiving mail

I find that many companies do not or cannot enforce storage limit policies by disabling the user functionality. If your company falls into this category, you will need to regularly check up on your user mailbox sizes. This is necessary because if you neglect to follow up on your users, they will disregard the system messages they receive and abuse your messaging system. This will result in the inefficient use of disk space (possibly resulting in purchases of additional disks to compensate for the waste) and will affect your backup and restore process.

If you are working for a small company (fewer than 500 users), you probably don't need to check user storage limits more frequently than once a week. On the other hand, larger companies should take a look at mailbox resources daily since this environment lends itself to very large database size—typically due to the huge installed user base. Daily checkups can allow you to nip problems in the bud, and this is always better done sooner rather than later.

No matter which option you choose for enforcing storage limits, you can get a snapshot of mailbox resources by expanding the appropriate server object in the Administrator console and selecting the Private Information Store object. You will see an item called Mailbox Resources that lists all mailboxes that have been logged in to or have received mail, along with how many items the mailbox holds and how much space the mailbox is taking up. You can configure these columns to suit you on the View menu if you want to add information, such as what the storage limit for each user is defined as. This is a good way to quickly scan for abusers on an ad-hoc basis.

Another way to get a snapshot of storage limits—which I would highly recommend—is to use Crystal Reports. Seagate Software sells a Crystal Reports module that can be used to query a ton of useful parameters from your Exchange server. Use the Mailbox Admin Table in Crystal Reports to create a report identifying user mailbox ID correlated with the current mailbox size and limit information. Do this by inserting property fields for Mailbox, Storage Limit Information, Total Message Size (Byte), Issue Warning Storage Limit (K), and Prohibit Send Storage Limit (K). The report can be formatted in columns to make it easier to scan these values for limit violators. You'll find an evaluation copy of Crystal Reports on the BackOffice Resource Kit, Second Edition.

Enacting a "Clean Mailbox" Policy

In addition to using storage limits, you will need to clean out your users' mailboxes regularly for them. I find that many administrators do not clean their users' mailboxes, although they understand the obvious benefit of controlling user disk space usage. What many administrators do not realize is that the clean mailbox functionality should be utilized not only to train your users to keep only important information on the server, but also to optimize your server as a whole.

Over time, you will obviously find that your Private Information Store grows larger. What you may not realize is that this database gets bigger when new documents and messages are received, but it does *not* get smaller when documents and messages are deleted. Instead, the System Attendant performs an online defragmentation of PRIV.EDB every night and marks pages of the database available for Exchange to use again in the future. This means that space is cleared for Exchange's usage only, and will not be seen as free when you look at the free space reported on your disk object. Exchange 5.5 Service Pack 1 causes event 1221 to be written to your Event Viewer, which tells you how much space you can reclaim if you do an offline defragmentation. Unfortunately, this means you have to stop your server to do the defrag. The impact this has on you can best be observed in the following example.

Al has 200MB of space being utilized by his mailbox. The administrator gets a report of users abusing the server storage limits and finds that Al's name repeatedly comes up. The administrator finally persuades Al to delete some of the unnecessary items out of his mailbox. Al deletes 50MB of data. The administrator expects to see that PRIV.EDB is 50MB smaller as a result but instead finds that there has been no change to PRIV.EDB's size. What happened? Exchange reclaimed that space for itself, and you can't get it back without doing an offline defragmentation (which we will discuss further in Chapter 11, "Periodic Proactive Troubleshooting").

You can minimize this problem in your environment by cleaning out everyone's mailboxes for them every night. By doing this, your users will be unlikely to have large amounts of data that need deleted all at once. You can do this for individual users or groups of users by using the **Ctrl** key and selecting those users that need your intervention from within the Administrator GUI. Under **Tools** you will find **Clean Mailbox**. This is the manual tool that you can use periodically to help the storage limit violators control the size of their mailboxes.

Automatic Clean Mailbox

The best way to optimize the Private Information Store in many instances is an automatic solution. I prefer the Clean Mailbox utility (MBClean.exe) that you will find on the BackOffice Resource Kit 2 CD. Installing this utility causes an agent to be installed in the container you specify during installation (don't use the recipients containers, or your users will see the agent in the Global Address List (GAL)). This agent object can subsequently be configured to delete items older than a certain number of days in user mailboxes, and can also purge the Deleted Items folder. Additionally, some mailboxes can be excluded from the procedure if necessary. A word of caution: don't be overly aggressive with your clean mailbox procedures, or you may find yourself having to recover user data from backup more often than you care to imagine.

This automated utility does have a few drawbacks, which in many cases cause it to be unusable. One of the drawbacks is that MBClean uses a different property than auto-archive for cleanup. As a result, a user can modify a document or move it to another folder, which results in the *modified date* getting updated. This affects auto-archive, but not MBClean. The end result is that MBClean cleans out items based on creation date, including modified items that have not been archived yet because the archive timing was reset with the modification. Your users will be highly irate when this happens to them. The other drawback I've found is that using Clean Mailbox causes mailboxes to get logged in to by the service account. This can throw a wrench into your ability to detect and remove mailboxes that are no longer being used.

Optimizing the Public Information Store

Optimizing the Public Information Store means controlling the amount of data stored in the PUB.EDB database. You will find this database in the same location as PRIV.EDB: either on the drive you specified as the installation location or on the drive that the Performance Optimizer determined was the best choice for random access calls in the \exchsrvr\mdbdata directory. The Public Information Store contains any data your users store in public folders. What you may not have realized is that it also stores system folder data. Depending on the server you are administering, this can include all of your users' free and busy calendar data, the offline address book, your forms library, and scripts defined for public folder and mailbox events. Controlling the Public Information Store includes controlling the size of these public and system folders.

Optimization of the Public Information Store can be accomplished in many ways. You must determine what the best solution is for your environment, because these options are only appropriate in certain situations. Options include the following:

- Creating a dedicated public folder server for your site
- Setting storage and age limits on public folder contents
- Optimizing the location of the data in newly created public folders

The Service Pack and the Manual Clean Mailbox Utility

Before using the manual Clean Mailbox utility under Exchange 5.0 or 5.5, apply the latest service pack. Without the Exchange 5.5 Service Pack 1 or Exchange 5.0 Service Pack 2, this utility will wipe out data in all of the users' server-based folders (not just the Inbox).

Creating a Dedicated Public Folder Server for Your Site

Creation of a dedicated public folder server is a good idea in environments in which your users are heavy public folder users. The dedicated server allows you to offload the data that would ordinarily be found on your users' home server onto some other server. This helps improve performance on the mailbox server.

To create a dedicated public folder server, you need to move all mailboxes defined on the public folder server to a mailbox server, then delete the Private Information Store (select it and click the **X** icon on the toolbar). After you have finished this, run the Performance Optimizer to allow Exchange to reconfigure your memory and system settings. A dedicated public folder server does not pass any user interpersonal messages (IPMs) to other servers. It is responsible only for the replication of the hierarchy and folder content (if you configure it) and directory updates with other servers in the site (or other sites, if you make it a bridgehead).

Setting Storage and Age Limits on Public Folder Contents

Regardless of whether you use dedicated public folder servers or not, you should always configure age limits and storage limits in general at the server level, which should be overridden only when necessary at the folder level. The purpose for this is similar to the reason for cleaning user mailboxes: it just isn't necessary to keep every single document in many types of public folders. Defining age limits will expunge old, obsolete data out of the Public Information Store and free up space for other types of data.

With storage limits, the folder owner is notified when the folder is at a point that cleaning might be warranted. Because folder storage limits are not enforceable within Exchange (the owner only gets a warning message) it is up to you to regularly check the amount of space your folders are taking up so that you can personally encourage the folder owner to clean the folder out.

Optimizing the Location of the Data in the Newly Created Public Folders

In addition to controlling how much space your public data occupies, it is important to control where the data will be stored. Top-level public folders are created on the Public Information Store of the user creating the folder. Subfolders are created in the same location as the parent folder. Therefore, if you control where the top-level folders are created, the subfolders will naturally follow suit.

As part of your deployment, you should have identified who will be responsible for creating your public folder hierarchy. If the individuals identified are on multiple servers, you should now take a look at where the home server is for the folders they created and verify that their location makes sense with regard to the location of the users that will access them. If not, use replication to move the folders to an appropriate server.

After the top-level folders are where you want them, newly created subfolders will store their data on that same server. If this is not the behavior you want, you will need to periodically check your folder home servers or you may wind up with more network traffic than you expected.

Optimizing the Directory Database

Whereas optimization of the Public and Private Information stores involves controlling your users, optimization of the Directory Database involves controlling your server. The Directory Database is stored in a database file named `DIR.EDB`. You will find this database in the `\exchsrvr\dsadata` directory on the drive you identified during installation or where the Performance Optimizer determined was the best location.

The Directory Database contains every object and the associated properties defined in your Exchange organization. It is a complete copy of your organization's Exchange directory. This is the case for every Exchange server in your Exchange organization. In other messaging systems, the Directory only contains mailbox definitions, foreign user accounts, and the identification of other post offices in the messaging system. This is not true in Exchange—in addition to the aforementioned objects, in Exchange the Directory contains global properties you define at the site level (such as whether message tracking will be enabled), in addition to server-specific properties (such as the schedule defining when the Information Stores will be defragmented).

Because the Directory Database contains all the definitions for objects in an organization, you will find that it gets pretty big over time. There are a few places you can go to optimize the way the Directory utilizes your disk resources. Things you can do to optimize include the following:

- Deleting unused mailboxes
- Deleting tombstones periodically
- Utilizing offline defrag

Deleting Unused Mailboxes

You might have unused mailboxes if your IS department is not regularly informed of personnel changes. Unused mailboxes take up space in both your Private Information Store and your Directory Database. We will be discussing how to find unused mailboxes in Chapter 10, "Reporting." After you've identified unused mailboxes and determined that the mailbox should be slated for deletion, delete it. This creates a tombstone that instructs other servers to delete the mailbox object from their directories.

Configuring Tombstone Removal

When an object is deleted from the database, it is removed from the local server and marked for deletion by remote servers with what is called a *tombstone*. The tombstone replicates to the remote server and instructs that server to remove the object from its local directory.

Because tombstones are just markers for deleted objects, you should get rid of them periodically. Therefore, tombstones have a lifetime that you can configure. At the end of the tombstone lifetime, the tombstone is flagged for purging. The default tombstone lifetime is 30 days, but this is probably more than you need. You should identify a lifetime that corresponds with the maximum amount of time a server or network link is likely to be down. The catch is that you don't want to make the lifetime too short or tombstones may not replicate to other servers in your site or across connectors to other sites. This will result in objects you have deleted continuing to appear in the directories of remote servers. We will discuss this "orphaning" problem further in Chapter 13, "Troubleshooting Your Exchange Server."

If your tombstone lifetime is too long, on the other hand, you will wind up wasting disk space on objects that are not needed by your system. Tombstones will be removed from the Directory Database during the next garbage collection interval after tombstone expiration (the default is every 12 hours).

Utilizing Offline Defrag

Because online defragmentation of the Directory Database only marks free space to be used by Exchange, you may need to do an offline defragmentation periodically. *Online defragmentation* clears out the expired tombstones and *offline defragmentation* reclaims the space previously occupied by tombstones for other system data. Exchange versions 4.0 and 5.0 are not optimized for defragmentation the way version 5.5 is, and therefore will need to be periodically defragmented using EDBUTIL. In Exchange 5.5, use of ESEUTIL for offline defragmentation should generally only be necessary after moving large numbers of users to another server, or removing a large amount of data. Both EDBUTIL and ESEUTIL will be discussed in Chapter 11.

Orphaned Objects Resulting from Inappropriate Tombstone Lifetimes

Since purging tombstones too early can cause orphaned objects to remain in remote directories, I don't recommend changing this parameter unless you are having severe disk space utilization problems and have a very dynamic Directory. Generally, I decrease the tombstone lifetime at companies where the servers are connected over a LAN and have a short downtime, and I only do that if I have a compelling reason, such as disk space problems.

Optimizing the Directory Synchronization Database

The Directory Synchronization (DirSync) database is used by Exchange to manage the directory data that has already been synced with MS Mail. If you have never completed a DirSync with MS Mail, the XDIR.EDB file will not exist. The XDIR.EDB file contains a list of objects that have been sent to the MS Mail post offices by the Directory Synchronization service on Exchange. When DirSync runs, the service checks the XDIR.EDB file to determine if a given object has been sent during a previous cycle. There are four values stored for each object listed in XDIR.EDB: USN-Changed, Display Name, Email-Address, and Obj-Dist-Name. The XDIR.EDB database will grow larger over time and will need to be periodically defragmented. Exchange does not do an online defragmentation of this database, so you will need to stop the DXA service and use ESEUTIL to do an offline defragmentation.

Optimizing the Key Manager Database

The Key Manager Database is where your user's security keys are registered if you have installed the Key Manager component of Exchange. Optimization of this database is not as much about disk resource utilization as it is about security. This database needs to be secured. Although it is encrypted, it is better to be safe than sorry. It would be extremely difficult, but it is technically possible, for someone to break into the Key Manager database and gain access to your users' keys. The server that maintains this database should be in a locked room with limited access. The people who back it up and have restore rights should be highly trusted, and the backup tapes should be secured.

Transaction Logging

All Exchange databases use transaction logging to keep track of what transactions have been performed and committed to the databases. The amount of disk space these logs take up is dependent on your circular logging settings and the type and frequency of your backups. We will be discussing circular logging in more detail in Chapter 12, "Planning for Disaster," and backups in Chapter 6, "Backing Up Your Server." At this point, suffice it to say you have two logging options: circular logging can either be enabled or disabled.

The default setting for Exchange is to have circular logging enabled. This is to prevent the transaction log files from overpopulating your hard disk. If you have left circular logging enabled, then there is no further optimization required as far as disk resources are concerned. However, this limits your options if you have to recover from a disaster. I do not recommend that you leave circular logging enabled, and will explain more specifically why in Chapter 12, when we discuss server configuration.

After you have disabled circular logging, Exchange will create a new 5MB transaction log file automatically after the current log file is filled, and rename the filled current log file to a previous log file. You can see how this can quickly become a problem if you don't address how to purge these previous log files. If you do a full, online backup of your server using NTBackup or another backup program that uses the Exchange Backup API, then the log files that have been previously committed to the databases will be purged automatically at the end of the backup. If you do offline backups, the log files will not be automatically purged. Transactions in the log files will be committed to the appropriate database when the corresponding service is stopped. This means that you can safely delete them manually after stopping the service. I would recommend backing them up first, just to be safe. If you do offline backups and don't remove the log files, they will take up all of the available disk space and cause your services to shut down. When this happens, you will see events in your application event log indicating the problem. The events will reflect Event ID 49, 1113, or -529.

Archives

Whereas transaction logs may be an issue for you if you don't plan for them, archives exist only if you enable them. There are two archives to be aware of: protocol logging archives and message archives. Exchange will not maintain any archives by default, but if you do elect to archive data, you will need to know where these archives are stored so that you can manually purge the data Exchange puts there. I have been to customer sites where an administrator enabled archiving and then either forgot or didn't tell his successor. This resulted in disk space problems that had to be addressed because the administrator didn't understand how protocol and message logging would affect the server.

Protocol Logging Archives

You can enable server-side *protocol logging* for troubleshooting so that the entire session established between any remote client and your server is recorded in a log file. This will impact your server performance, so logging should only be configured if you are attempting to identify a specific problem. For example, if you are having difficulty establishing an SMTP session between your Internet Mail Service (IMS) and a remote SMTP host, enabling protocol logging for SMTP can help point you to the problem. This can be accomplished for SMTP under Diagnostics Logging on your server properties, or in the Registry for IMAP4, POP3, and NNTP. In all cases, text files are created that keep an account of the data transmitted between the two machines. Over time, these files will take up huge amounts of space if you don't clean them out.

After protocol logging is enabled, log files are created as detailed in the following list:

- **SMTP.** Enable protocol logging and stop and restart the IMS. A file called `L000000#.log` will be created in the `exchsrvr\imcdata\log` directory on the corresponding Exchange server. You will see additional log files created as new sessions are established with your server. You should delete the log files you find in here periodically to prevent them from taking up too much space on your disk.

- **IMAP4, POP3, and NNTP.** Enable logging in the Registry and stop and restart the IS service to cause the Information Store to create a file called `L00000#.log` in the path you specify in the Registry (`exchsrvr\mdbdata` by default). These log files are created as sessions are established using the associated protocol. To delete them, reset the logging level to 0 to allow them to close. As with SMTP, you should delete these log files regularly so that you don't wind up with disk space problems.

Message Archives

Message archiving is a term used to describe two distinct activities: the maintenance of a copy of messages transferred through the IMS and the necessity of your users to remove messages from the server and store them in local PST files. Both of these activities will be addressed in this section.

To enable message archival for the IMS, use the diagnostics logging feature in the Administrator Program. Set the level for Message Archival to medium or maximum to cause each message sent or received by the IMS to be stored in its own text file. You will find these messages in the `\exchsrvr\imcdata\in\archive` folder if they were being routed inbound or in the `\exchsrvr\imcdata\out\archive` folder if they were being routed outbound. These files can be used to troubleshoot problems because they will allow you to see message header information associated with the message.

Enabling Protocol Logging

IMAP4, POP3, and NNTP protocol logging is enabled under HKEY_LOCAL_MACHINE\SYSTEM\ CurrentControlSet\Services\MSExchangeIS\ParametersSystem. In here, you will find keys defining the path to the file location and keys to define the level of logging. Generally, use levels 1 through 4 to define minimum to maximum log levels. Logging can be enabled to a level 6; however, this can cause excessive system overhead and should not be enabled except in extreme troubleshooting scenarios.

Permanently Enabling Protocol Logging

My feeling about protocol logging is that it should only be used for troubleshooting. I have run across companies that like to leave it on all the time even though they don't use the log files for anything on a regular basis. Because protocol logging requires you to stay on top of log file purging, I recommend that you leave it disabled until you need it.

Whereas message archives are maintained on the server and will require you to manually purge them, user archives are stored on your clients and are controlled by the client's settings. Because you will be configuring and enforcing storage limits on your user mailboxes, you will undoubtedly need to maintain PST files for your user mail archives. The maintenance of manually created PST files is in addition to any autoarchive files that are controlled by the Outlook client.

PST Files

Your users may also have PST files defined to archive their messages manually. I have come across many companies that have their users store these PST files in their home directories on the server so that they get backed up. My feeling is that this is counter-productive, since it does away with Exchange's ability to store a single copy of a message for multiple user access. If your users keep their PST files on the server, then you will have difficulty with your server disk space utilization.

As far as disk resources are concerned, archive files and regular PST files both consume more space per message than PRIV.EDB. As a matter of fact, PSTs actually store two copies of each message—one in rich text format and the other in plain text. Because the storage in PSTs is so much less optimized than Exchange's database storage, I believe that unless your users roam to other systems, PST files belong on the local workstation if you use them at all. If you need to include them in your backup routine, they should be stored in a predefined path on the user's drive and backed up to tape across the network.

Autoarchive Files

Outlook 97/98 has an autoarchive feature that moves data from your server folders to a local archive file after a specified period of time. The folders that are affected and their archive periods are shown in Table 5.1.

Table 5.1 **User Data Archived Every 14 Days**

Folder	Time	Action
Calendar	6 months	Moved to archive file
Tasks	6 months	Moved to archive file
Journal	6 months	Moved to archive file
Sent Items	2 months	Moved to archive file
Deleted Items	2 months	Purged from system
Inbox		Not archived
Notes		Not archived
Contacts		Not archived

The archive file used by autoarchive is called `C:\WINDOWS\Profiles\Username\` `Application Data\Microsoft\Outlook\archive.pst` by default. Because this is part of the user profile, it will be stored on the server if you enable server-based profiles. Otherwise, it stays local to your users' workstation. The setting can be changed in Outlook98 by accessing the **Tools**, **Options** menu. Click the **Other** tab and select **AutoArchive** to configure the file location and archive time period (14 days by default), determine whether to prompt before archiving, and choose whether to delete expired items.

To configure individual folder archive periods, right-click the appropriate folder and choose **Properties**. The AutoArchive tab has the settings you can configure. We will discuss backup issues as they pertain to archive files in Chapter 6.

Journaling

As mentioned earlier, Message Journaling is a feature added with the release of the Exchange 5.5 Service Pack 1. It allows you to define a recipient that will receive a copy of every message handled by the MTA on a given server, on all servers in a site, or organization-wide. The intended use is to allow you to comply with government regulations that may require you to retain email for a period of time. This is important in that it allows you to comply with these regulations without relying on your users to keep copies of their email.

Because Journaling is keeping a copy of every single message passed by the MTA in a single mailbox, the disk resources on the server on which the mailbox is defined can become a real administrative issue. I find that the best solution is to use a dedicated server for this task. Create only the one mailbox on that server to be used as the Journaling recipient. I also prefer to delete the Public Information Store so that no folder-related traffic is processed by the Journaling server. Be sure to run the Performance Optimizer on this server configured with the following options selected:

Message Archival for Troubleshooting Only

I had a customer at one point complain to me that he was almost out of disk space. Upon further examination, I determined that someone had enabled Message Archival to maximum. None of the administrators were aware that all of their Internet messages were being stored. I disabled the setting for them and purged the useless data out of the archive folders. The point I'm trying to make is that, like protocol logging, Message Archival is a troubleshooting tool, and should not be enabled as a standard practice.

Enabling Message Journaling

Message Journaling is enabled through the Registry. See Appendix B, "Exchange Registry Tuning," for the Registry settings. Also, see the Exchange Server 5.5 Service Pack 1 Release Notes for more information.

- Users on this server: Less than 500
- Type of server: Private Store

Limit the amount of memory used only if the Journaling server is also running as a controller or an application server, and select the appropriate option button for the number of users in your organization. If you find that your server performance is not acceptable with these settings, you may need to rerun the Optimizer with a larger number of users defined on this server. This can happen if the message load being routed to your Journaling recipient is very high.

Tracking Logs

Message tracking logs—another important tool for managing disk resources—allow you to keep track of what messages have been generated or handled by servers in your organization. This function is enabled at the site level for each site individually by checking the appropriate box on the MTA and Information Store objects. Message tracking can also be enabled for messages passed through connectors. In all cases, the System Attendant logs the tracking information to a file named for the date on which the traffic occurred, which you can later view using the Track Message tool in the Administrator Program. These files are stored in the \exchsrvr\tracking.log directory on the disk the Performance Optimizer determines is best for sequential reads and writes.

The default for message tracking is that it is not enabled at all. If you do decide to enable it, the default retention period for tracking logs is seven days. This setting is configurable on each individual server, such that it is possible to find that some servers retain information about a message being delivered or handled, while other servers that handled the same message no longer maintain the fact in their tracking logs.

My opinion is that you should enable message tracking, and you should also come up with a standard retention time for the log files. Without message tracking enabled, you will be unable to identify at what point a message being transferred may have become stuck. Tracking should be enabled with the same settings in all sites and on the same objects, and the logs should be maintained for the same amount of time on all servers. This can make support a lot easier. I like to enable it on all objects (MTA, IS, connectors, and so on) and maintain the logs for at least the default of seven days. This way, I can look for messages stuck at any location for up to a week. In some cases, keeping the logs longer is warranted. I find that keeping logs for fewer than seven days is sometimes not sufficient because users may not realize there is a delivery problem within that time period.

Summary

In this chapter, we addressed the data you will find in various locations on your hard disks, and the steps you can take to optimize your disk resources. Optimization includes controlling the data stored in the Private Information Store, Public Information Store, and Directory Database, as well as managing the disk usage of your message journaling server, message archives, protocol archives, and transaction and tracking logs. We also addressed some of the security considerations of the Key Manager Database. Now let's take a look at Chapter 6 to see how best to back up these resources.

6

Backing Up Your Server

ESSAGING IS PROBABLY THE MOST CRITICAL application your business runs. It is therefore crucial for you to understand how to back up your Exchange server and to know what data is backed up with each type of backup. In this chapter, we will address backup types, which Exchange and NT data needs to be backed up, and how to perform backups optimally, with an eye to disaster recovery. See Appendix A, "Maintenance Schedule," for a complete administration schedule, and Chapter 14, "Disaster Recovery," for more information on disaster recovery.

Backup Types

The backup types you can choose from are the same regardless of what product you use to perform your backup. In this section we will look at the pros and cons of offline versus online backups, as well as the differences between full, differential, incremental, and copy backup types.

Online Versus Offline Backup

The Exchange databases can be backed up while the Exchange services are running (online) or not running (offline). There are a few really great advantages to backing up an Exchange server online rather than offline:

- Users can still receive and send email while the backup is running.
- Online backups actually can help you detect database corruption.

Any backup program that uses the Exchange Backup API (sold as an Exchange backup agent) has the ability to back up Exchange online.

In many companies, it is becoming more and more difficult to schedule server downtime. Too many employees require access to the server during off hours, because they are either dialing in from home or staying late at the office. As a result, the online backup functionality is key to the ability of these users to continue to do their job. Exchange accomplishes online backups by allowing database transactions that occur while Exchange is being backed up to be posted to a patch file rather than to the Exchange database. This patch file is then applied to the database at the end of the backup so that any new mail received or modifications users have made to their mailboxes will be committed from the patch file to the database correctly. We will be talking about the patch file in more detail later in this chapter. The following are some things to keep in mind as you choose when to use online and offline backup:

- Online backups are affected by your circular logging settings.
- Online backups can back up your Private Information Store, Public Information Store, Directory Database, and transaction log files.
- Online backups can help alert you to corruption in your database.
- Offline backups are necessary if you don't use NTBackup and you don't have the Exchange module for the backup program you do use.

One of your primary considerations should be to decide on your circular logging settings. In addition to affecting your fault tolerance ability, your circular logging settings will affect the types of online backup you can perform. As we discussed in Chapter 5, "Managing Disk Resources," circular logging is enabled by default in Exchange to prevent transaction logs from completely taking over your hard disk. This means that with circular logging enabled, as transactions are committed to the appropriate database, your transaction log files are free to be overwritten. How this affects your backup will be discussed a bit later in this chapter. Circular logging and fault tolerance will be discussed in detail in Chapter 12, "Planning for Disaster."

In addition to planning your backup strategy around your circular logging settings, you will also need to consider what additional data needs to be backed up. Online backups can back up your Private Information Store, Public Information Store, Directory Database, and transaction log files. They may not back up files that could be accessed by other services if those services are open during the backup. As a result, you need to stop the corresponding services to back up files used by foreign connectors. This includes the PC MTA used to connect to MS Mail, the MS Mail Directory Synchronization service, and the MS Mail Schedule+ Free/Busy Connector service. Online backups will also not back up your Key Manager Database, so you will need to take steps to back that up offline in addition to your nightly online backups.

Once you are performing regular online backups, you will be in a good position to notice corrupt databases. In some cases, doing online backups can help alert you to corruption in your database. When this happens, you will see an error in your Event Viewer notifying you that your backup has failed. Generally, the amount of data backed up before the failure will be the same and will indicate the area of the database that is corrupt. This can happen before you or your users suspect there are any problems with the server. By regularly going through the event logs after online backups are performed, you can be made aware of the problem and attempt corrective actions before the problem becomes catastrophic. We will discuss identifying these errors in the event log in Chapter 7, "Daily Proactive Troubleshooting," and how to repair corrupt databases in Chapter 14.

Although online backups are best, offline backups are necessary if you don't use NTBackup and you don't have the Exchange agent for the backup program you do use. You will need to schedule downtime with your users so that you can stop the services without causing them to lose data prior to performing the backup. I don't recommend using offline backups as your nightly backup because it is not as straightforward to restore from an offline backup as it is from an online backup. You also can't detect corruption offline, and your users may be inconvenienced by having to disconnect for the backup.

Both online and offline backups are an important part of your backup schedule. If possible, you should perform nightly online backups and weekly offline backups. This combination will allow you to keep up-to-date information on tape for the best recovery of Exchange databases, and also allow you to perform a full-server rebuild if necessary. Weekly offline, full-server backups are best in terms of recovery options, but may not be possible in large companies due to the amount of down time required.

Bear in mind that online backups may not back up all of your data, so if you run additional services, as discussed earlier in this section, you need to make arrangements to back up that data as well. Also, if your databases are too large to allow you to do nightly full backups, differential backups are the next best thing in terms of ease of recovery. Use incremental backups between full backups if your transaction logs are populating your hard disk too quickly and you need to purge them more often than your full backup schedule allows. Chapter 14 will address recovery from backups.

Backup API Enhanced for Version 5.5

The Exchange Backup API was enhanced for Exchange version 5.5 such that, with sufficient hardware, it is possible to back up as much as 30GB of data per hour. Be aware that although your backup is faster, your restore rate may be limited to 10GB per hour.

Microsoft's Disaster Recovery White Paper

Do yourself and your company a favor: Print out a copy of Microsoft's Exchange Disaster Recovery white paper. You can find a copy on TechNet or on the Microsoft Web site. Keep this white paper near each server that you back up as an easy reference for both backup and recovery guidelines.

Full Backup

Ideally, you should be performing full, online backups every night for best Exchange recoverability and for best disk resource management. A full, online backup will back up your databases in addition to your transaction log files, as you can see in Figure 6.1. At the end of the backup, your files will be marked as archived and the transaction log files that had already been applied to the database will be purged from your server. This is the best way to get rid of your transaction log files. If you have circular logging enabled, this is the only type of online backup you can perform.

If you use NTBackup, configure a batch file so that your backups are consistent. The command to include in the batch file for a full, online backup of a server named ORLANDO is as follows:

```
Ntbackup backup DS \\ORLANDO IS \\ORLANDO /a /v /t normal /l
c:\logs\mcoexch.log /tape:0
```

This command will back up the directory and information store databases and transaction logs on the ORLANDO server. The backup will be appended to any existing backups already on the tape and files backed up will be verified. The backup will be logged to `c:\logs\mcoexch.log` and will be stored on the tape drive identified as number 0 in the Registry of the server performing the backup. At the end of the backup, the transaction logs that had been committed to the database prior to the start of the backup will be purged from the server.

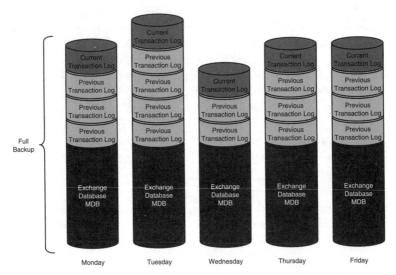

Figure 6.1   Because full, online backups include the Exchange databases and transaction log files, recovery from a crash requires only one backup set.

Although online backups will purge your log files, offline backups will not. If your company does offline backups only, you must manually purge your transaction log files after your backup is complete (given that you have circular logging disabled, which I think is a must). Because there is no way to tell which log files have been committed to the database and which ones haven't just by looking at them, you should *never* just go in there and delete log files. This can cause an unrecoverable inconsistency in your database. To safely purge your log files manually, the procedure is as follows:

1. Stop the Exchange services and other NT services if necessary (such as Server).

2. Back up the entire server, including the Registry.

3. Verify that all databases and transaction log files have been backed up.

4. Delete all transaction log files named `*.log` from the `exchsrvr\mdbdata` and `exchsrvr\dsadata` directories.

5. Start the Exchange services.

If for some reason your services won't start back up, restore the transaction log files from your backup tape and attempt to restart them again.

You should also periodically do a full, offline, file-based backup of your Exchange server. As we indicated previously, offline backups ideally should be performed once each week. If your company cannot schedule that much down time, perform full, offline backups monthly and plan for backups of other data that might be missed in the online backup. Use NET STOP and NET START commands to stop and restart the Exchange services. A batch file for an offline backup of the ORLANDO server running the Internet Mail Service in addition to the core Message Transfer Agent, Information Store, Directory Service, and System Attendant services might look like this:

```
net stop MSExchangeIMC
net stop MSExchangeMTA
net stop MSExchangeIS
net stop MSExchangeDS
net stop MSExchangeSA
ntbackup backup c:\ d:\ e:\ /a /v /d "ORLANDO File-based Backup" /b /l
c:\logs\mcofb.log
net start MSExchangeSA
net start MSExchangeDS
net start MSExchangeIS
net start MSExchangeMTA
net start MSExchangeIMC
```

This file could be run using AT or WinAT. It will stop the appropriate Exchange services; back up all files on drives C, D, and E; and append the backup to any existing backups on the tape. It will also verify files, name the backup "ORLANDO File-based Backup," back up the local Registry, and log the backup to `c:\logs\mcofb.log`.

Differential Backup

If your database is too large to allow you to do full, nightly backups, you may find that differential backups are a good alternative solution. Unlike full backups, *differential* backups don't set the archive bit on files they back up. Because differential backups will back up files that don't have the archive bit set, you will be backing up the same data with each backup. This causes the backup duration to incrementally lengthen each night, but the time to restore is much shorter than with incremental. Obviously, the quickest restore is from a full backup.

Online differential backups will back up your transaction log files and other files that don't have the archive bit set, but not your databases, as you can see in Figure 6.2. In order to recover your server from backup, you will need to first apply the tape with the databases on it and then the differential tape set to get the transaction logs. Because only the log files are backed up, you will not be able to perform a differential backup if you have circular logging enabled. This makes sense, if you think about it. Since those transactions log files get overwritten as data is committed to the database, they wouldn't do any good anyway.

Companies Performing Only Offline Backups

I have run across a few smaller companies that do offline backups only. Typically, the profile for these companies is that they have fewer than 250 users and they run Exchange on the same server as other applications. They feel that they can easily schedule downtime, so they take the whole server down every night and do a full backup.

Although this is an acceptable solution, because you can recover data if you need to, the recovery is not going to be as straightforward and you are needlessly inconveniencing your users. Even if you don't want to invest in the Exchange backup agent for your third-party backup program, you can still use NTBackup for this one piece of your backup regimen.

Stopping Services in the Batch File

To stop any NT service in a batch file, you need to know the correct name for the service. Services are defined in the Registry in HKEY_LOCAL_MACHINE\SYSTEM\CurrentControlSet\Services. All Exchange services are prefaced with the string MSExchange.

Upgrading Your Tape Device

Although data can be restored just as completely from multiple tapes as from a single tape, the restore process is much smoother when you don't have to juggle multiple tapes in a tape set. To improve your restore productivity, consider purchasing a new tape device that will allow you to back up your data to a single tape.

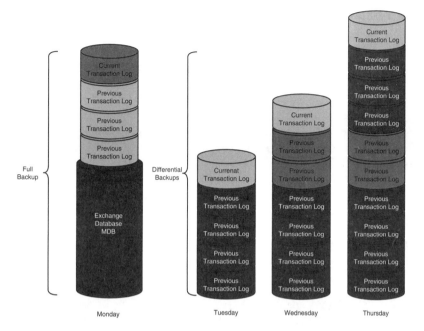

Figure 6.2   Because differential backups include just the Exchange transaction log files, the last full backup set and the current differential backup set are required to recover from a crash.

The command to include in the NTBACKUP batch file for an online, differential backup of a server named ORLANDO is as follows:

```
Ntbackup backup DS \\ORLANDO IS \\ORLANDO /a /v /t differential /l
c:\logs\mcoexch.log /tape:0
```

This command will back up all transaction logs for the directory and information store on the ORLANDO server that have been modified or added since the last full backup. The backup will be appended to any existing backups already on the tape, and files backed up will be verified. The backup will be logged to c:\logs\mcoexch.log and stored on the tape drive identified as number 0 in the Registry of the server performing the backup.

Disk Space on your Transaction Log Drive

In order to perform a restore, you need to have enough space on your transaction log drive to hold all of the transaction logs that have not yet been applied in addition to the logs on the tape. If you don't have enough disk space to recover the transaction logs, you won't be able to restore your data.

Incremental Backup

Another option that you have other than a full or differential backup is to use incremental backups between your full backups. Similar to differential backups, online incremental backups do not back up your databases. Online incremental backups include only the Exchange transaction log files that have changed since the last full or incremental backup (see Figure 6.3). In addition to files that do not have the archive bit set, all transaction log files will be backed up to tape. At the end of the backup, the archive bit will be set and transaction log files that have been committed to the database will be purged. If your database is too large to back up every night and differential backups are not sufficient because they don't purge transaction logs, I recommend doing incremental backups between full backups. Restore will be sticky (see Chapter 14 for details) but you won't have transaction logs taking up too much space on your drive.

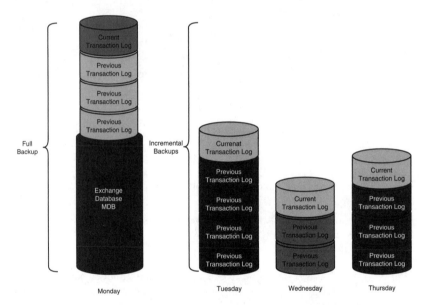

Figure 6.3 Because online incremental backups include only Exchange transaction log files that have changed since the last full or incremental backup, you will need to apply the last full backup set and then each subsequent incremental backup set to recover from a crash.

Avoid Mixing Incremental and Differential Backups

Don't mix incremental and differential backups. This can make recovery really confusing. If you can't do full backups every night, use differentials in between. If differentials are a problem due to the log files, use incrementals rather than differentials in between full backups.

Like differential backups, online incremental backups can not be performed if circular logging is enabled. Because only the transaction log files are backed up with an online incremental backup, and we know those files are being overwritten as the data they contain is committed to the database, it doesn't make sense to back up the log files in this way.

The command to include in the NTBACKUP batch file for an online, incremental backup of a server named ORLANDO is as follows:

```
Ntbackup backup DS \\ORLANDO IS \\ORLANDO /a /v /t incremental /l
c:\logs\mcoexch.log /tape:0
```

This command will back up all transaction logs for the directory and information store on the ORLANDO server that have been modified or added since the last full or incremental backup. The backup will be appended to any existing backups already on the tape and files backed up will be verified. The backup will be logged to c:\logs\mcoexch.log. The backup will be stored on the tape drive identified as number 0 in the Registry of the server performing the backup. At the end of the backup, the transaction logs that had been committed to the database before backup began will be purged from the server.

Copy Backup

Copy backups are just like full backups, except that files are not marked as archived and transaction logs aren't purged at the end. This is a good way to back up your data before performing unusual tasks, such as applying service packs or upgrading. Because you should not be performing copy backups as part of your regular backup program, you will not need a line in your NTBackup batch file to perform one.

I don't recommend copy backups normally because you will have to purge your transaction log files manually at the end of the backup, and you don't get the benefit of faster backup that is obtained with incremental or differential. Because it is best not to interrupt your regular backup procedure by performing unscheduled full, online backups, use copy backups for special occasions. Adding an unscheduled full backup can cause problems if you need to restore data because your documented restore procedure will be incorrect. Any time you want to do an extra backup, use the copy backup type in order to keep your regular backups on track.

From my experience, I've found that the best schedule is full, online backups performed every night with a full offline backup performed every weekend. The offline backup will get any data not picked up as part of your online backup, and will be usable in a disaster in the event your online tape set is damaged. It is also useful if you miss the event log errors indicating halted online backups and you need to restore a corrupt database for repair attempts in the lab. Regardless of how you perform your backups, the most important thing is to have a well-documented procedure that is followed for every backup and every restore. There should be no question as to how to restore data during a disaster recovery. See Chapter 12 for sample standard operating procedures. Use AT or WinAT to schedule backups using a batch file so that they are always performed the same way.

Exchange Data

Let's take a look now at the types of data Exchange stores that need to be backed up. This data includes the server databases, transaction log files, user data, and Exchange system files.

Databases

There are three main databases that must be backed up in all situations: the Private Information Store, the Public Information Store, and the Directory Database. Depending on how your Exchange organization is configured, you may need to back up the Key Manager Database or the Directory Synchronization Database as well.

Private Information Store

The Private Information Store database (`PRIV.EDB`) is located in the `\exchsrvr\mdbdata` directory by default, as noted in Chapter 5. Because this database contains all of your private user data, it is critical that you back it up regularly. Use either NTBackup or a third-party utility such as the Cheyenne MS Exchange Database Agent for ARCserve 6.5 for Windows NT. I recommend this particular agent because it allows you to perform a "bricks-level" backup of your user data. This is particularly important if you find yourself needing to recover individual user data regularly. Individual mailbox recovery is one of the most lamented areas of Exchange. The reason it is a problem is that all of your user data is in a single database file. To recover one small section of it traditionally requires that you restore the entire database.

To get access to the individual mailbox, you must rebuild the entire server. This is a huge pain, and we will talk about it further in Chapter 14. Anyway, the Cheyenne Exchange Agent backs up Exchange in such a way as to make recovery of a single inbox possible using what is called a *bricks-level* backup. Drawbacks to this process are as follows:

- Backups at the bricks-level are significantly more time consuming than a regular online backup would be. (This is the most prohibitive drawback.)

- With this process, you cannot do a bricks-level backup or restore of the Calendar, Contacts, Journal, Notes, or Tasks folders.

- You won't be able to recover private folders that have forms associated with them.

- System mailboxes can't be backed up or restored in this way either. *System mailboxes* include those associated with connectors and Exchange components, such as the Private or Public Information Store, Directory Service, System Attendant, and connectors.

Keep in mind the limitations of bricks-level backups. You will need to have a database-level backup in order to effectively recover a whole server should it become necessary. Bricks-level backups are good only for mailbox recovery, not server recovery. As a result, I recommend them only for companies that do a lot of individual mailbox recovery, and only for the most critical users. If you do decide to do bricks-level backups, you should do them nightly to get the most recoverability. If you do them any less frequently, you'll find yourself rebuilding a server in the lab to recover more recent data than is stored in the bricks-level backup.

Public Information Store

You need to back up the Public Information Store (PUB.EDB) so that you can recover an entire server if necessary. This includes individual public folders and individual documents that were stored in public folders.

You will find PUB.EDB in the \exchsrvr\mdbdata directory, as noted in Chapter 5. By default, there will be one on every server in your site. If you have elected to use dedicated public folder servers, this database will be found only on those dedicated servers. In this database is all of your user-shared data. This includes public folders you and your users create, in addition to system information such as Schedule+ Free/Busy data, the offline address book, the organizational forms library, and scripts that have been written to run against folders and mailboxes.

As was mentioned earlier in this chapter, full, online backups of the Public Information Store are best for recovery. In addition to these, you may want to do a periodic bricks-level backup so that you can recover individual public folders without having to recover the entire server first. Just keep in mind the limitations we discussed for bricks-level backups in the section "Private Information Store." As mentioned earlier, you will need a database-level backup to be able to recover your server, so be sure that you don't replace full backups with bricks-level backups.

Directory Database

In addition to backing up your Private and Public Information Stores in order to recover user data, you must back up your Directory to recover system data. The Directory Database (DIR.EDB) is located in the \exchsrvr\dsadata directory by default. Every server in your organization will maintain a local copy of the Directory tagged specifically to the local server. This is an important concept to grasp because you might think that a corrupt directory on one server can simply be restored from a backup of a different server's directory.

Back up DIR.EDB so that you can recover an entire server if necessary. You may also need to recover the Directory if you accidentally delete a directory object and need to recover it. This actually results in some special circumstances that we will discuss in Chapter 14.

Key Manager Database

If you have installed the Key Manager to facilitate digital signatures and encrypted messages, you will find the database in your \exchsrvr\security directory if you are running versions 4.0 or 5.0 or in the \exchsrvr\kmsdata directory for version 5.5. Online backups do not back up the Key Manager Database—you must do this offline.

The Key Manager service uses a startup disk to provide a password at service start-up. The password on the startup disk is assigned during installation of the Key Manager Database and is not the same as the service account password or the administrator password. If for some reason this password should become unavailable or the floppy disk should become corrupt, you will need to have a backup to regain access to the database. For Exchange 4.0 or 5.0, you can re-create the startup disk by creating a file called KMSPWD.INI, in which the contents of the file are as follows:

```
[config]
  pwd=your-password
```

The variable *your-password* is the 14-character password assigned during installation.

For Exchange version 5.5, the password is stored in a file called kmserver.pwd. Enter the 15-character password in the first line of the file. Note that there is no square-bracket section header preceding the password in kmserver.pwd as there is in kmspwd.ini.

Directory Synchronization Database

If you coexist with a Microsoft Mail environment, then you probably are using the DXA Service in Exchange to synchronize address lists between the two systems. As we discussed in Chapter 5, XDIR.EDB contains the objects that have been sent from Exchange to MS Mail. If you want to avoid having to redo directory synchronization from scratch, you need to back this database up. Unfortunately, XDIR.EDB will not be backed up during an online backup. You must stop the DXA service on the Exchange server to gain access to the file offline and back it up. Keep in mind that the worst case scenario when you lose the XDIR.EDB file is that you have to rerun an entire DirSync between your MS Mail network and your Exchange organization. Although this can potentially take a long time and make your users unhappy, you will not actually lose any unrecoverable data.

Transaction Logs

Before any transaction is committed to an Exchange database, it is first recorded in a *transaction log*. Exchange uses these files for fault tolerance and to increase performance, and you can use them for disaster recovery if you have configured your system appropriately. We will look at the optimum configuration in Chapter 12. Now let's discuss the log files themselves, checkpoint files, and patch files.

Log Files

Every single thing you or your users do in Exchange is written to a transaction *log file* before it is committed to the database. Each database has an associated transaction log. By default, the log files are found in the same directory as their associated database. The current log file is always named EDB.LOG. EDB.LOG is always 5MB in size, and when it becomes full, Exchange renames it EDB*XXXXX*.LOG, where the XXXXX is a sequentially incremented hexadecimal number ranging from 00000 to FFFFF.

In order to recover fully from a server crash, you will need one of the two following things:

- An offline copy of your databases
- An online copy of your databases, along with the transaction log files

The backup tape created during an online backup will have a copy of transaction logs that had not been committed to the database as of the beginning of the backup.

Checkpoint Files

The checkpoint files are called EDB.CHK and are found in the same directory as their corresponding log files. The checkpoint files are used by Exchange to determine which transactions have been committed to their database. As transactions are committed, the pointer in the checkpoint file is incremented. This allows Exchange to recover at the point at which it left off in the event of a power failure or hard reset.

Before a full or incremental online backup is performed, the checkpoint file is first processed to identify which transaction logs have not yet been backed up. Online backup will back those logs up to tape and purge the logs that the checkpoint file indicates have been committed to the database.

Security of Your Key Manager Backups

Because this database includes your security keys, the decision of who backs it up should be carefully considered. I recommend that this particular right be assigned to one of the administrators who has Permissions Admin rights to your Site and Configuration containers. Additionally, the backup tape should be secured to minimize the likelihood of unauthorized access through restores. Although extremely diffi-cult, it is technically possible to crack the 128-bit key used to encrypt the database. Therefore, you need to prevent intruders from gaining access to your tape backup so that they can't subsequently restore the database to another server where their break-in attempts go unnoticed.

Using the Key Manager Startup Floppy Disk

During Key Manager installation in Exchange 5.5, you will be presented with a choice to enter the pass-word in manually at service startup or use a startup floppy disk. Do yourself a favor and use the startup floppy. Entering the password in manually every time can get pretty tiresome.

Patch Files

Patch files are used by Exchange to keep track of transactions that occur during the course of an online backup. The databases that can be backed up online include `PRIV.EDB`, `PUB.EDB`, and `DIR.EDB`, and their corresponding patch files are named `PRIV.PAT`, `PUB.PAT`, and `DIR.PAT`. The patch file is created at the beginning of an online backup when the database application locks the database file. Transactions that cannot be committed to the database during the backup are written to the patch file. At the end of the backup when the database is unlocked, the patch file is written to the backup tape, and the patch file transactions are posted to the current Exchange database. The patch file is then deleted from your Exchange server.

User Data

In addition to managing all the server-based data, you should consider your user data when you determine your backup scheme. User data quite often resides on your user workstations, so in some cases you'll have to decide whether to back up across the network or have your users save their files on the server. User data to be aware of includes autoarchive files, `.PST` files, `.OST` files, and `.PAB` files.

Autoarchive Files

As mentioned in Chapter 5, Outlook97 and Outlook98 both have an *autoarchive* feature that downloads data from your users' server-based mailboxes to local `.PST` files. When your users attempt to access information that has been archived, Outlook automatically loads the data from the archive file. This activity is invisible to your user. The thing to consider is that after information is archived to the archive file, it is no longer on the server and is no longer being backed up. You should include this file in your backups at least weekly. The good news is that if you have enabled roving user profiles in your environment, the `archive.pst` file will be uploaded to the server into your user profile directory. The bad news is that this can involve a lot of network overhead and server disk space for large archive files.

`.PST` Files

In addition to depending on autoarchiving, your users may also be moving mail off the server into local `.PST` files. These are pretty obvious; your users need to add the Personal Folder service to the local profile before a `.PST` file can be created. As with autoarchive files, the data in a local `.PST` has been removed from the server and will not be backed up unless you take action specifically to back it up.

I recommend you do network backups at least weekly. Have your users store their `.PST` files in a predetermined local directory that your backup program connects to and backs up for your users. If you fail to do this, you cannot recover items that are lost due to user error or hardware malfunction.

.OST **Files**

Offline storage files are used to synchronize data from the Exchange mailbox and/or public folders to a local file to be used when the user is not connected to the Exchange server. If you fail to back them up and a user loses his local profile or his .OST file becomes too corrupt to repair, the worst thing that will happen is that you will have to re-create the .OST file and resynchronize with the server. This can be a problem if the user's mailbox is huge, but restoring across the network will present the same problem. I would not personally worry about backing up user .OST files.

.PAB **Files**

It is of the utmost importance that you back up all of your users' .PAB files. I have found that when users lose email they become somewhat irate, but when they lose their personal address books they become downright furious. It is very frustrating to have to repopulate a new personal address book, especially if it held a lot of foreign addresses and distribution lists.

The default location for the .PAB file is C:\WINDOWS\Profiles\Username\ Application Data\Microsoft\Outlook\mailbox.PAB. Like archive.pst, the .PAB file default location is part of your user profile and will be on the server in the profile directory if you have enabled roaming user profiles.

Be sure to back up the profile directory on your server to safeguard autoarchive files and .PAB files if you have roaming user profiles. If you don't have roaming user profiles, connect to your user workstations to do a network backup of this data. The command line for a network backup for the user profile directory is as follows:

```
ntbackup backup \\userworkstation\c$\WINDOWS\Profiles /a /v /l
c:\logs\user.log /e
```

This command will back up all data stored in c:\windows\profiles on the user's workstation. The data will be appended to any existing backup sets and verified. Exceptions will then be logged to c:\logs\user.log.

.PST **Files on the Server**

I have been to numerous customer sites where the local powers-that-be insist upon having their users store .PST files on the server for backups. This is counterproductive; the primary purpose of .PST files is to minimize server disk resource utilization. If you feel that .PST files should be on the server, you should not be using them at all. Exchange native data storage is far more efficient due to the nature of the database and single copy message storage.

Backup of the NT Registry and SAM

I do a lot of consulting for small companies, and I find that many of them are too small to require a dedicated server for Exchange. In fact, it is not uncommon to find that Exchange is installed on the PDC along with SQL or some other application. If this sounds like your company, you absolutely *must* have a backup of your server's Registry and SAM database, or you may not be able to regain access to your Exchange server.

Exchange System Files

In addition to the databases and logs, you need to back up the system files found in the \exchsrvr directory. Of particular importance are the files in the mtadata, imcdata, and tracking.log directories.

The \mtadata directory contains the following files:

- MTA database stored as DbXXXXXX.dat
- MTA crash state files stored as *.DMP
- Event log files stored as EV*
- Calls.out file for troubleshooting

The most important data is stored in the DbXXXXXX.dat file, since this is the actual queued message data. I would recommend backing up the troubleshooting files as well, simply because you never know when the information they contain will become useful.

If you have diagnostics logging configured to archive incoming an outgoing Internet mail, the archive is found in the \imcdata directory. You need to back up this directory to recover the archives in the event of a server crash.

The tracking.log directory contains a log file for each day a message is processed by services that have tracking enabled. This could include the MTA, Information Store, and various connectors. If you lose this directory you will not be able to track messages processed by your Exchange server.

Windows NT Data

Ideally, Exchange should be installed on a dedicated member server. If Exchange is on a dedicated server and you lose the entire server, recovery of NT could be a matter of simply reinstalling the operating system. If, however, your Exchange server is running on the only controller in your NT domain, it is critical that you back up your NT configuration information. This includes the Registry (particularly the portions relating to Exchange configuration) and the Security Accounts Manager (SAM) database.

Summary

Backing up your server regularly according to a Standard Operating Procedure is critical. In this chapter we discussed the options you have for backups and the data that needs to be backed up in order for you to have a successful recovery. The next chapter addresses the tasks that should be performed daily in order to minimize the necessity of your actually having to use your backup to restore your Exchange server.

7

Daily Proactive Troubleshooting

AN OLD SAYING STATES THAT "An ounce of prevention is worth a pound of cure," and nowhere is that more true than with networking. So far in Part I we have addressed tasks that need to be done regularly in order to provide current functionality to your users. This is not enough, however. You need to take steps every day to minimize the likelihood of a disaster, and to minimize the damage a disaster may create. In this chapter, we will address the things you can do every day that will help you keep your Exchange server up and running in the long run. These tasks include using event logs and backup logs to find problems early on, implementing Server Monitors and Link Monitors that will alert you to performance problems, and utilizing Performance Monitor to track workload trends. You can make the performance of these tasks easier by using an automatic reporting tool such as Crystal Reports.

Windows NT Event Logs

Because Exchange components run as services in the background of NT, problems that the services have are logged to the Event Viewer's Application Log. In addition to STOP errors, you will find a wealth of information in the event logs that can help you optimize your Exchange server. Let's take a look at the types of storage-related events and performance events that can help you discover problems before they become catastrophes.

Disk Space Events

You will find some interesting information related to storage space issues if you check your event logs. Significant events to take note of involve disk space being used by the Information Store and the Internet Mail Service (IMS). You need to keep track of your available disk space because if you run too low, your services will stop.

Information Store

Exchange's online defragmentation of the Information Store only marks pages of the database as free for subsequent use by Exchange—it does not actually release the disk space. Therefore, you can often benefit by periodically using ESEUTIL or EDBUTIL to perform an offline defragmentation, which frees space for use by other applications.

Exchange 5.5 is much better about not wasting space in the Information Store than versions 4.0 or 5.0 were, an improvement that minimizes the need to do regular offline defragmentations. You will probably still want to do offline defragmentations in version 5.5 if you have recently moved or deleted a lot of data from the Information Stores, or if you are becoming concerned about the amount of disk space you have available. If you are running version 5.5 using the single-server edition, you are still limited to 16GB database sizes. If you are creeping up on that limit you may want to run ESEUTIL to buy yourself a little more time to address the problem.

Service Pack 1 for Exchange 5.5 has a handy new feature that records events in your application log to tell you how much disk space you can recover by performing an offline defragmentation of your Information Store. After you apply the service pack, each night an informational event will be recorded in the application event log's General category that reads as follows: "The database has *XX* megabytes of free space after online defragmentation has terminated." This information can help you determine whether you can benefit from an offline defragmentation.

The event this new feature records is particularly helpful in environments that don't enforce storage limits. I find that quite often in environments in which storage limits are not enforced, users are asked to clean out their mailboxes only when the administrator is already having disk space problems. This frequently leads to considerable disk space becoming available, which you probably wish to have released for use by programs other than Exchange. You must perform an offline defragmentation in order to reclaim the space, and because offline defragmentation requires free space available equivalent to the current size of the database being defragmented, this can become a real problem. You can help yourself out by checking the Event Viewer for storage information events and acting upon them as soon as possible.

> **Exchange Version and Event IDs**
>
> Be sure that you are viewing the event logs on a computer that is running the same version of Exchange as the one logging the events; the event descriptions vary with each version of Exchange.

There is an argument about the benefits of ESEUTIL in Exchange 5.5 that any space you reclaim will eventually be used again later, and that doing an offline defragmentation just forces Exchange to spend resources growing the database again later. However, my experience is that in many cases there is an immediate need to reclaim that space. ESEUTIL will allow you to identify a separate drive for the temporary database it creates, so you can use it to shrink the size of your database without having to use an equal amount of disk space on the same drive. If you are running Exchange versions 4.0 or 5.0, online defragmentation is not optimized, and therefore will leave you with the responsibility of performing periodic offline defragmentations using EDBUTIL.

Unfortunately, there is not an Event ID for version 4.0 or 5.0 to alert you as to how much space can actually be recovered by an offline defragmentation, so you should build offline defragmentation using EDBUTIL into your maintenance schedule for versions 4.0 and 5.0. Do an ESEUTIL in version 5.5 only when you have a compelling reason to do so.

Internet Mail Service

The Information Store is not the only component of Exchange to worry about as far as disk storage is concerned. If the drive that houses your IMS runs out of disk space, you will receive warning errors in your Event Viewer that inform you the IMS is going into Flush Mode.

Flush Mode means the IMS is not accepting any new messages from either the Internet or from internal Exchange users via the MTS-OUT queue for processing until the amount of space available on the drive increases above a predefined value. This isn't too big of a deal for your internal users because their outgoing messages will queue up in MTS-OUT until the IMS is ready to resume routing. It can, however, be a problem for incoming messages if you don't have multiple mail exchangers (and DNS MX records) defined for your email domain.

For example, HTS.COM has only one IMS defined with an MX record in DNS. When the server that hosts the IMS runs low on disk space on the drive where the IMCDATA directory is stored, the IMS stops receiving incoming mail. Because there is no other IMS defined in DNS, message delivery will fail until Flush Mode ends. If Flush Mode remains enabled for longer than the transfer timeout defined at the sending host, messages addressed to HTS.COM will be bounced back to the sender.

The IMS checks the amount of space available every 15 seconds, so you won't have much time to prevent Flush Mode from starting. By default, the threshold value for starting Flush Mode is 10MB, but you can change this by editing the Registry key HKEY_LOCAL_MACHINE\SYSTEM\CurrentControlSet\Services\MSExchangeIMC\ Parameters\DiskSpaceLowWaterMark. The default value of 10MB is expressed as a hex DWORD of 0x00A00000 bytes.

When the IMS determines that the available disk space has dropped below the defined limit, you'll get a warning error in the event log in the Message Transfer category that reads as follows:

"The available disk space on the spool drive has dropped below 1000 kilobytes. The Internet Mail Connector will not accept messages for inbound and outbound conversion. Inbound and outbound message conversion will continue when the available disk space has increased above 1000 kilobytes."

As soon as the IMS determines that the available disk space has increased sufficiently, Flush Mode will be disabled and you'll see another warning error for the Message Transfer category that reads:

"The available disk space on the spool drive has increased above 1000 kilobytes. The Internet Mail Connector is once again accepting messages for inbound and outbound conversion."

Performance Events

Now that you are aware of storage related events, let's take a look at some events you might find that indicate serious performance problems. The events we will discuss in this section relate to the Message Transfer Agent, system time, Performance Optimizer, and database corruption.

Message Transfer Agent

As you do your daily analysis of the event logs, you may run into events that indicate performance problems with the Message Transfer Agent (MTA). The Exchange MTA has a limit of 10 associations allowed between itself and a remote MTA. This includes nine regular associations to handle normal priority mail and one additional association to handle urgent messages. By default, Exchange attempts to create a new association for every 50 messages queued for a remote host. If your environment generates so much message traffic that the limit of 10 associations is exceeded, you'll see an Event ID 57 in the application log that reads as follows:

Changing the IMS Low Disk Space Threshold

I don't recommend decreasing the threshold value for the IMS in general because 10MB is not much of a window to work with. It is better for the IMS to not respond for a period than for it to crash altogether, potentially resulting in lost data. However, I do recommend increasing this value in environments in which there is substantial SMTP traffic being passed through the IMS.

Editing the Registry Incorrectly

If you accidentally cause problems in your environment by editing the Registry incorrectly, you may have to reinstall or restore your server from backup. Don't go in there unless you know what you are doing, and for goodness sake, back up the Registry first!

"The limit on the number of associations allowed to and from entity *destination-server* has been reached. The limit is 9."

The variable *destination-server* reflects the X.500 name of the server your local MTA is trying to deliver mail to. This server could be another server in the same site or in another site accessible via either site connector or X.400 connector.

It is my experience that this error typically indicates a network problem. Because Exchange is unable to deliver mail as fast as it wants to due to bandwidth problems, it dedicates more and more local resources to the mail transfer, usually just adding to the problem. Eventually, the resource threshold is reached and the event is written to the log. To solve the problem, you may need to upgrade your network connection to the remote server.

System Time

In addition to the MTA association problem, you should be aware of delivery problems due to incorrect system time. The MTA compares the date and time stamped on the message by the message sender with the local system's date and time during message routing. If the time difference is greater than the maximum time for delivery (24 hours by default), the MTA returns the message to the sender as nondeliverable and logs a warning event to the Event Viewer that reads something like the following:

"The default latest delivery time for the message *[message ID]* has expired (*XXXXX* minutes after a submission). A non-delivery report has been generated with reason code unable-to-transfer and diagnostic code maximum-time-expired."

You are less likely to encounter this error than other errors mentioned in this chapter during administration because time errors cause a multitude of other problems in an NT network. I have encountered only this one in the lab, although I have heard of it happening on one or two occasions in the field. To prevent time synchronization problems, you can either use a Server Monitor within Exchange to fix the discrepancy, or you can use a time server. I recommend a time server with which every server in your organization (or time zone) is synchronized at startup using the NET TIME command.

MTA and Event 9156 Errors

There is a bug in the MTA Winsock code for Exchange versions 5.0 and 5.5 that may result in event 9156 errors being logged when the MTA attempts to send mail across an X.400 connector. If you are getting these errors, contact Microsoft Product Support Services for the fix. Their phone number can be found at the following Web site:

http://support.microsoft.com/support/supportnet/default.asp

Performance Optimizer

Aside from message delivery events, you should also be aware of events that prompt you to run the Performance Optimizer. You probably remember that after you installed Exchange Server, you were prompted to run the Performance Optimizer. Hopefully you did so at the time and continue to use the Performance Optimizer to analyze your system resources and configure system variables appropriately, based on information you provide about your current messaging environment. Performance Optimizer usage will be discussed in Chapter 8, "Managing Server Resources."

Ideally, the Performance Optimizer should be run whenever any of the following is true:

- An Exchange server's functions have changed
- Users have been added to the server
- Users have been added to the organization
- Resources (such as memory) have been added to the server

I have seen the following error in companies where the administrator elected to not run the Performance Optimizer after installation and in companies in which the Performance Optimizer was not re-run regularly with the expansion of the messaging system:

"The total number of threads (XX) configured for the Information Store is too low. Assuming YY threads."

The value for XX is smaller than the value for YY, indicating that Exchange decided for itself in real-time that it could not operate sufficiently under the current conditions. This error indicates that you need to re-run the Performance Optimizer.

More often than not, companies that get this message in the event viewer tend to ignore it because it is not a STOP error and Exchange appears to be self-optimizing. This is a bad practice; although Exchange is attempting to repair itself, it is by no means optimizing itself on the fly. I have also seen this error during upgrades in which, occasionally, the Exchange server will fail to start correctly as a result of the problem. If this happens to you, and you are unable to run the Performance Optimizer, you can try editing the Registry value `HKEY_LOCAL_MACHINE\SYSTEM\CurrentControlSet\Services\MSexchangeIS\ParametersSystem`. Change the value for Minimum Threads to a larger number. Remember to always back up your Registry before editing anything!

Database Corruption

The worst performance event you can find is one that indicates a corrupt database. As we mentioned in Chapter 6, "Backing Up Your Server," database corruption can be identified during online backups as well as during online defragmentation. The reason for this is that both of these processes read pages from the database in order to perform their jobs. As these pages are read, the backup and defragmentation routines perform a comparison of the checksum stored in the page header to the checksum returned by the read request. If these two checksum values are not the same, a Jet error is returned and logged to the Event Viewer that reads something like the following:

"The database engine has stopped the backup with error -1018."

Other errors you may see are addressed in Table 7.1.

Table 7.1 **Error Messages Indicating Database Corruption of the Private Information Store**

Event	Error Message
Database Page Cache	"Direct read found corrupted page (*XXXXX*) with error -1018. Please restore the databases from a previous backup."
Online Defragmentation	"Online defragmentation of database 'E:\exchsrvr\ MDBDATA\PRIV.EDB' terminated prematurely after encountering unexpected error -1018."
Database Cache	"Synchronous read page checksum error -1018 occurred. Please restore the databases from a previous backup."

I have seen variations of these errors on occasion, and in most cases the data was recoverable because the problem was discovered early. This particular set of errors is one of the reasons I recommend doing full, online backups regularly.

If you have a corrupt database, you will continue to receive these errors during every online backup or every online defragmentation until you fix the problem. Repair options include ESEUTIL/EDBUTIL, moving users to a different server, and restoring from a backup. We will be discussing disaster recovery in detail in Chapter 14, "Disaster Recovery."

Windows NT Backup Logs

In addition to daily parsing of your event logs, you need to be on top of your backup logs. Daily perusal of the backup logs can alert you to problems such as corrupt databases or incorrectly backed-up files before the problem becomes a disaster. You should always verify the backup as part of your standard operating procedure. I also recommend creating a log file to be printed out and stored in a three-ring binder at the end of each backup. When it comes time to recover something from backup, the log file can help you determine when and where the data can be found.

Crystal Reports

Now that you know what to look for in your log files, you're probably thinking about what a pain it is going to be to have to go through all of that stuff manually. Well, there is an easier way. Although there are several reporting tools available on the market, I really like Seagate Software's Crystal Reports. Not only is Crystal Reports a great tool that you can use to create reports based on Exchange data and on the log files generated by your system, but its use is quite widespread. Because Crystal Reports is so commonly used, you will find lots of books to help you master it, in addition to widely offered instructor-led classes and newsgroups such as `www.crystaluser.com`.

The best place to start with Crystal Reports is by using the canned reports that come with the BackOffice Resource Kit. The mailbox and public folder reports are great because they give a detailed account of the resources being used for each mailbox or folder. In addition to reporting on server statistics, you will also want to run Crystal Reports against your event logs. Bear in mind that the version of Crystal Reports found on the Resource Kit is limited. You will have to purchase the full version from Seagate Software in order to get all the bells and whistles.

Monitoring Exchange

Going through logs is a good way to stay on top of your Exchange environment, but it tends to be reactive rather than proactive. Because it's always better to prevent a fire rather than having to put one out, do yourself a favor and take advantage of Exchange's self-monitoring features. Exchange's ability to self-monitor is definitely one of its best features.

You'll notice that the Monitor's container in your site's Configuration container has no monitors configured by default. In this section we will look at how to configure and use both Server Monitors and Link Monitors. At the end of this section we will also discuss configuration and management of Performance Monitor logs. For detailed information on the Performance Monitor counters and how they can be used to troubleshoot, please see Chapter 13, "Troubleshooting Your Exchange Server."

Planning Server Monitors

Server Monitors are used to verify whether a predefined service is running on an Exchange server. You can use Server Monitors to monitor any service that's running on the server. You are not limited to Exchange services. Let's take a look at planning your Server Monitors and, subsequently, how to configure them according to your plan.

Before you begin creating Server Monitors, it is important for you to plan what servers will be monitored, what services on them will be monitored, and what actions you will be taking in the event one of the monitored services is found to be stopped. This involves determining which servers are critical to your messaging topology and what indispensable services those servers run. After you've identified the services, you will also need to decide what, if any, action will be taken automatically to correct the problem.

A Server Monitor will query the services once during each polling interval until a service is found to be stopped. Subsequent queries will be made at the rate you define in the Critical Sites field on the monitor. Consider carefully what actions you will define and the polling interval for your monitors. The best way to plan your Server Monitors is to create a table for yourself like Table 7.2. Keep in mind that this table is just an example—you should make your own determinations based on your environment.

Table 7.2 **Planning Your Server Monitor Topology**

Server Name	Services Monitored	First Attempt	Second Attempt	Third Attempt	Poll	Critical Sites Field
FLHub	MSExchangeDS	0	1	2	30	10
	MSExchangeMTA	0	1	2	30	10
	DHCPServer	0	1	2	30	10
	Wins	0	1	2	30	10
TAMPA	MSExchangeDS	0	1	1	30	5
	MSExchangeIS	0	1	1	30	5
	MSExchangeMTA	0	1	1	30	5
MIAMI	MSExchangeDS	0	1	1	30	5
	MSExchangeIS	0	1	1	30	5
	MSExchangeMTA	0	1	1	30	5
NYHub	MSExchangeDS	0	1	1	30	5
	MSExchangeMTA	0	1	1	30	5
	DNS	0	1	1	30	5
	PC MTA	0	1	1	30	5
	MSMI	0	1	1	30	5
	MSExchangeIMC	0	1	1	30	5
NEWARK	MSExchangeDS	0	1	1	30	5
	MSExchangeIS	0	1	1	30	5
	MSExchangeMTA	0	1	1	30	5
ALBANY	MSExchangeDS	0	1	1	30	5
	MSExchangeIS	0	1	1	30	5
	MSExchangeMTA	0	1	1	30	5

0=Take no action, 1=Restart the service, 2=Restart the computer

You'll notice that Table 7.2 gives a longer time between polls for the FLHub server. This is because the actions defined include forced restart of the computer. Because a restart can take several minutes (and you don't want the monitor to be attempting to fix a problem during a corrective restart), it is important to configure the polling interval so that a restart can successfully complete before the next corrective attempt will be made. I have seen incorrectly configured monitors do more harm than good.

After you have planned your server monitor strategy by determining the information in Table 7.2, you need to decide where the monitor will be run from. Deciding what server will be running the monitor is very important. This decision requires just as much planning as determining what servers to monitor in the first place. You need to be careful not to run monitors that monitor the same services on the same server from two different servers. In other words, don't create a monitor on the ALBANY server that monitors the MSExchangeDS on the NEWARK server if there is already a monitor configured to do so on the NYHub server. Obviously the problem is that both monitors will generate notifications and attempt corrective action independently of the other and you may wind up with conflicts. Table 7.3 is an example of the information you need to collect in order to plan where your monitors will be run.

Table 7.3   **Determining What Server Will Run Which Monitor(s)**

Monitor Name	Monitored Server(s)	Monitoring Server
FLHub	FLHub	MIAMI
FLUsers	TAMPA and MIAMI	FLHub
NYHub	NYHub	NEWARK
NYUsers	ALBANY and NEWARK	NYHub

In this example, the NYHub is being monitored from NEWARK because the NYHub server is physically located in Newark. The same is true of the FLHub server and MIAMI. The only limitation you should consider when determining where a monitor should be run is that the monitor uses RPCs to query the services of the remote server. For that reason, you should make sure that the network between the monitored and monitoring servers supports RPCs. You might also notice from the table that in two instances a single monitor is responsible for monitoring more than one server. You should take advantage of the ability of a monitor to monitor multiple servers. You can have the monitor query as many servers as you want, as long as the actions being taken for stopped services are the same.

Creating Server Monitors

Exchange can monitor its own services, so you should configure it to do just that. To create a Server Monitor, access the Administrator Program and select **File**, **New Other**, **Server Monitor**. A set of property pages will pop up allowing you to define how the monitor will operate. Table 7.4 defines what properties are available to you.

Table 7.4 **Server Monitor Configuration Properties**

Property	Method of Configuration
General	Define a log file on the **General** tab so that you can peruse the monitor status at your leisure. This is helpful if you are being notified only when an Alert is generated but you are interested in seeing how often Warnings are generated. The polling interval section is where you define how often the monitor will query your servers during normal operation, and how often the query will be generated when a service is found to be stopped.
Notification	Define who will be notified, how they will be notified, and when they will be notified on the **Notification** tab. You can use this to create either NT alerts or email messages. If you have a product that allows you to send a page message from a command line, you can enter the command line into the notification configuration fields.
Servers	Use the **Servers** tab to identify what servers will be monitored from this monitor. After you have picked the servers, use the **Services** button to select the services to be monitored on each server. You will notice that there is a default set of services that pops up. This list is defined on the server's property pages for each server. By editing this list on each server, you will allow monitors created in other sites to monitor the correct services by default.
Actions	Define what actions the monitor should take when a service is found to be stopped. These actions are performed when the moniter determines the service has stopped. You probably want the monitor to take different actions the third time it checks and finds a service stopped than it did the first time.
Clock	As we mentioned earlier in the "Windows NT Event Logs" section, system time problems can cause real performance issues with Exchange. You can configure your monitor to compare the local time with the time on the monitored server. If the time discrepancy becomes large enough (based on your threshold values defined on this tab) the monitor can generate a Warning or Alert message and can optionally be configured to change the time on the remote, monitored server to synchronize with the local time.

Planning Link Monitors

Whereas Server Monitors are used to verify whether a predefined service is running on an Exchange server, *Link Monitors* are used to verify the performance of the physical connection between an Exchange server and a remote server. You can use Link Monitors to monitor the connection between Exchange and any other type of server. You are not limited to using it only between two Exchange servers. In this section we will discuss planning your Link Monitor strategy.

Like Server Monitors, before you begin creating Link Monitors you will need to plan which servers will be monitored, what server will be doing the monitoring, and what is an acceptable bounce time for messages to and from the remote server. Create a table for yourself like Table 7.5, which helps you consider the availability and bandwidth when determining bounce times. As you formulate your plan, determine what acceptable bounce times are for each of your monitored links in addition to what action will be taken if and when a link is found to be non-functional.

Table 7.5   **Link Monitor Strategy**

Monitored Server	Monitoring Server	Network	Warning	Alert
ALBANY, NEWARK, and FLHub	NYHub	T1	10 min	30 min
TAMPA, MIAMI, and NYHub	FLHub	T1	10 min	30 min
HTS.COM	NYHub	Demand/Dial-up	2 hrs	4 hrs
HEMPLE.EDU	NYHub	Demand/T1	30 min	60 min

Notice in Table 7.5 that one monitor is being used to bounce messages to three different servers—to ALBANY, NEWARK, and FLHub—while a second monitor is bouncing messages to TAMPA, MIAMI, and NYHub. You can use a single monitor to monitor the link between as many hosts as you want as long as the bounce times are the same for all hosts. A good rule of thumb is to combine monitors together that you connect to via the same network.

For example, before configuring these Link Monitors, I spoke to the administrator at HTS.COM and learned that HTS has a dial-up connection to its ISP that is active only once every hour. Because I know that my site's outgoing messages will be transmitted to their holding location virtually immediately, the bounce is limited only by their intermittent connection. On the other hand, HEMPLE.EDU has a T1 connection to the Internet. Although I expect to have much faster return than the bounce I defined on the monitor to HEMPLE.EDU, it is not critical that I have messages transfer faster than 30 minutes. Therefore, I elected to not configure the monitor for less than 30 minutes. If you find that your monitors are always in Warning or Alert states, you should either reevaluate your performance expectations and reconfigure your monitors, or purchase a better network connection.

The Link Monitor uses the System Attendant of the local Exchange server to generate an email message to the remote server. If the remote server is another Exchange server, the System Attendant of that server will respond to the incoming Link Monitor message. If, on the other hand, the remote server is a foreign host, you must create a custom recipient within Exchange to be used to send to the foreign host. You should always consult with the administrator of any foreign system that you do link monitoring with. If the custom recipient you create on your Exchange server does not exist on the remote system (such that you get non-delivery reports (NDRs) back as Link Monitor responses) then it is possible the remote administrator is being notified of the failure to deliver a message to her domain. If you want to create a custom recipient that corresponds to a real mailbox, then the remote administrator will need to configure the mailbox to auto-reply to your Link Monitor messages.

Each Link Monitor will send a message to the servers and/or recipients you identify once during each polling interval until a message reply is not received by the Link Monitor within the Warning state threshold. When a bounce exceeds the warning state, the local System Attendant will begin sending messages at the rate defined as a Critical site on the General tab. This will continue until the link is considered operational again.

Creating Link Monitors

To create a Link Monitor, access the Administrator Program and select **File**, **New Other**, **Link Monitor**. A set of property pages will pop up allowing you to define how the monitor will operate. Table 7.6 defines those properties available to you.

Table 7.6 **Link Monitor Configuration Properties**

Property Page	Method of Configuration
General	Use this page the same way you would for Server Monitors. The only difference is that the polling interval defines how often the local System Attendant will send messages to the defined servers and recipients during normal operation, and how often the message will be sent when the Warning bounce time has been exceeded.
Notification	Use this page in the same way you would for a Server Monitor.
Servers	Use the Servers tab to identify which Exchange servers will be tested from this monitor.
Recipients	Define the foreign custom recipients that will be tested.
Bounce	Configure the bounce time for both Warning and Alert states on this tab.

Planning and Configuring Performance Monitor Logs

In addition to using Server and Link Monitors to monitor your system in real-time, Performance Monitor can and should be used regularly to track system resource usage in order to plan for future upgrades. Companies that neglect to monitor system performance inevitably run into trouble with server response time. Performance Monitor has greatly helped these companies to identify increased workload and prepare for system resource upgrades.

To be most effective, you must take a baseline of your system during regular business hours. This baseline will later be used to identify performance thresholds and expectations. After you've identified the performance parameters you expect to see, you need to compare the baseline with regular Performance Monitor logs to identify trends in your workload and resource usage over time.

Workload Trends

Workload trends are related to how your users are using the features of your Exchange system. What I find happens in most companies is that the workload increases over time regardless of whether there is an increase in the installed user base. This appears to happen because, as users become more familiar and more comfortable with the available features, they will use them more. The problem is that you as the administrator must identify these workload trends before they result in performance problems that are obvious to your users.

For example, in companies where the users did not have email before Exchange or had an older, less robust system, adoption of public folder usage was slower than in companies that were already heavy email users. My experience has been that companies with inexperienced email users were unable to accurately predict server usage prior to deployment because they simply didn't know how users, administrators, and so on would take advantage of Exchange's features beforehand.

Task-Specific Resource Usage

You also need to keep track of resource usage as it corresponds with specific Exchange tasks. For example, it is not enough to know that your %Processor Time is increasing. You need to correlate that increase with the tasks that the Exchange server is performing at that time. By tracking both sets of data, you will be able to pinpoint the processes that users are taking better advantage of and subsequently prepare to offload some of that processing to another server when bottlenecks begin to occur.

See Table 7.7 for a listing of some of the counters that you can use to help you identify increasing workload and decreasing performance trends.

Increased Workloads Indicate Increased User Satisfaction

Keep an eye out for increases in the number of messages being sent and the inclusion of message attachments. I've seen both of these variables increase dramatically as users become more comfortable with the messaging system.

Table 7.7 **Workload and Server Performance Trends**

Object	Counter	Description
MSExchangeIS	User Count	The number of clients currently connected to either the Private or Public Information Store.
	Active User Count	The number of clients who have actively accessed data in the IS in the past 10 minutes.
MSExchangeIS Private	Messages Submitted/min	The average number of messages submitted to the Private Information Store each minute.
	Message Recipients Delivered/min	The average number of messages delivered by thePrivate Information Store each minute.
	Send Queue Size	The number of outbound messages waiting to be processed by the Private Information Store. This value should be zero during normal activity.
	Average Time for Delivery	Number of seconds it takes for the Information Store to deliver a message.
MSExchangeIS Public	Messages Submitted/min	The average number of messages submitted to the Public Information Store each minute.
	Message Recipients Delivered/min	The average number of messages submitted by the Public Information Store each minute.
MSExchangeIS Public	Send Queue Size	The number of outbound messages waiting to be processed by the Public Information Store. This value should be zero during normal activity.
	Average Time for Delivery	Number of seconds it takes for the Public Information Store to deliver a message.
MSExchangeMTA	Messages/sec	The number of messages the MTA processes per second.
	Messages Bytes/sec	The number of bytes the MTA processes per second.
	Work Queue Length	The number of messages queued for the MTA to process. Work Queue Length should be zero under ordinary circumstances.

In addition to workload and resource counters, you should also be keeping track of system counters in order to identify where bottlenecks are occurring. See Table 7.8 for some useful bottleneck counters.

Table 7.8 **Performance Monitor Counters that Can Be Used to Identify Bottlenecks**

Object	Counter	Recommendation
System	% Total Processor Time	On multiprocessor systems, this counter reflects the total combined processor usage. Optimum is around 60% × the number of processors, such that a dual processor system should reflect 120% or less during peak workload.
Process	% Processor Time	Monitor over long periods of time. Optimum is around 60% utilization to provide for workload peaks.
LogicalDisk	Disk Bytes Written/sec Disk Reads/sec Disk Writes/sec Avg. Disk Queue Length	For all disk counters, compare the values you obtain from the Performance Monitor with the specifications provided by your disk's manufacturer. Your disk may be a bottleneck if the logs reflect numbers very close to the disk specifications.
Memory	Pages/sec	If this value is high, you could benefit from the addition of more memory to your Exchange server. It's important to monitor paging in conjunction with the disk counters since your disk activity will increase as your paging increases.
Network Interface	Bytes Received/sec Bytes Sent/sec Packets Received/sec Packets Sent/sec	Install the NT Resource Kit to obtain these network counters. Compare the figures you obtain via logging with the vendor specifications of your network card. If your data is very close to the vendor specifications, consider upgrading your network.

Performance Monitor Alerts

In addition to creating performance logs, consider implementing the Alerts functionality in Performance Monitor as well. You can use the Alerts to notify you when certain thresholds are exceeded, such as too many messages queued up or too many requests awaiting processing. You can then quickly react to a problem before it degenerates into a disaster and becomes an issue with your users.

I am a big fan of performance monitoring. If I were a consultant for your company's installed Exchange organization, one of the first things I would do is make sure you have a performance baseline, and create one for you if you didn't. After you have that baseline and have identified your personal performance thresholds, set up Performance Monitor logging to run regularly during the week. A data collection frequency of 15–30 minutes is enough for average performance trend analysis, and will prevent you from having data overload.

Summary

In this chapter, we addressed what I feel to be the most important part of administration: preventive action. Your use of event logs and backup logs will help you catch problems before they become true disasters, and your implementation of Server and Link Monitors will alert you to immediate performance problems. Finally, one of the most important actions you can take to optimize your Exchange environment is to use the Performance Monitor to create a performance baseline and subsequent performance logs, which can be used to identify workload and resource usage trends and bottlenecks.

This chapter concludes the daily administration section of this book. Let's move on to some of the tasks you will need to do periodically in order to keep Exchange up and running. We will start with managing server resources.

Periodic Administration

8

Managing Server Resources

So FAR IN THIS BOOK WE'VE TALKED about the things you really need to at least look at every day as an Exchange administrator. This chapter marks the beginning of Part II, "Periodic Administration." To start with, we will address the resources used in Exchange Server, what they are used for, and how to optimize them. We will then discuss how to manage growth in your organization as well as see how the Performance Optimizer can be used to help you get the most out of your Exchange server.

Upgrading Hardware

At some point during your resource management routine you will find that you need to upgrade your Exchange server hardware. Perhaps your users are complaining about response time, or you find yourself low on disk space. Whatever the reason, hopefully you have implemented the Performance Monitor, as discussed in Chapter 7, "Daily Proactive Troubleshooting," and your upgrade is a thoroughly considered, planned upgrade rather than a bucket of water on an out–of–control fire. I highly recommend planning for upgrades even if your studies indicate that your load will not increase to bottleneck level; it is a lot easier to upgrade systems that have a lot of expansion capabilities. For example, if you are buying a RAID array, purchase one that you can easily add more disk drives to in the future. Hardware upgrades involve the following:

- Adding memory
- Adding or upgrading processors
- Adding hard disks
- Replacing an entire server

We will discuss all of these options for Exchange organization scaling in this chapter.

Adding Memory

"You can never be too rich or have too much RAM" is what I always say when asked how much memory Exchange *really* needs in a production environment. When it comes to hardware upgrades, there is nothing that will improve the performance of your Exchange server more than memory. Obviously this is a slight exaggeration, as you could be experiencing a bottleneck in another area, but the basic premise is true. Let's look at the operations within Exchange that are such memory pigs and see what you can do about them.

Memory Usage

In my experience, memory is almost always the first thing that needs to be upgraded. The reason for this is that so much data is loaded into memory during Exchange runtime, if you don't have enough memory you will wind up having disk problems due to excessive paging. Memory is used for the following tasks:

- Exchange uses a memory buffer cache to hold data destined for the transaction log files and the Private and Public Information Stores.
- Since Microsoft improved the MTA's performance in Exchange version 5.5, the MTA is much more memory intensive. Messages queued for MTA transfer are now stored in memory instead of in the file system, and are only moved to the file system during shutdown.
- The Exchange Directory is loaded into memory when Exchange starts up. This allows for faster processing of user GAL requests, but takes up considerable memory resources.
- All foreign connectors queue messages in memory while awaiting transfer.

Exchange on Non-Dedicated Servers

I have been to lots of small companies that run Exchange along with other applications. If you are administering a multifunction server, your analysis of resource usage should take into account whatever jobs the other applications are doing. For example, if you are running Exchange on a BDC, then it is not enough to be aware of the Exchange-related processing that is increasing over time. You must also keep track of the amount of memory the BDC uses to load the domain SAM and the processor usage for account logon.

- Exchange loads as much of the Private Information Store into memory as it possibly can. If the virtual memory in your Exchange server exceeds the size of your Private Information Store, then your entire Private Information Store is probably loaded in memory.

It's easy to see how memory can become such a problem, given the amount of data Exchange attempts to load at startup and during runtime.

Optimizing Memory

Now that you are aware of what is actually using up all that memory, you probably would like to optimize. Unfortunately, there's not too much you can do other than add more memory to your Exchange server to improve Exchange's usage of memory. Exchange will pretty much use all the memory available on your Exchange Server, although you can limit this by using the Performance Optimizer. There is an entire section entitled "Performance Optimizer" later in this chapter. Consider performing one or more of the following tasks to improve Exchange's usage of memory:

- Add RAM to your Exchange server.
- Configure your server to **Maximize Throughput for Network Applications** in the Network Server Service properties.
- Configure a page file of at least 125MB plus the amount of RAM you have in your system. For example, if you have 128MB of physical RAM, your virtual memory should be set to at least 253MB.
- Run Exchange on its own dedicated server.
- Offload some of the services your Exchange server is running to another Exchange server. For example, create a dedicated connector or public folder server.
- Offload some of your user mailboxes to another server.

As part of Exchange implementation, I always set the Maximize Throughput for Network Applications setting and configure a page file per the preceding recommendations. I have found that most small companies cannot afford to run Exchange on a dedicated computer or purchase another server to offload some of the services. In these cases, the only remedy for memory problems is to add more to your system. For this reason, you should always purchase servers that have more memory expansion slots than you think you will ever need.

Adding and Upgrading a Processor

Now that we've discussed memory additions and optimization, it is time to take a look at processor upgrades. As you already know, you have two options: Replace your existing processor or add another processor to your multiprocessor computer. Because some tasks require more processor time than others, let's look at what exactly

Exchange is doing with your processor and how you can improve processor utilization.

Processor Usage

As with system memory, there are several Exchange-related tasks that use processor resources. Knowledge of the tasks being performed can help you determine what steps to take to improve your processor performance. Tasks to be aware of include the following:

- Client requests for mailbox contents or public folder contents and directory queries, which can be either via RPCs or the supported Internet protocols POP3, IMAP4, HTTP, LDAP, and NNTP.

- Messages clients send to foreign systems, such as SMTP and MS Mail. Connector usage causes processor utilization for message queuing, content conversion, and message transfer.

- Messages clients send to users on other Exchange servers. The MTA requires processor cycles to queue messages in memory while awaiting transfer, as well as to establish and maintain connections to remote Exchange servers.

- Changes made to the Exchange Directory are propagated to other servers in the same site within five minutes via RPCs, and to other sites on a schedule via message transfer. Both methods require processor time, but should not be debilitating to the processor in most environments.

- Public folder replication requires processor time also. Your users will notice performance degradation during the actual creation and incorporation of replication messages.

Although in my experience, the processor is the last thing you will need to upgrade, you should still plan for changes in your environment that will eventually warrant the upgrade. This includes purchasing servers that support the addition of more processors, even if you don't think you will ever need to add them.

Optimizing Your Processor

Although Exchange will function if you elect to not optimize your processor usage, you can realize considerable performance improvements if you take some of the following advice:

- Install the fastest processor available. If you're already running the fastest available processor, consider installing additional processors on systems that support multiple processors. I have found that upgrading a processor provides more of a performance benefit than adding another, slower processor.

- Offload some of your services, mailboxes, or folders to another server. This includes the creation of dedicated connector and public folder servers. User perception of performance is defined by how long an application appears busy rather than by how long it takes to actually transfer a message to another server. Moving connectors and routing calculation tasks to hub servers can improve user perception of server performance.

- Run Exchange on a dedicated server. Other applications running on the same server will obviously slow response time for your users' messaging requirements.

- Configure your Exchange server so that there is no **Performance Boost for Foreground Applications** on your System Properties. Because the server side of client/server applications is always run as a background process, this will improve performance. No one should be running client applications on the actual Exchange server; this will compete with user resource requirements. I have also seen companies run OpenGL screen savers on the server. Don't do this for obvious reasons.

- Increase the size of your L2 cache. More L2 cache means less waiting for information to be read out of RAM for processing. The less time your processor has to wait for information, the faster your system as a whole will be.

In addition to following these recommendations, use the Performance Monitor to predict and determine when your processor is causing bottlenecks.

Adding a Hard Disk

In addition to memory and processor upgrades, you will inevitably find yourself in need of more disk space. Exchange does try to help you out in this area by providing a really efficient storage environment and using a single-copy message store philosophy. However, I find that because disk space is cheap, a lot of places don't want to try to curtail their users' usage of it by setting storage limits. This leads to space issues. Let's evaluate and optimize the components of Exchange that are using up your disk space.

Exchange and Multiple Processors

Don't bother installing more than two processors in Exchange servers running versions 4.0 or 5.0, or more than four processors in systems running Exchange 5.5. Exchange won't use them enough to make the expense worthwhile.

The Effects of Rules, Views, and Forms on Your Server

Although rules, views, and forms are defined by users and stored on the server, their use has virtually no effect on the server in production environments. In testing, I've seen rules affect server processing only when nearly everyone has several rules set up to affect every incoming message. Similarly, Exchange caches views that have been used recently, so the user may experience a minimal delay when accessing a less heavily utilized view. Forms are downloaded only the first time a user accesses one or if the form design has changed, and subsequently they have little effect on Exchange after the form is cached on the user's local computer. Therefore, the use of rules, views, or forms should not have a significant impact on most resource planning that you do.

Disk Usage

There are a lot of things you should be aware of in terms of Exchange's usage of your disk resources. Some of these items are as follows:

- Most actual disk space is used by the Private Information Store, Public Information Store, Directory Service, and their associated transaction log files.

- Disk I/O is required for both public and private folder access. Disk I/O is affected by how often users access the public folders and mailboxes, how often public folder content is changed and subsequently replicated, how often messages are created and read, and (to a small extent) which views users define on the folders.

- Messages read and posted to the Information Stores first go through the buffer cache. If the cache is not optimized, data will be prematurely flushed from the cache to make room for newly accessed data. When the flushed data is requested later, Exchange will have to read it back out of the database on disk.

  For example, suppose Piper is looking for an old message in her inbox. As she pulls up old messages for review, the message data is loaded into the cache. She continues to load messages until the cache fills and purges data that hasn't been accessed in a while. When Piper returns to messages she accessed earlier, they are no longer in the cache because the system flushed them out. Exchange will have to reload this data from the database. This scenario can cause excessive disk I/O, which can be improved with the addition of memory and subsequent optimization of the buffer cache.

- If you have NNTP access to your Exchange server, you will probably have considerable numbers of foreign users accessing data on your Exchange server, which will affect disk I/O, in addition to the massive amounts of disk space that many newsgroups occupy on your Public Information Store disk.

Disk usage is almost always an issue with mailbox servers. While disk space is an easy parameter to consider when planning Exchange upgrades, it is easy to overlook disk I/O. You should consider both factors when attempting to optimize your disks.

Optimizing Your Hard Disks

Because your hard disks will be so heavily utilized, you will invariably run into disk resource bottlenecks requiring your attention. I have seen misinformed administrators respond to poor system performance by adding memory without adequately analyzing the bottleneck problem. Since it is really just as likely that you will run into disk-related bottlenecks as memory bottlenecks, here are some suggestions for improving the performance of your disks:

- Add faster hard disks to your system. Sequential access time is important for transaction logs, and random access time is important for your database disks.

- Place the Information Stores on hardware-configured stripe sets with parity that support hot-swappable drives.
- Place the transaction logs on their own dedicated hard disks. You can really optimize the I/O on the transaction log disks if there are no other applications using the disk. Because the files are read from and written to sequentially, the disk heads will not have to spend a lot of time seeking data.
- Use disk mirroring to provide fault tolerance for the transaction log files.
- Use fast disk controllers with read caching and battery-backed write caching for all disks. Be careful about this—if you don't have battery-backed write caching, you need to disable the write cache feature. I have seen more than one database become corrupt when the Exchange server crashed at a point when data was cached but had not yet been written to transaction logs.
- Group the users who communicate most on the same server to take advantage of Exchange's single copy message store and to prevent unnecessary MTA utilization.
- Enforce storage limits on your users and implement a clean mailbox policy. We discussed this in depth in Chapter 2, "Administering Users."
- Use age limits on your public folders. We discussed age limits in Chapter 3, "Administering Public Folders."
- Put a pagefile on the stripe set that holds the Information Store if memory paging is an issue. Better yet, add more memory.

Replacing a Server

Sometimes the best thing to do when it comes to server resource utilization is to just replace the existing server with a new server. This requires a lot of very careful planning on your part; otherwise, it could become a huge nightmare. In this section we will address the steps you need to take when replacing an existing server in order to have minimal user disruption. These steps are as follows:

1. Stop the Exchange services and back up the original server's Exchange data to tape.
2. Delete the original server from the NT domain using Server Manager. (Do *not* delete the Exchange server from the organization using the Exchange Administrator!)

Optimizing Your Disks Based on Current Performance

If your Performance Monitoring indicates that you have more database reads than writes, optimize the disks that store PRIV.EDB and PUB.EDB. If, on the other hand, Performance Monitor indicates that you have more writes than reads, optimize the Information Store transaction log disks.

3. Install NT on the replacement server using the original server's NetBIOS computer name.

4. Join the NT domain.

5. Install the latest NT service pack and applicable hot fixes.

6. Install your backup software.

7. Install Exchange in a new site with the same organization and site names as the original server. Do not use `setup /r` for the installation unless your original server did not have any Exchange service packs installed on it.

8. Install the Exchange Service Packs and/or hot fixes that were installed on the original server.

9. Stop all of the Exchange services except for the System Attendant.

10. Delete the new `EDB.CHK`, `EDB.LOG`, and any `EDB*.LOG` files.

11. Recover the `PRIV.EDB`, `PUB.EDB`, and `DIR.EDB` databases from the original server's backup tapes.

12. Run ISINTEG -patch and then start the Exchange services.

13. Verify that the Exchange server is functional.

Replacing a server is a very touchy area that is rife with potential disasters. The most important step in this series is the first one—to back up your data. The best part of replacing Exchange servers is that if something goes wrong with the replacement, you can go back to using the original server until you work out the problem.

Scaling Your Organization

Now that we have discussed hardware upgrades, it is time to discuss the actual load changes you will experience over the years. Growth will affect your Exchange server resources in different ways, depending on what aspect of your organization is growing. In this section, we will look at how adding mailboxes to your server affects the local resource usage as opposed to adding mailboxes to other servers in your organization, such as when you are migrating a remote site. You will also find that adding services such as Outlook Web Access to your organization affects performance and resource utilization. We will discuss all of these results of scaling in this section.

Adding Users to Your Server

When it comes to scaling an Exchange organization, the most common increase in server resource usage results from the addition of users to a server. This may take place insidiously over time, or you may be adding several users at a time through a migration. In any event, you will find that the first components of a mailbox server requiring your attention after users are added are generally hard disks and memory. In some cases processor upgrades can help mailbox server performance as well.

Disk Resources

Disk resources are heavily utilized on any server that houses user mailboxes. In addition to the obvious storage space requirements, there are a lot of random I/O calls that the disk must fulfill. Obviously, both storage space requirements and I/O calls will increase as new users are added because the new users will be sending and receiving mail. For example, when Bill receives a new message, the IS must store it in the Private Information Store. When Bill accesses the new message, the disk must locate the message data and load it into memory. After Bill is finished reading the message, the IS must mark the message as having been read and update the unread message counters in the database. All of these pieces of data are stored in different locations in the database. This results in disk seeking taking up a lot of disk time. The more users your server houses, the more work it will have to do to provide messaging services as a whole.

As we mentioned before, you can improve your disk performance by storing the actual PRIV.EDB and PUB.EDB files on stripe sets with parity while keeping transaction log files on a separate mirror set. Keeping the databases on stripe sets with parity provides fault tolerance in addition to better read performance; data can be read from more than one disk simultaneously in servers that have multiple disk controllers. Similarly, you will have better performance out of your transaction log files if you put them on mirror sets with disk duplexing because Exchange can read and write to them simultaneously.

Memory

In addition to disk resources, you'll find memory in short supply on many Exchange servers. Memory resources are committed for loading user data from the Private Information Store for faster read access, so as you add users to your server you will find that your memory is utilized more. Exchange will use all available memory for Information Store buffers. As we mentioned in our earlier example, when Bill accesses his mailbox, Exchange loads his messages into memory. Similarly, when Bill opens his calendar, Exchange caches his schedule into memory. All of this memory usage can ultimately lead to disk *thrashing*, whereby too much data is being moved to and from the page file. The best thing you can do when this happens is to add more memory.

Processors

It is possible that the addition of users to your server over time will cause your processor to become a bottleneck. Interestingly, performance is not much improved by adding processors in mailbox servers because the bulk of resource utilization is found in memory and disk utilization. If you run other services on the server, such as IMS or Directory Bridgehead service, then you can realize significant performance improvements by adding processors to your server.

The method by which clients access the server also affects the resources the server must dedicate to client data requests. Different access types include MAPI,

POP3/IMAP4, and HTTP. The resource usage trends you can expect to see with each of these protocols are described as follows:

- **MAPI.** Because 32-bit MAPI clients allow the most access to Exchange features, their use results in the most processing on the Exchange server. The more your users take advantage of features such as views, rules, and forms, or of services such as scheduling and contact management, the more processor load you will notice on the Exchange server. This is one of the reasons it is so important to plan for more growth than you expect, since users are notoriously inaccurate at guessing their future usage of new features.

- **POP3/IMAP4.** POP3 and IMAP4 are used to download mail from the mailbox server. All mail sent from these clients goes through your IMS server, so if you are using dedicated connector servers you will find that the load on your mailbox server is considerably reduced for POP3 and IMAP4 users, whereas the load on the IMS is considerably increased. You will also get better server disk performance when using POP3 clients because, generally, POP3 users download messages from the server and access them from a local message store. After the data is moved to the client's local store, future processing will not affect the Exchange server at all.

- **HTTP.** The Outlook Web Access (OWA) client uses HTTP to communicate with Exchange via IIS. Use of OWA clients currently does not create as much of a load on the server because the OWA client doesn't have access to the same features and services as the 32-bit Outlook client. This, however, changes with each release of Exchange and with each service pack, so don't count on this to always be the case. Because the OWA client must send data requests through an Internet Information Server, you will find that IIS performance is more important than Exchange performance for the OWA users. Ideally, IIS should be on a dedicated, multiprocessor server.

Most companies I work with use the 32-bit MAPI client primarily with OWA for remote users. I find that memory is generally the first bottleneck, with disk space right behind it. I recommend purchasing as much memory as possible when rolling out Exchange, and installing Exchange on a server that has a lot of RAM expansion capabilities.

Running Exchange and IIS on the Same Server

Although you can run Exchange and IIS on the same server, I don't recommend doing so except in the smallest installations, or if you have a specific functional requirement, such as NTLM authentication. Performance is generally terrible for both components when they are run on the same server.

Adding Users to Your Organization

The addition of users to your organization will most affect the servers that provide access to the Schedule+ Free/Busy system folder. We discussed the Schedule+ Free/Busy folder in Chapter 3 in terms of what functionality it provides. You also should be aware of the resources Exchange utilizes to provide that functionality.

The Schedule+ Free/Busy folder is stored on the first server you install in each site. Client access to it is defined by the same rules that define client access to any other public folder, such that clients in each site will not be able to view calendar data belonging to users in other sites unless you configure replication or affinities to those sites. When the load becomes too much for the first server in each site to handle all the schedule requests, you should consider adding an additional Schedule+ server to the site and configuring replication. I recommend creating dedicated Exchange servers to provide calendar data to your users so that user access to schedule data does not affect access to other Exchange server resources, such as mailboxes. You should be careful about the settings for location of user calendar data. There are two things to be aware of: PST files and primary calendars.

PST files

Although having users use PST files for the primary delivery location for incoming messages will considerably improve server Information Store performance, you will suffer a huge loss in functionality. The only case in which I've seen this successfully implemented was in a company that formerly had all UNIX clients running POP3 messaging clients. Because the UNIX users were accustomed to having all data stored locally, they used PST files for all message storage. Although this prevented them from sharing calendars, they had great server performance. As far as adding users is concerned, this company had no problems with calendar access because they didn't use the Schedule+ Free/Busy folder anyway. You, on the other hand, will probably eventually have real problems with the server that houses this folder if your company grows appreciably. I recommend at least one dedicated server per site for this folder in most medium to large companies.

Primary Calendars

Whether a user uses his calendar primarily on the server or primarily on the client will also have a huge impact on server performance. The default setting for Outlook is to work primarily on the client. This means that schedule changes made by the users are actually made to the local calendar and then updated to the server periodically. Because the client is not constantly accessing the server, server performance is improved.

On the other hand, Outlook Web Access now has support for scheduling. Unfortunately, OWA cannot store information locally for any great period of time (outside of caching); therefore the client must work primarily on the server. Every change made to the calendar is run through the IIS as the change is committed. This can have a significant impact on your Exchange server performance. If you have a lot of OWA clients you may want to consider offloading the Schedule+ Free/Busy system folder to another server.

Adding Services to Your Organization

At some point you will likely experience bottlenecks due to the addition or increased utilization of Exchange services as opposed to the addition of users. To remedy this, you will need to scale your organization. In addition to simply moving some of the mailboxes off the overloaded server, this scaling can take place by adding a dedicated server to function as one of the following:

- Public folder server
- Connector server

Public Folder Server Access

Dedicating a server to provide public folder access can significantly improve the performance of your mailbox servers. This is because, like mailbox access, access to public folders is extremely disk I/O and memory intensive. The actual performance improvement will vary depending on how heavily utilized the public folders are in your environment. Use the Performance Monitor, as described in Chapter 7, to determine whether public folder access is causing bottlenecks on your Exchange server. Factors that affect this should include not just client access of the folders, but also the number of replicas you have and the frequency of content changes and the replication schedule. If your folders are changed often and replicated often, the servers that maintain the replicas will reflect delayed response time during replication.

For example, creation of a dedicated public folder server is probably a good idea if your users access several folders each day and make a lot of changes to them that get replicated to other servers. On the other hand, if you are administering a small organization and the only folders your users access are system folders, a dedicated public folder server will probably not improve system performance appreciably. If you do not use Performance Monitor to alert you when your folders are becoming more heavily accessed, you will be made aware of the situation by user complaints. If and when this happens, you should consider the move to dedicated public folder servers.

Connector Server Access

Dedicating a server to connector functionality is also a wise move. Connectors use a lot of memory and processor resources, so they will contribute to bottleneck problems on already overloaded mailbox servers. Additionally, connectors periodically have problems that may affect your clients if the mailbox is on the same server as the connector. In addition to gaining performance improvements, dedicated connector servers are great for their inherent ability to be taken offline without a lot of user interaction.

I generally try to get medium to large companies to dedicate servers in each site to connector functionality. This helps with server response time to client requests and makes it easy to do offline work on the connector server.

Performance Optimizer

Because you now have added or upgraded hardware, added users, or added services to your Exchange server, it is important to reconfigure the way Exchange allocates resources for the services it uses to do its job. As we mentioned in Chapter 7, an inaccurately configured Exchange server can not only result in substandard performance but also generate events that will be logged to your Application log. You should be in the habit of running the Performance Optimizer after adding users, adding services, and adding hardware to your server. In this section we will address Performance Optimizer usage, including how to run it, how to use its command line switches, how to configure it, and what the memory and processor settings actually do.

Running the Performance Optimizer

Many administrators only run the Performance Optimizer after an Exchange installation. This is such an unfortunate waste because the Optimizer can and should be run every time new services are added to the Exchange server, every time you add several users to the local server or organization, and every time you make changes to your hardware configuration. The Performance Optimizer is located in the \exchsrvr\bin directory, along with `admin.exe`. You can run it manually by accessing the Microsoft Exchange Optimizer shortcut in the Microsoft Exchange program group, or you can run it from a command line or batch file. If you choose to run the Performance Optimizer from a command line or batch file, there are a few switches you can use to customize the way it runs.

Silent Mode

Running the Performance Optimizer from a batch file or command line in *silent* mode is a wonderful way of reconfiguring your Exchange settings off-hours. It is especially useful if you would like to change your resource settings before a scheduled task is to be run but want the settings restored after your task is run. Simply add the `perfwiz` command before the nightly task to optimize Exchange for the upcoming task, and then rerun it at task completion to restore the original settings.

The Performance Optimizer can be run in silent mode by using the command line `perfwiz -f`. You will need to create a data file from which the Performance Optimizer can read your configuration settings. Follow these steps to run Performance Optimizer using a data file:

1. Create the data file containing your Performance Optimizer settings.

2. Run `perfwiz -f INF_filename`, in which *INF_filename* contains the path and name of the data file you created in step 1. For example, suppose your data file is called `import.inf` and is located in `D:\datafile\exchange`. The command line would read `perfwiz -f D:\datafile\exchange\import.inf`. I find it easier to just leave the .INF file in the same directory as the `perfwiz` executable.

The format for the data file is quite straightforward. As with other .INF files you will encounter, there is a single square-bracket section that contains the relevant variables. The Performance Optimizer data file needs to read as follows:

```
[Perfwiz]
Users=[0¦1¦2¦3¦4¦5]
Org Users=[0¦1¦2¦3¦4]
Server Type=sum of server values
Dont Restart=[0¦1]
Analyze Disks=[0¦1]
Move Files=[0¦1]
Limit Memory Usage=Number in MB
```

Table 8.1 shows how you can use a data file to set environment variables for Performance Optimizer to use in silent mode.

Table 8.1 **Variables and Values Used to Create the Data File**

Variable	Usage	Value	Value Definition
Users	The number of users hosted on this server	0	1–25 (default)
		1	26–50
		2	51–100
		3	101–250
		4	251–500
		5	More than 500
Org Users	The number of users in the organization	0	Fewer than 100 (default)
		1	100–999
		2	1,000–9,999
		3	10,000–99,999
		4	100,000 or more
Server Type	Server Functionality	1	Public Information Store
		2	Private Information Store (default)
		4	Connector/Directory Import
		8	Multiserver
		16	POP3/IMAP4/NNTP only

Variable	Usage	Value	Value Definition
Don't Restart	Elect to restart services after	0	Services are restarted (default)
	optimization	1	Services are not restarted
Analyze Disks	Elect to analyze disks for access times	0	Disks are not analyzed
		1	Disks are analyzed (default)
Move Files	Elect to move	0	Files are not moved
	files automatically per recommendations	1	Files are moved (default)
Limit Memory Usage	Number between 32 and amount of physical RAM	x	Elect to limit the amount of memory Exchange can use.

The `Server Type` parameter is definitely unusual. To determine the value to assign to this parameter in the data file, add the numbers listed in the `Server Type` section of Table 8.1 that correspond with the functions your server will provide. For example, if your server has both a Private and Public Information Store and is running in a multi-server site, but does not have any connectors installed on it, the `Server Type` value will be 2 + 1 + 8, for a total of 11. Following is a sample data file:

```
[Perfwiz]
Users=[3]
Org Users=[2]
Server Type=14
Dont Restart=[0]
Analyze Disks=[0]
Move Files=[0]
```

perfwiz -s

You can also run the Performance Optimizer as `perfwiz -s` for silent mode. I never use this option because this switch always runs the Optimizer with the same .INF file, and I generally need to be able to define the .INF file to use for the current run.

Limiting Memory Usage in Exchange

Technically you can limit memory to 24MB. Functionally, less than 64MB is not enough for most production environments.

This sample Performance Optimizer data file can be used to optimize a server with 200 local users and 2,000 users in the organization that both communicates with other servers in the local site and runs an IMS. The services will restart after the Optimizer completes, but the disks won't be analyzed and files won't be moved.

You should take note that the values in the data file do not correspond with the Performance Optimizer interface. For example, the Optimizer has settings for users hosted on the local server as high as 50,000 or more, whereas the data file only allows for a setting of 500 or more. Therefore, you can tune your Exchange server to a much finer degree than the Performance Optimizer interface, a situation you should take advantage of.

Verbose Mode

In addition to running Performance Optimizer in silent mode, you can also elect to run it in *verbose* mode. The command to launch verbose mode is `perfwiz -v`. Verbose mode provides a series of windows that display the current settings for Exchange resources compared with the new settings, based on information you provide in the introductory screen. You probably won't have cause to use verbose mode very often because you generally will want to run the Optimizer after hours (perhaps using a batch file) and you can easily view the changes the Optimizer makes in the `perfopt.log` file.

Verbose mode allows you to change the fine points of Exchange resource settings if you want to, but because this is a very delicate area, you really should just try to avoid having to do it. I almost never use verbose mode because it is really only good for extreme fine-tuning and troubleshooting. I *never* recommend just going in there and changing values. This is analogous to randomly editing the Registry, and you can do real damage to your Exchange performance by altering values without understanding the effects. There are a lot of parameters that should only be changed in conjunction with other variables. For example, the `Maximum # of concurrent read threads` is a subset of the `# of directory threads`. As a result, changes you make to `Maximum # of concurrent read threads` that aren't reflected in the `# of directory threads` can cause real directory performance problems.

Using the Performance Optimizer to Move Exchange Files

Although the Performance Optimizer can move your files for you, I don't recommend it. Use the Optimizer to determine the best location for files for your information, but place your files in the best location for performance and backup/restore purposes as determined by your own system analysis. Move files manually using the Exchange Administrator Program's server object for the server on which you want to move files.

JET Buffer Settings

Exchange allocates JET buffer resources after all other resource values are set in order to maximize Exchange's usage of system memory. Because the JET buffers are already taking up all remaining memory, you should never manually set the JET buffers higher than the values assigned by the Exchange Performance Optimizer.

Read Only Mode

Read only mode is provided so that you can get a look at the values Exchange assigns to resources without actually stopping the services and changing anything. This mode gives you a snapshot of the Registry settings that correspond to Exchange performance. I use `perfwiz -r` quite frequently to see how Exchange resources are configured.

Resource Settings

The Exchange Performance Optimizer affects over 40 parameters in addition to optimizing the location of your databases and log files. Many of these parameters have a considerable impact on your system. Table 8.2 summarizes the most important parameters the Optimizer adjusts and gives my suggestions on when and when not to edit the values manually.

Table 8.2   **Recommendations on Editing Parameters**

Parameter	Description	Recommendation
`# of information store buffers`	Area of memory allocated for loading of private and public data. Typically the most heavily utilized resource on an Exchange server.	You should never set this value higher than the Performance Optimizer sets it.
`# of directory buffers`	Area of memory allocated for loading directory information. Heavily utilized on Directory Replication bridgehead servers.	You should never set this value higher than the Performance Optimizer sets it.
`Minimum # of information store threads`	The minimum number of threads allocated for client requests to the Exchange server.	You should never change this setting.
`Maximum # of information store threads # of directory threads`	The maximum number of threads allocated for client requests to the Exchange server. Total number of threads Exchange allocates for directory processes such as replication and address book queries.	Small tweaks can improve client access performance, but large alterations can contribute to client performance problems. Alter this manually only when necessary; there are other variables that depend on this setting.

continues

Table 8.2 **Continued**

Parameter	Description	Recommendation
Maximum # of concurrent read threads	Number of concurrent threads used for directory replication.	This value is a subset of # of directory threads, so if you edit it to be too large, your clients will have slow directory parsing.
# of background threads	Number of threads allocated for background processes such as message tracking, Exchange link/ server monitoring, storage limit checking, online defragmentation, message expirations and garbage collection.	Be careful about setting this too high; you might run out of memory and prevent the IS from starting.
# of private information store send threads	Number of threads Exchange allocates for sending messages to the local MTA.	Tweaking this higher can sometimes help with queue problems. This value is a subset of # of background threads, so if you raise it, you will affect Exchange's ability to perform background tasks.
# of private information store delivery threads	Number of threads allocated for sending messages from the MTA to the local IS.	Tweaking this higher can sometimes help with queue problems. This value is a subset of # of background threads, so if you raise it, you will affect Exchange's ability to perform background tasks.
# of public information store send threads	Number of threads Exchange allocates for sending public folder replicas through the local MTA.	Raising this can sometimes help with queue problems. This value is a subset of # of background threads, so if you raise it you will affect Exchange's ability to perform background tasks.
# of public information store delivery threads	Number of threads Exchange allocates for transferring public folder replica messages from the MTA to the local IS.	Raising this can sometimes help with queue problems. This value is a subset of # of background threads, so if you raise it you will affect Exchange's ability to perform background tasks.

Parameter	Description	Recommendation
# of information store gateway in threads	Number of threads the IS allocates for incoming messages from foreign systems.	Raising this can sometimes help with queue problems. This value is a subset of # of background threads, so if you raise it you will affect Exchange's ability to perform background tasks.
# of information store gateway out threads	Number of threads the IS allocates for messages sent from Exchange to foreign systems.	Raising this can sometimes help with queue problems. This value is a subset of # of background threads, so if you raise it you will affect Exchange's ability to perform background tasks.
# of submit/ deliver threads	Number of threads allocated to the MTA for message transfer.	Because this value corresponds with IS send/deliver threads, both parameters should generally be edited at the same time. This thread is also a subset of # of background threads, so editing it may cause problems with Exchange background task processing.
Max # of RPC calls outstanding	Number of RPC requests that can be unacknowledged before logging an event to the event log.	Typically, RPC problems indicate network trouble rather than Exchange server trouble.

You can see from the preceding table that Exchange Performance Optimizer is working hard to make your Exchange server perform at its best. The most productive thing you can do is run the Optimizer after significant server changes with accurate environment information. As a rule, don't edit any of these settings manually.

Summary

In this chapter we looked at the things you can do to manage your server resources periodically. This includes upgrading hardware, scaling your organization for growth, and optimizing the performance of your Exchange servers. Now let's move on to discuss management of communication and data replication between sites.

9

Managing Intersite Communication and Replication

NOW THAT YOU KNOW WHAT KINDS of resource utilization you can expect to find with your Exchange server, let's take a look at some of the services that will require your periodic attention. If you are an administrator for a multiple-site environment, you will need to stay on top of your connectors. For example, you need to be aware of communications problems between sites that prevent user message transfer in addition to problems that may affect system messages. These problems can relate to native Site and X.400 Connectors, the Internet Mail Service, MS Mail Connectors, and any third-party connectors you might have installed. You also need to keep an eye on directory replication between sites. Since Chapter 4, "Queue Management," has already addressed managing your queues, here we will just be focusing on connector issues such as performance and security that you should periodically address.

Site Connector

The Site Connector is the easiest connector to configure, and is very popular as a means to connect two sites that have a high bandwidth connection between them. Connections made between sites using the Site Connector, when configured with the default settings, function exactly like connections made between servers in the same site. For example, suppose Greg is a user defined on the SEATTLE server in the

North America site. Mark is a user defined on the VANCOUVER server, the only server in the Canada site. When Greg sends a message to Mark, the message flow is as follows:

1. The SEATTLE MTA evaluates the message routing and determines the recipient is in Canada.

2. The SEATTLE MTA creates a connection to the VANCOUVER MTA.

3. Using RPCs, the SEATTLE MTA transmits the message to the VANCOUVER MTA.

If, on the other hand, Greg sends a message to Angie, who is defined on the BELLEVUE server in the North America site, the message flow is as follows:

1. The SEATTLE MTA evaluates the message routing and determines the recipient is on the BELLEVUE server.

2. The SEATTLE MTA creates a connection to the BELLEVUE MTA.

3. Using RPCs, the SEATTLE MTA transmits the message to the BELLEVUE MTA.

You can see that these processes are virtually identical. Even if you identify a bridgehead server for the Site Connector in each site, the actual transfer of messages to and from the bridgehead will be exactly like a single site, except for the added hops. As a result, Site Connector administration is exactly like administering the communication between multiple servers in a single site environment.

Management

As for managing Site Connectors, I find that because they function just like MTA communication in a single site, many of the steps that need to be taken to administer them are covered in the daily administration of the Exchange MTA. For example, you should use Performance Monitor to keep track of your MTA communications. Because the Site Connector functionality is built into the MTA, the same counters should be tracked for Site Connectors as for the MTA. Refer to Chapter 7, "Daily Proactive Troubleshooting," for Performance Monitoring suggestions that will enable you to keep track of your MTA and Site Connectors.

In addition to the MTA counters listed in Chapter 7, track the LAN Receive Bytes/sec and LAN Transmit Bytes/sec counters on the MTA Communication object. These counters reflect the amount of data sent and received per second via the MTA. If either number drops significantly below the baseline, you could have MTA or network problems. If either number increases considerably over the baseline, you should consider creating a dedicated connector server or adding an additional connector to the site.

These counters will give you statistics for the communication between the local MTA and each remote MTA for which there is a session established. This includes the servers defined in the local site in addition to any servers to which the local MTA is connected in other sites via the Site Connector.

When you daily peruse the MTA queues, as discussed in Chapter 4, you will see messages destined for other users in your site as well as other sites via the Site Connector. Similarly, the data you collect in the Performance Monitor using the MTA and MTA Connections counters will include Site Connector information.

Optimizing Performance

Site Connector performance is fast. As soon as the MTA has a message queued for another site that is accessible via Site Connector, the MTA will create the connection and transmit the message. Because there is no content conversion or other processing necessary to send the message, transmission is just as fast between sites as within a site (limited only by available bandwidth between sites). This performance comes at the cost of administrative options. I like to compare the Site Connector to NetBEUI; both are really easy to get working, but have almost no options for isolated tuning or optimization. We'll be looking at some of the performance trade-offs in this section.

Site Connector Performance Versus Configuration Control

Although there are almost no isolated tuning options, there are options you can configure that will alter the way the MTA in general connects if you need to address transmission problems. Unfortunately, changes you make to affect the Site Connector will also affect the way the MTAs within your site connect to each other.

For example, SEATTLE and BELLEVUE are in the North America site. The North America site is connected to the Canada site via a Site Connector. Beth, the administrator, is unhappy about the number of nondelivery reports (NDRs) the users in North America are receiving when sending messages to Canada. She changes some of the default values on the MTA Site Configuration property pages and is happy to note that the NDR problem has been solved. Unfortunately, now her users are complaining that local message delivery is slow. If you find yourself in this boat and can't afford to upgrade your WAN connection, you will have to determine for yourself which is the lesser of two evils.

Site Connector Problems

The Site Connector is not my favorite way of connecting two sites. I personally feel that the difficulty with distinguishing Site Connector problems from MTA problems makes it somewhat difficult to work with. This is exacerbated in scenarios in which companies allow any server in the local site to connect to any server in the remote site. Although message tracking can help, pinpointing problems can be a real headache because Exchange will automatically reroute to other servers. I have had to use Performance Monitor to identify problems with the Site Connector because I couldn't determine what the problem was by using just Exchange administration tools.

In most cases, I believe slower local delivery is better than too many NDRs. What I would recommend to Beth in this scenario is to get rid of the Site Connector altogether and use X.400 Connector instead. We will be discussing X.400 Connectors in the "X.400 Connector" section, later in this chapter.

Altering Connection Properties

The biggest drawback to using the Site Connector is the lack of configuration options specific to the connector. To alter the connection properties of the Site Connector, you will have to alter the properties for all MTAs within your site. Do this by accessing the MTA Site Configuration Messaging Defaults property page. My suggestions for optimization are listed in Table 9.1.

Table 9.1 **Controlling Communication Parameters for All MTA Connections**

Section	Parameter	Description	Recommendation
RTS values	`Checkpoint size`	The amount of data the MTA transmits before inserting a checkpoint.	On reliable networks you can increase this value to get better performance. On slow networks, decrease this value to prevent the MTA from having to resend too much data for every unacknowledged checkpoint.
	`Recovery timeout`	After an error occurs, the MTA waits the `Recovery timeout` before resending data from the problematic transmission. The amount of data re-sent is defined by the Checkpoint size.	I generally don't alter this value.
	`Window size`	The number of checkpoints that go unacknowledged before the sending MTA stops transferring messages and restarts from the beginning.	I generally don't change this value.

Section	Parameter	Description	Recommendation
Connection Retry values	`Max open retries`	This value defines the maximum number of times the local MTA will attempt to open a connection to the remote MTA.	If you wish to attempt connections for more than 144 retries, increase this number. For example, if you are running a Dynamic RAS connector and receiving a lot of busy signals, increasing this number will give the connector a better chance of connecting.
	`Max transfer-retries`	Once the MTA establishes a connection, this value defines the number of times the MTA will attempt to transfer data to the remote MTA.	Increase this number if your MTA seems to be successfully connecting to the remote host but network problems are interfering with the transmission. This will prevent the MTA from disconnecting and waiting for the `Open interval` to pass before retrying the connection.
	`Open interval`	`Open interval` defines the number of seconds the MTA will wait before retrying an unsuccessful connection. The default is 10 minutes.	Increase this value if you seem to have trouble in short bursts during the day, such as during peak production times. Decrease this value if you don't have regular connection problems and want the MTA to retry again immediately when an intermittent problem does occur.
	`Transfer interval`	This value defines the number of seconds the MTA waits to transfer data across an open connection if the last attempt failed.	I wouldn't change this number as a remedy for most problems.

continues

Table 9.1 **Continued**

Section	Parameter	Description	Recommendation
Association parameters	`Lifetime`	An association defines the commitment of resources to send and receive data. Once a connection is established, an association is created in order to transmit messages.	Since Exchange uses two-way associations in order to allow the remote host to send mail back to the originating host, the `Lifetime` value is necessary for the originating host to know how long to wait for the remote host's message transfer. Normally this number should not need to be altered.
	`Disconnect`	Once the MTA is finished transferring data and has waited the `Lifetime` value, a disconnect request is sent. If the disconnect is unacknowledged, Exchange will disconnect anyway at the end of this time period.	You should not need to change this value to optimize your system.
	`Threshold`	`Threshold` defines the number of messages queued for a remote host that cause an additional association to be created. It is intended to force Exchange to try harder to transmit mail.	I increase this number to remedy network problems since generally the problem across a WAN link is not Exchange's failure to dedicate resources so much as it is a limited bandwidth problem.
Transfer timeouts (sec/K)	`Urgent`	Amount of time an Urgent priority message can wait in the associated queue before being returned to the sender.	You may want to increase this value if it seems that most Urgent messages are returned as undeliverable due to connection speed.

Section	Parameter	Description	Recommendation
	Normal	Amount of time a Normal priority message can wait in the associated queue before being returned to the sender.	Increase this only if network problems prevent successful connections/transmissions and you are getting a lot of NDRs.
	Non-urgent	Amount of time a Non-urgent priority message waits in the associated queue before being returned to the sender.	Since these messages are not urgent, I generally don't recommend changing this value.

X.400 Connector

Like the Site Connector, the X.400 Connector is used to connect two Exchange sites together. It can also be used to connect Exchange to other X.400-compliant systems. Connectivity can be established either over an X.400 public network or over the Internet. The X.400 Connector also supports TP0/X.25 and TP4/CLNP transport protocols. We discussed the X.400 Connector's queues in Chapter 4. Now let's take a look at some of the periodic administrative tasks you should perform to keep your X.400 Connector up and running.

Management

As with Site Connectors, managing X.400 Connectors is similar to managing MTA communication in a single site. This is because the Exchange MTA is natively X.400 compliant. For example, you should use Performance Monitor to keep track of your MTA communications. When you daily peruse the MTA queues, you will see messages destined for other users in your site as well as other sites via the X.400 Connector. As we discussed in Chapter 4, you should be analyzing your queues every day.

I like the X.400 Connector a lot better than the Site Connector. Although it is much more difficult to configure, there are many more options that enable you to control things such as when the connector will be available, maximum message size, and who is allowed to use the connector. Plus, it functions over slower network links than Site Connectors do. Except for a few very limited circumstances, I invariably configure X.400 Connectors to connect two sites together.

Security

The X.400 Connector can run over a leased line, or you can elect to run it over the Internet. This is called *backboning* and presents some security problems that you should be aware of.

We know from our earlier example that the MTA and Site Connector both use RPCs to transmit messages. Within a single site, the MTA will use encrypted RPCs for the transmission. Microsoft Windows NT supports 40-bit RPC encryption out of the box, but you can get 128-bit support by installing NT Service Pack 2 or later. Although the X.400 Connector uses the Exchange MTA, and X.400 support is provided natively by the Exchange MTA, the X.400 Connector does not use RPC encryption. This means that no data transmitted via X.400 Connector over the Internet will be secure.

As a result, you should implement an advanced security feature, such as Microsoft Exchange's Key Management Server, and require your users to encrypt their own messages. Microsoft Exchange's Key Management Server allows the administrator to define the level of encryption. You can select encryption levels that use 40-bit, 56-bit, 64-bit, or 128-bit keys.

How Encryption Works

I think the mathematical operation behind data encryption is really interesting. Although encryption in Exchange and NT is a lot more complicated than simply XORing two data streams together, it is always fundamentally based on one or more exclusive OR (XOR) operations. When two inputs are XORed together, the outputs are as follows:

```
    Inputs     Output
    0    0     0
    0    1     1
    1    0     1
    1    1     0
```

Because ultimately all the data you transmit is encoded as a series of ones and zeros, it can be encrypted by XORing it bit by bit against an encryption key. For example, consider the following data file:

```
    0011101011
```

Consider also the following 10-bit encryption key:

```
    1010101010
```

The encrypted data will look like this:

```
    1001000001
```

Obviously the receiver will not be able to open the encrypted data without the decryption key. As long as the receiver has your 10-bit key, he will be able to perform an additional XOR with the encrypted data and the encryption key to get the original data back out. Pretty cool, eh?

Optimizing Performance

The performance of X.400 Connectors is almost as good as that of Site Connectors. There is a little extra overhead associated with routing to and from bridgehead servers as well as message content conversion, but generally you should not experience noticeable differences in response time between these two connectors. As with Site Connectors, the X.400 Connector can be run over the Internet as well as over leased lines and public network providers. In this section we'll discuss two main areas of X.400 Connector optimization: performance monitoring and property configuration.

Performance Monitoring

Although you can expect message transmission speed to be fast given there are no network bandwidth problems, you really still should monitor your performance statistics with the Performance Monitor. In addition to the counters we discussed in Chapter 7, there are a few counters specific to intersite connectors that you should use to track connector performance. For the X.400 Connector, track the following counters as applicable on the MTA Connections object:

- TCP/IP Receive Bytes/sec
- TCP/IP Transmit Bytes/sec
- TP4 Receive Bytes/sec
- TP4 Transmit Bytes/sec
- X.25 Receive Bytes/sec
- X.25 Transmit Bytes/sec

Use these counters the same way you would use the LAN Transmit Bytes/sec and LAN Receive Bytes/sec counters discussed in the earlier "Site Connector" section.

Obviously you will track only the counters that correspond with the transport you use for your X.400 Connector. For example, if you run the X.400 Connector using a TCP/IP MTA Transport Stack, you would track the TCP/IP specific counters.

Configuring X.400 Connection Properties

You may need to periodically alter your X.400 properties based on network performance. For example, your leased line may have had plenty of bandwidth available when you first rolled out Exchange, but since then you've rolled out a SQL application and added over 100 users to your network that utilize the WAN daily.

To determine when it is appropriate to tweak your X.400 Connector, you should be comparing your Performance Monitor data with the baseline data. If you find that messages are transferring more slowly than your baseline threshold, it may be time to consider a few small changes to your X.400 configuration. In general, the changes you make to your X.400 Connector should be temporary. In other words, if your network bandwidth is a problem, you should attempt to purchase additional bandwidth rather than slow the operation of your network applications.

The X.400 Connector has a multitude of property pages. The property page labeled Override has the same properties as the MTA Site Configuration Messaging Defaults page discussed earlier in this chapter in the "Site Connector" section. Changes you make to X.400 Override page affect only the X.400 Connector—they don't affect the communication of the Site Connector or the MTAs within your site. Refer to Table 9.1 for recommendations on property optimization.

Internet Mail Service

Like the X.400 and Site Connectors, the Internet Mail Service (IMS) can be used to connect two Exchange sites together in addition to connecting to foreign SMTP hosts. In addition to evaluating IMS queues regularly, there are a number of other issues you should be aware of when it comes to managing the IMS. These issues are discussed in the following sections.

Management and Performance Optimization

When it comes to managing the IMS, I find that one of the most important and beneficial things you can do is monitor it with the Performance Monitor. Exchange provides the `MSExchangeIMC` object, with which you can obtain a wide variety of applicable data. I would recommend the counters listed in Table 9.2.

Table 9.2 **Recommended Counters for IMS**

Counter	Description	Recommendation
Queued Inbound	The number of messages currently waiting to route into Exchange from the IMS. This queue is part of the file system.	Keep an eye on this queue because a significant drop in the number of inbound messages could be a result of IMS failure, such as Flush Mode becoming enabled (Refer to Chapter 7.)
Queued Outbound	The number of messages sent from Exchange users to SMTP users that are awaiting final transfer out. This queue is part of the file system.	Pay attention to increases in the average number of messages queued outbound. A large increase could indicate network problems, DNS problems, or a breach of security where an external user is utilizing your SMTP host to send mail. Security issues are covered later in this section.
Queued MTS-IN	The number of messages originating from the IMS that are currently queued in the Information Store's MTS-IN directory	Pay attention to the number of messages queued as incoming. A significant number could indicate a security breach. We will

Counter	Description	Recommendation
	awaiting delivery to Exchange users.	discuss this further in this section.
Queued MTS-OUT	The number of messages sent from Exchange users to SMTP users who are currently queued in the Information Store's MTS-OUT directory awaiting content conversion by the IMAIL Process.	Remember that if the number of messages begins to increase dramatically, you may have disk space problems that are causing the IMS to stop receiving mail. (Refer to Chapter 7 for details about Flush Mode.)

These counters will give you statistics for the communication between the Information Store and the IMS on the server that runs the IMS. You should create a performance baseline with which to compare your production data so that you can become immediately apprised of detrimental situations.

Security

IMS performance can best be optimized using the Exchange Performance Optimizer, as discussed in Chapter 8, "Managing Server Resources." By providing accurate environment information you will allow the Optimizer to configure your resource allocation appropriately for your environment. As far as optimization is concerned, I am a huge advocate for security. My interest with customers is less about performance and response time of the IMS as it is with preventing unauthorized access. You need to take steps to prevent the following:

- **Incoming viruses.** The introduction of destructive code via email sent to your users. For example, many viruses find their way into the corporate network as executable attachments. The unsuspecting recipient simply double-clicks the attachment, allowing the virus to infiltrate your network.

- **Mailstorming.** An attack of incoming mail sent at a high rate in an effort to bring your server down. This is a popular way for attackers to express dissatisfaction (for whatever reason), since there are lots of programs available that will automatically keep sending mail until the attacker wants to stop.

The Dynamic RAS Connector

The Dynamic RAS Connector can be used to connect two Exchange sites across a dial-up connection. This connector is not covered here because I almost never run into it in the field. The Dynamic RAS Connector is more difficult to configure and administer, and as a result I generally recommend that the Internet Mail Connector be used instead. If you are running the Dynamic RAS Connector and need help, see the Microsoft support Web site at http://www.microsoft.com/support.

- **Sniffing.** The use of network-monitoring software in an attempt to collect or modify message data while on the wire. Most Internet traffic is not encrypted, just encoded, and can be easily deciphered by a knowledgeable hacker.

- **Spoofing.** Sending messages using someone else's name such that the recipient believes the message originator is another person. It is easy to put any name you want in the configuration fields of POP3 messaging clients. This can trick your users into thinking a message actually was sent from someone else.

- **Spamming.** Using your Exchange server to send hundreds of thousands of junk messages to other SMTP users outside your organizations. Since SMTP is open, all a spammer has to do is find an SMTP host that isn't protected to send "spam" around the world until the server is disabled.

- **Hacking.** The attempt to gain access to your corporate network through your IMS, which needs to be available to the Internet in order to perform its job.

Fortunately, the Exchange IMS object has a number of options you can configure that promote security. These options are listed in Table 9.3.

Table 9.3 **IMS Security Options**

Tab	Property	Recommendation
Connections	`Accept Connections`	Usually you will want to accept SMTP connections from any host since you can't predict the source of acceptable incoming mail. However, if you use the IMS to backbone two Exchange sites or only communicate with authorized hosts, configure this property to identify the IP address of the authorized host.
	`Clients can only submit if homed on this server`	If you administer a small, single-server company, consider selecting this box. Outside SMTP users will be prevented from using your server to send SMTP mail.
	`Message Filtering`	If you have identified users or domains that have been problems in the past, add them to the `Message Filtering` list. If you enable message filtering, consider moving messages

Tab	Property	Recommendation
		from unauthorized locations to the Turf directory where you can later inspect them.
General	`Message size`	Identify a maximum size for messages you will both send and receive through this connector. Controlling the size of incoming messages can prevent an attacker from flooding your server with huge files and causing you to run out of disk space.
Internet Mail	`Advanced options`	Leave the default setting Disable Automatic Replies to the Internet intact. An attacker who learns which users are not in the office can attempt to spoof using the absent employee's account. You can always override this setting for specific, trusted email domains.
	`Enable message tracking`	Check this box to cause the System Attendant to track all messages to the daily log file in the `tracking.log` directory. This can help you both troubleshoot problems and identify problematic internal users.
Security		By adding email domains to this list, you can cause Exchange's IMS to encrypt the data transferred to users of that domain as long as the destination server is also an Exchange 5.5 IMS. This will prevent attackers with sniffers from easily picking off your data and deciphering it.
Delivery Restrictions		By controlling who has permission to send SMTP

continues

Table 9.3 **Continued**

Tab	Property	Recommendation
		mail you can prevent troublesome employees from launching their own denial of service attacks against outside SMTP hosts.

In addition to the GUI options for configuring the IMS, there are a few Registry settings that you may want to take advantage of, which are listed in Table 9.4.

Table 9.4 **IMS Registry Security Options**

Parameter	Description	Recommendation
Reverse Resolution	The IMS automatically resolves the name of sending SMTP hosts to put in the message header. This process takes time and you can improve IMS performance by disabling it.	I don't recommend disabling this parameter because the header information is useful for troubleshooting. If you want to disable reverse resolution, add a value named `DisableReverseResolve` with `REG_DWORD` Data of 1 to `HKEY_LOCAL_MACHINE\System\CurrentControlSet\Services\MSExchangeIMC\Parameters`.
User Name Resolution	The IMS resolves the FROM name in an SMTP header against the local GAL.	If you are running Exchange 4.0 or upgradedfrom 4.0, you probably still have username resolution enabled. Disable it in the Registry at `HKEY_LOCAL_MACHINE\System\CurrentControlSet\Services\MSExchangeIMC\Parameters` by adding a `REG_DWORD` value named `ResolveP2` with Data 0.
Verify Request	`Verify Request` allows the sending SMTP host to verify the recipient's address on the receiving host.	Disabling this parameter can prevent attackers from obtaining the mailbox and full names of internal users through the SMTP port, but some systems (such as some DNS registration offices) require `VRFY` to be enabled to verify the existence of certain accounts on the server. It is disabled by default in Exchange. If you need to enable it, add to the `HKEY_LOCAL_MACHINE\System\CurrentControlSet\Services\MSExchangeIMC\Parameters` key a

Parameter	Description	Recommendation
		`REG_DWORD` value named `EnableVRFY` with Data 1.

MS Mail Connector

If you are coexisting with MS Mail users then you will need to administer the MS Mail Connector (MSMC) on at least one server in your organization. The MS Mail Connector architecture is unique, so its administration is a little bit different than that for the IMS or third-party connectors. Unlike other foreign connectors, Exchange's MS Mail Connector actually has a Microsoft Mail post office component, which is sometimes referred to as a *shadow post office*. The MS Mail/PC MTA connects to the shadow post office and to the MS Mail post office to deliver mail back and forth. Because the exposed component of Exchange is actually an MS Mail post office, Exchange is treated like an MS Mail post office by other MS Mail post offices. In this section we will look at management and performance optimization of the MS Mail Connector in addition to administering the PC MTA and Directory Synchronization services you may be running to support the connector.

Internal Versus External Security Breaches

Your biggest worry when it comes to security is actually your internal users and not external users, as Hollywood and the media would have you believe. Most network problems and security breaches are a result of poorly educated users and/or bad policies, which allow users to email secure data or alter it in some way.

Why Exchange 5.5 Doesn't Enable User Name Resolution

A somewhat humorous example using User Name Resolution occurred at Microsoft, where an outside user identified himself as Bill Gates and sent messages to internal Microsoft employees. The Microsoft Exchange server resolved the sender's name to Bill Gates in the Exchange Directory so that the recipients were led to believe the message was actually from Bill Gates himself. Because of this, Exchange 5.0 and later do not enable User Name Resolution.

Additional Network Security

In addition to the security steps we discussed in the earlier "Internet Mail Service" section, there are a number of other things you can and should do to provide a high security network to your employer. These include proper firewall, proxy server, and packet filter configuration, in addition to enforcing strict NT account policies with logon auditing and utilizing NTFS security with file access auditing.

Management

After the MS Mail Connector is up and running, about the only thing I do other than watch the queues is configure a Link Monitor. As we discussed in Chapter 7, *Link Monitors* can be used to verify the physical link between an Exchange server and any foreign server in addition to other Exchange servers. To configure a Link Monitor to connect to MS Mail, create a custom recipient in Exchange that reflects an invalid MS Mail address. The MS Mail post office will be unable to deliver the message because the address is invalid and will generate an NDR. The speed at which the NDR is returned will notify you of potential link problems.

Optimizing Performance

After the MSMC is configured, optimize your server using the Performance Optimizer. Identify the server as a Directory Import/Connector server in addition to other roles the server fills. After the server has been optimized, use the Performance Monitor to create a performance baseline and track performance over time. I recommend using the objects and counters listed in Table 9.5.

Table 9.5 **Recommended MSMC Objects and Counters**

Object	Counter	Recommendation
MSExchangeMSMI	Messages Received	This is the total number of messages received by Exchange from MS Mail since the service started. I usually suspect a problem if this value plateaus, since that indicates no messages are coming in.
MSExchangePCMTA	File contentions/ hour	Compare this with the baseline to see if an unusual number of file contentions are occurring. If so, you may have too much traffic on one of your post offices. This happens frequently on hub post offices.
	LAN/WAN messages moved/hour	Compare this value with your baseline to see if you have an unusually high or low number of messages passing between Exchange and MSMail. If so, you may have a network problem, or it may be time to add another connector or create a dedicated connector server to provide load balancing.

As we mentioned earlier, be sure to create a baseline of values you expect to obtain in performance monitoring. This is the only way you can know if there is an upcoming problem.

PC MTA

Because the PC MTA is Exchange's replacement for the native MS Mail MTA (external.exe), you will need to keep an eye on its performance as well. The biggest problem you are likely to have with your PC MTA is that it doesn't move mail at a fast enough rate. This will be evidenced by increasing queue lengths while the LAN/WAN messages moved per hour counter is stuck at its peak value. This should not be a major problem for you if you are in the midst of migrating because there is a point in every migration when the connector load peaks. However, if you are going to coexist for a long period of time you will want to take steps to offload some of the processing from the connector server.

What you should try to do is add another instance of the MS Mail Connector to your site. It is tempting to add additional PC MTA instances to your connector server, but unfortunately there is a limit to the number of instances a server can host. Generally, you won't be able to run more than seven MS Mail related services on a given server due to memory limitations. This seven-instance limitation includes the PC MTA, MSMI, Schedule+ Free and Busy Connector, and Directory Synchronization service.

Directory Synchronization

As with the PC MTA, DirSync with MS Mail is a process you will have to keep an eye on. Unlike replication within Exchange, directory synchronization in MS Mail is a huge pain, and adding Exchange to the mix is not going to fix anything for you. Before you begin DirSync with Exchange you need to fix any weird problems you are currently experiencing in your native MS Mail environment.

After you have MS Mail DirSync problems resolved to the best of your ability, configure Exchange as a DirSync requestor. Although you can obtain some benefits by reconfiguring your whole MS Mail DirSync topology to include Exchange as a DirSync server, the effort is not worth the payoff if you are just going to migrate everyone to Exchange. If you are planning to coexist for a time period then it may be worthwhile to port your DirSync server functionality to Exchange.

Unfortunately, there aren't any DirSync-specific counters that you can use in the Performance Monitor to keep track of your DirSync. The best way is to weekly go through the log files generated on the DirSync server and the DirSync requestors to identify whether all post offices have sent and received updates.

Accidental DirSync of Link Monitor Recipient

Be sure to assign a trust level to the Link Monitor recipient that is higher than your DirSync trust level to prevent it from showing up in the MS Mail GAL.

Third-Party Connector Performance

In addition to managing Site Connectors, X.400 Connectors, IMS, and MS Mail Connectors, you may also need to keep an eye on third-party connectors. Third-party connectors allow Exchange to transmit mail to a foreign system, and require just as much attention on your part as Exchange's native connectors. Unfortunately, although they all share a common architecture, there is not necessarily anything else common about them. For this reason, you will need to obtain as much information as possible about the connectors you purchase from the vendor that sold them to you. Most of the foreign connectors that Exchange supports were developed by LinkAge, and therefore share some common administrative features. LinkAge was purchased by Microsoft; hence, all of the connectors now ship with the Exchange 5.5 Enterprise CD.

One of the best ways to improve performance of any connector is to add another connector to provide some load balancing. Exchange will automatically update its routing tables to reflect the additional connectors, which you can further customize by editing route costs. Keep in mind that most foreign connectors cannot automatically take advantage of the addition of another connector, so you will probably have to edit the routing in the foreign system in order to achieve return message load balancing.

After you have your connector configured and functioning, there are a few things you will need to do regularly to keep it running. The first is to routinely analyze the queues. We discussed the queues in Chapter 4, because you need to be looking at them every day. I prefer to use the MDBVU32 tool to see messages queued in the MTS-IN, MTS-OUT, READY-IN, and READY-OUT queues because the LinkAge Queue Viewer alphabetizes the messages in the queue, making it hard to figure out which message has been in there the longest.

In addition to managing the queues, you should also be going through the LinkAge log file. Because all LinkAge connectors are controlled by the same NT service (LinkAge Controller) you will find message traffic information pertaining to all locally installed LinkAge connectors in the same log file. For example, if you happen to have both the Notes and the PROFS connectors installed on the same connector server, information relating to both connectors will appear in the same log file. This log file is a great resource if you are having problems; you can get details on how severe the event was, what process created the event message, and even the line of the source code that was executing when the event was logged. You can peruse the log file by using the Log Browser.

Directory Replication

Now that we've discussed the physical connectors that actually move messages, let's look at the logical Directory Replication Connector. Managing directory replication within an Exchange organization is actually not too difficult, at least compared with other systems, such as Microsoft Mail. There is no configuration or management at all in a single site environment. After you start adding sites, you will need to add

Directory Replication Connectors. These connectors define the sending and receiving servers responsible for compiling changes in the local site and incorporating changes received from the remote site.

In addition to replication between Exchange sites, you may also need to provide directory synchronization between Exchange and a foreign system. We will discuss this issue in the "Foreign Directory Synchronization" section later in this chapter.

Management

The way you manage directory replication depends entirely on how replication is configured to occur. For example, replication management within a single Exchange organization is different from managing it between organizations, or between Exchange and a foreign system. We will look at all these scenarios in this section.

Native Exchange Replication

Fortunately, Exchange directory replication is easy to set up and get working. It uses your existing messaging topology, so as long as messages are being sent successfully, replication can be configured to function correctly as well. As a result, there are only a few things to be aware of in terms of periodic administration. These are forcing an update, checking knowledge consistency, optimizing the replication schedule, and monitoring performance.

Forcing Updates

Force directory replication between sites by accessing the appropriate Directory Replication Connector in your site's Directory Replication container. You will find a Sites tab that lists on the left all sites that your site receives updates from. Select the site that has the changes you want to see reflected in your site and click the **Update** button.

When forcing updates, you should be careful to request only changed items from the remote site, not the entire directory structure. Obviously you can cause a lot of network problems if you do a full synchronization during normal business hours.

> **Planning Your Directory Replication Topology**
>
> Directory Replication in Exchange must be configured such that no site can be made aware of another site through more than one route. For example, if North America has a replication connector to South America, and South America has a replication connector to Europe, then North America cannot have a replication connector to Europe because it knows about Europe through South America. As a result of the topology, North America receives all updates from South America, even if they originated in Europe. If a change is made in Europe that the administrator of North America wants to see replicate to his local site, the change must first show up in South America. Therefore, selecting Europe from the connector's list will not bring in updates that have not yet reached the directly connected site.

Forcing a Knowledge Consistency Check

In addition to forcing updates, you may also periodically want to force a knowledge consistency check. The *Knowledge Consistency Checker (KCC)* is used by Exchange during replication to determine whether any new sites have been added downstream. It runs every time you restart an Exchange server and every three hours thereafter. If you know that a new site has been added and want to see it in your own site's directory, force replication with a site that already has knowledge of the new site's existence and then perform a knowledge consistency check.

For example, suppose a new site named Canada has been added to your organization. Canada directly connects to North America, whereas North America directly connects to South America. The replication topology maps to the actual network connections such that in order for South America to learn about Canada, North America will have to add Canada to its local directory. To that end, the administrator of North America forces a replication with Canada. After Canada shows up in North America's directory, the administrator of South America forces an update with North America. At the end of the update, Canada does not show up in South America's directory. To force Canada to be added to South America's directory, the administrator must force a knowledge consistency check. The KCC button is available on the Directory Service object of the replication bridgehead server.

Schedule Optimization

In addition to being aware of the KCC, you must be aware of the effects your schedule selection can have on your Exchange server and on your network. Be careful about the schedule at which you define directory replication to occur. Because replication is email based, your bridgehead will request an update based on the schedule you define on the Directory Replication Connector. The receiving bridgehead will respond to every request it receives, so it is important to not configure the schedule so that more requests are sent than are necessary. This is especially important if you have intermittent network problems: Messages will queue up until the network is back up.

When the network is backed up, the messages will be sent, potentially causing problems on the receiving bridgehead server. For example, the replication between North America and Canada is set to Always (every 15 minutes). Every 15 minutes, North America requests an update from Canada and Canada requests an update from North America. All is well until the ISDN connection between the two sites fails. The connection is down for six hours, allowing 24 replication messages to queue up on either side. As soon as the connection is reestablished, the replication requests are transmitted to the bridgeheads on the other side of the connection. This causes the bridgeheads to slow processing due to their having to respond to all of the incoming requests. You should configure your schedule to be frequent enough for functionality, but not so frequent that it can cause problems.

Performance Monitor

After your replication connector is configured and functioning, you will want to keep it that way. Because it is easy to not notice the addition or modification of users in the directory, you should keep track of your intersite replication using the Performance Monitor. I recommend tracking the following counters to the MSExchangeDS Object:

- **Pending Replication Synchronizations.** This value gives the number of synchronization messages that the local server has sent out to other servers that have not yet been processed. If this value seems to never drop to zero, you probably have your schedule configured too frequently for the connection. If this value increases above your baseline, you may have a network problem or a problem with one of your Directory Services.

- **Remaining Replication Updates.** This value gives the number of changes received in the current update message that have not yet been incorporated into the local directory. This value should be at zero until a request is sent out. Shortly after the request is made, this value should peak and then fall back to zero.

Foreign Directory Synchronization

In addition to internal directory replication, you may need to administer directory synchronization with a foreign system. Many foreign connectors will include a directory synchronization module that you should use to update the directories on each system. You also can elect to use ADSI/LDAP to get data out of and into the Exchange Directory. I have run into several scenarios where two companies with installed Exchange organizations have merged into one company and wanted to see all employees of the newly created company in the directory. There is now a tool that allows you to move servers between organizations, but I find that is not always an option that companies want to adopt. If you need a way of synchronizing two Exchange organizations, you might be able to use the InterOrg tool available on the BackOffice Resource Kit.

LinkAge Directory Exchange

In addition to InterOrg, there is a utility called *LinkAge Directory Exchange (LDE)* that can be used to synchronize the directories of two Exchange organizations. LDE is not available to the general public, but is supported by PSS, while InterOrg is not. You should use LDE instead of InterOrg only if you need to sync custom attributes, proxy addresses, or if you don't have SMTP connectivity between the organizations. Contact Microsoft PSS for more information.

The InterOrg tool works a lot like MS Mail DirSync. Like MS Mail, InterOrg has you identify a Master server responsible for compiling directory updates into a JET database. The Master server processes all of the updates it receives and then sends them back to Requestors via the Internet Mail Service. InterOrg is a great tool for performing both updates and full synchronizations with external Exchange organizations. You can configure trust levels to prevent specific objects from replicating, and you can even identify which container to import into and export out of.

As far as managing InterOrg is concerned, you will need to keep a close eye on the mailboxes defined for the Master and Requestor servers. These mailboxes send and receive all directory updates, and because they actually are mailboxes they will fill up over time if you don't clean them out.

Optimizing Performance

Like any physical connector, performance of the logical directory replication connector can be optimized by running the Performance Optimizer on the bridgehead servers. Each replication bridgehead server should be configured with both the Connector/Directory import and Multi-server options selected to optimize resource allocation for directory updates as well as the connection to other servers. If you are running dedicated bridgeheads, be sure to uncheck the Public and Private Information Store options to prevent Exchange from allocating resources to processes such as client connections that don't occur on the bridgehead.

Summary

Intersite communication and replication is a critical component of Exchange administration. In this chapter we addressed the native Site and X.400 Connectors, Internet Mail Service, MS Mail Connector, and general third-party connectors before moving on to directory replication management. In addition to managing communication, it is important to periodically obtain reports about server performance. Lets take a look now at the reports that you should be generating each week.

10

Reporting

I N ADDITION TO MONITORING YOUR MESSAGING connectors and replication functionality, you also need to generate reports so you can keep track of system usage and can
better plan for future growth. You should generate and review reports weekly so you
can act on the information they obtain in a timely manner. Additionally, you can get a
better feel for the general trends in your organization if you compile your weekly
reports into monthly and semi-annual reports as well. In this chapter we will discuss
the manual creation and interpretation of usage reports, status reports, and help desk
reports.

Usage Reports

Usage reports are intended to provide information about the way the Exchange
servers in your organization are being used. Two of the most useful reports you create
are for server disk usage and downtime.

Server Disk Usage

The first usage report we are going to address is the Server Disk Usage report. In
addition to paying attention to how much disk space is available to keep from running
out of disk space, you need to know how disk space is being utilized to optimize your

disk resources. Knowledge of what data is occupying disk space can help you identify services that perhaps would perform better on another server, for example. Table 10.1 gives a list of the parameters that you need to collect each week and lets you know how the information can help you.

Table 10.1 **Creating Weekly Server Disk Resource Usage Reports**

Server Disk Parameter	Recommendation
DISK DATA	
Available disk space for all disks	Trends in Private and Public Information Store growth allow you to predict when additional disk resources should be purchased. For example, if you know you have 1.2GB of available disk space and see the number dwindling by 30MB per week, you could have as few as 40 weeks before you need to add storage.
MAILBOX DATA	
Total number of messages stored in mailboxes	This information helps you identify the total number of new messages added to the Private Information Store. This value should increase by the same average amount each week, so large jumps outside of the norm could indicate a problem requiring additional investigation.
Total amount of disk space occupied by mailboxes	Comparing the total amount of disk space occupied by user mailboxes with the disk space used by other Exchange services can help you determine if and when a server should become a dedicated mailbox server or public folder server. If the total disk space used by mailboxes and public folders is growing rapidly at the same time, consider offloading the folders to a dedicated public folder server.
Total number of messages stored in each user's mailbox	Use this information to identify users who may be the recipients of mail storms or other attacks. Large increases from the norm indicate abnormal activity that perhaps requires your intervention.
Total amount of disk space occupied by each user's mailbox	This data is especially valuable if you enable but don't enforce storage limits. Use this to notify you which users are exceeding the limit so you can take action.
Names of mailboxes that haven't been logged into for 90 days or longer	If a mailbox hasn't been logged in to for this long, it probably can be removed from the server. See Chapter 2, "Administering Users," for details about correct removal procedures.

Server Disk Parameter	Recommendation
PUBLIC FOLDER DATA	
Total number of messages stored in public folders	Use this value to track the number of new messages posted to public folders. This value should grow fairly linearly each week, so if you see a sudden surge, you may want to investigate to determine which folder grew and why.
Total amount of disk space occupied by public folders	Like mailboxes, this value can be used to determine the percentage of disk space used by the Public Information Store. It can help you decide if and when to create a dedicated public folder server.
Total number of messages stored in each public folder	Use this value to keep track of individual public folder growth. When folders become too large, you might decide to replicate them to another server.
Total amount of disk space occupied by each public folder	Although Exchange will send warnings to the folder owners and contacts if their folder exceeds storage limits, there is no way to enforce this. You should be notified when folders grow too large so that you can personally address the problem.
Names of folders that don't have owners or contacts	As people leave the company, their folders will be left without owners. If you have folders without owners or contacts, you should remedy this by assigning one or more users to manage the orphaned folders.
CONNECTOR DATA	
Total and average (during peak times) of the following:	
Amount of data both in and out of your Exchange site through each connector	Use these values to identify increases in the number of messages and amount of data sent and received by your local users.
Number of messages transferred both in and out of your Exchange site through each connector	This can help you identify trends in workload so you can plan to offload services to other servers. For example, if your average throughput during peak periods exceeds your baseline on a regular basis, you should consider adding another connector server to your site.

The Exchange 5.5 Administrator Program has a really useful feature to allow you to collect mailbox and public folder usage data into a comma-separated value file (.CSV) without too much work. Although you'll have to go through these steps each week, the file format will always be the same, so you can easily cut and paste data into reports you design in Excel, for example, to get quick summaries of the output. To obtain mailbox data per the recommendations in Table 10.1, follow this procedure:

1. Expand the server name that you wish to obtain statistics for in the Exchange Administrator Program.

2. Expand the Private Information Store Container.

3. Select the **Mailbox Resources Container**.

4. Select any mailbox listed in the Mailbox Resources Container to make the listing active.

5. Select **Save Window Contents** from the **File** menu.

6. Identify a name and location for the .CSV file.

7. Open the .CSV file in a program such as Excel to manipulate the data.

Automatic Report Creation

I recommend purchasing Crystal Reports for creation of Exchange reports. You can use Crystal Reports to create your own custom reports, or you can use the built-in reports that ship with it. Either way, it is a very powerful tool that can make your administrative life a lot easier.

The Total Number of Messages and Connector Throughput

It's useful to compare the total number of messages in all mailboxes to connector throughput because these values together will give you an idea of what percentage of new mail is generated within the local site, as opposed to externally. For example, if the total number of messages in mailboxes grows by 12,000 messages each week, and your total connector throughput identifies 3,000 incoming each week, then you know that 9,000 were generated within your site. On the other hand, if you see 9,000 coming in through the connectors, this could indicate a less than optimized environment, where local users communicate with users in other sites more than within their local site.

Data Manipulation

When it comes to data manipulation, I personally prefer to use charts. You can easily create spreadsheets that hold the data from your reports, and link this data to a chart. Additionally, I like to add information such as raw value increase and % value increase per week. You might also consider adding a threshold value that can be compared with the data on the report.

Follow this procedure to get a .CSV file containing public folder data as defined in Table 10.1:

1. Expand the server name for which you want to obtain statistics in the Exchange Administrator Program.

2. Expand the Public Information Store Container.

3. Select the **Public Folder Resources Container**.

4. Select any folder listed in the Public Folder Resources Container to make the listing active.

5. Select **Save Window Contents** from the **File** menu.

6. Identify a name and location for the .CSV file.

7. Open the .CSV file in a program such as Excel to manipulate the data.

To get connector traffic statistics as defined in Table 10.1, configure Performance Monitor logging for the objects and counters defined in Table 10.2. I recommend a logging frequency of no more often than every 15 minutes. It isn't necessary to collect data more often unless you are attempting to troubleshoot a problem.

Table 10.2 **Using Performance Monitor to Obtain Connector Information for Weekly Reports**

Object	Counter
MSExchangeIMC	Inbound Messages Total
	Inbound Messages/Hr
	Outbound Messages Total
	Outbound Messages/Hr
	Total Inbound Kilobytes
	Inbound Bytes/Hr
	Total Outbound Kilobytes
	Outbound Bytes/Hr
MSExchangeMSMI	Messages Sent
	Messages Sent/hr
	Messages Received
	Messages Received/hr
MSExchangeMTA Connections (for each appropriate instance)	Inbound Bytes Total
	Receive Bytes/sec
	Inbound Messages Total
	Receive Messages/sec
	Outbound Bytes Total
	Send Bytes/sec
	Outbound Messages Total
	Send Messages/sec

Use the data in your report to create charts showing trends over time. The chart should go back no further than one year, and should have your performance thresholds marked so you can see when your data values exceeded your thresholds.

Downtime Summary

In addition to disk resource utilization, you should be keeping track of your downtime. I believe that it is of the utmost importance that companies implement a scheduled downtime standard operating procedure so that planned maintenance—such as service pack installation, upgrades, and offline backups—can be performed without inconveniencing users. Unfortunately, not all downtime can be planned. If your server has a problem that requires you to bring it down outside of the schedule, this should be logged and reported on. Over time you may find that downtime is associated with other processes or certain timeframes. You will never figure out relationships between Exchange problems and outside influences if you don't keep track of your server downtime. Information to be logged should include the following:

- Which server went down
- Date and time the server went down
- How long the server was down
- Why the server went down
- The remedy for the problem
- Whether the server required a reboot or just a service restart

Also keep track of link and network problems. This information can help you determine if a secondary backup link should be purchased. Information to track on the link includes the following:

- Which component failed
- Date and time the component failed
- How long the link/network was down
- Why the component failed
- The remedy for the problem

Connector Counter Resets

Be aware that all "Total" connector counters discussed in Table 10.2 reset whenever the corresponding connector's service is stopped and restarted ("Average" counters do not). If your report data appears to be significantly under normal usage, you should double-check that there isn't a reset in the log file.

Use the data from your log files to generate weekly, monthly, and semi-annual reports. Your weekly report should summarize the events from the log file, whereas monthly and semi-annual reports can be generated automatically from multiple weekly reports. All reports should include all information from the log file except problem remedies because the problem fix is already documented in the log. A weekly report might look something like the example HTS Corporation Weekly Downtime Report.

HTS CORPORATION
WEEKLY DOWNTIME REPORT

Exchange Server Downtime Summary
April 18–24, 1999

Site: Central Florida

Server Name	Date/Time	Down Time (HR)	Component(B/S)
MCOEXCMBX01	N/A	0	N/A
Total MCOEXCMBX01 Downtime:		*0*	
MCOEXCPF01	N/A	0	N/A
Total MCOEXCPF01 Downtime:		*0*	
MCOEXCCON01	4/20 16:42	.25	IS (s)
	4/22 02:17	2	Disk (s)
Total MCOEXCON01 Downtime:		*2.25*	

The HTS Corporation Weekly Downtime Report indicates that of the three Orlando servers, only the connector server, MCOEXCCON01, had problems during the reporting period. The mailbox and public folder servers did not even require service restarts during the week of April 18–24. The connector server required that the Information Store service be restarted on April 20, with a total downtime of approximately 15 minutes. On April 22, one of the hard disks on the connector server crashed, resulting in a partial restore from backup that took approximately two hours. Fortunately, the connector server was being monitored using a Link Monitor. The failure of the connector server to respond to the Link Monitor resulted in the IS on-call personnel to receive an alert, and enabled them to restore the server before the start of business the next day.

To create monthly and semi-annual reports, combine information found in the weekly reports in the same format shown in the HTS Corporation example. Look for problematic servers and/or services, as well as commonality in the timing of server problems.

Status Reports

Just like disk usage and downtime reports, status reports are an important component of proactive administration. At a minimum, you should create two status reports each week, with weekly reports being compiled into monthly and semi-annual reports. Reports to generate are as follows:

- Exchange server backup status reports
- User population reports

Server Backup Status

Server backup status reports are necessary to help you plan potential changes to future backup procedures resulting from growth. You should create weekly server backup status reports for each server in each site based on information found in your nightly backup logs. Table 10.3 lists the minimum information that should be included about each server in your weekly backup reports.

Table 10.3   **Using Data from the Backup Logs and Event Logs for Periodic Backup Reports**

Data	Recommendation
Number of MBs backed up this period	Compare the number of MBs backed up this period with the number backed up last period to illustrate the increased backup requirements for the period.
Number of MBs backed up last period	
Total size of databases last period	Although database size is reported in the disk usage report, I would add it to the backup report to indicate that the entire database is being backed up successfully.
Total size of databases this period	
Number of MBs restored this period	Use the restore values to get a big-picture view of how much restoration is necessary each week. Over time this value will enable you to decide whether steps should be taken to improve the restore procedure in place, or possibly use additional fault tolerance hardware at your company.
Whether any errors were reported	If errors were reported in the Event Viewer or backup logs, this fact should be annotated on the weekly report. Frequent backup errors are not normal. If your backup has errors on a regular basis you need to take corrective action to identify and fix the problem.

Your weekly backup report might look something like the following example HTS Corporation Weekly Backup Report.

HTS CORPORATION
WEEKLY BACKUP REPORT

Exchange Server Backup Summary
April 18–24, 1999

Site: Central Florida

Server Name	Total MBs Backed Up/Restored:			Total Database Size in MBs:		
	Current	Prev.	Restored	Current	Prev.	Errors
MCOEXCMBX01	756.2	734.8	0	687.5	658.5	N
MCOEXCPF01	512.3	486.3	0	459.5	445.9	N
MCOCONN01	478.5	461.7	265.5	437.7	425.8	N

Over time, the weekly backup reports will be compiled into monthly and semi-annual reports that you can use to see how much additional data your backup picks up on average each week. Use this to plan for backup hardware upgrades, to implement fault tolerance, or to redesign your backup procedures for growth. As with the disk usage reports, I like to chart the data from backup reports so I can more easily visualize the trends.

User Population Status

As do server backup status reports, user population status reports can help you plan for growth. We discussed the impact that different clients will have on your server resources in Chapter 8, "Managing Server Resources." Because each client has a different impact, you should attempt to keep track of the total number of users you add to your servers each week, as well as the protocol those clients will primarily use. This is a difficult estimate to make because some users will necessarily use both protocols due to the nature of their jobs. Even so, an estimate is a good starting point for mapping your user population. Your weekly user population status report should include the following information:

- Number of MAPI users added
- Number of POP3 users added
- Number of IMAP4 users added

- Number of HTTP users added
- Total number of users added

Use the weekly reports to generate monthly and semi-annual reports identifying your user population as a whole. For example, you know how many users were migrated when you first deployed Exchange. Because you also had to configure the messaging clients for your migrated uses, you also know how many users initially used each client. Use this information to create a chart of your user population each month. A sample monthly report might look like the example HTS Corporation Monthly User Population Report.

HTS CORPORATION
MONTHLY USER POPULATION REPORT

Exchange Server User Population Summary
April 1999

Site: Central Florida
Server: MCOEXCMBX01

Protocol	Previous Population	Current Population
MAPI	356	393
POP3	25	28
IMAP4	0	0
HTTP	57	69
Total Population	*438*	*490*

As you can see from the preceding example, HTS Corporation's Central Florida site is growing at a phenomenal rate. Total user population increased more than 10% in just one month. If this growth continues, the administrator should take a close look at Performance Monitor logs to see how the server is bearing up under the load.

Help Desk Reports

In addition to usage and status reports, you should also generate reports identifying help desk issues. Help desk reports can give you an idea of how often certain tasks need to be performed and allow you to document issues that perhaps could be alleviated by additional user training. You can also track how long it takes for help desk requests to be resolved in order to determine whether additional support personnel should be added to the help desk staff. The log file should be reviewed weekly, although entries should be made in it every day. Information that should be reported on includes the following:

- Number of times passwords have to be reset each day
- Username of the account holder requiring the password reset
- Account changes made
- Accounts unlocked each day
- Username of the account holder requiring account unlock

Your help desk personnel should be logging this information to the main help desk database as events occur. You should go through this database weekly to summarize the events of the week. Use the weekly reports to generate monthly and semi-annual reports that may help you identify areas that could use some work. A help desk report might look like the example HTS Corporation Weekly Help Desk Report.

HTS CORPORATION
WEEKLY HELP DESK REPORT

Exchange Server Help Desk Summary
April 18–24, 1999

Site: Central Florida

Task	Number of calls	Account Holder	Date/Time
Accounts Unlocked	2	James Taylor	4/19 08:52
			4/21 09:01
	1	John Bachinsky	4/19 08:23
	1	Julie Rice	4/19 13:12
Total Accounts Unlocked	*4*		
Passwords Reset	2	Kenneth Insco	4/19 09:07
			4/22 08:14
	1	John Bachinsky	4/19 08:25
	1	Julie Rice	4/19 13:15
Total Passwords Reset	*4*		
Accounts Changed	1	Susan Surloff	4/23 17:31
	1	Gwendolyn Hogan	4/23 17:31
	1	Nicole Sheehan	4/23 17:32
	1	Michele Nolan	4/23 17:32
	1	Steven Krupski	4/23 17:32
Total Accounts Changed	*5*		

You can see from the preceding sample report that user James Taylor had two account lockouts with no password resets. This could indicate a security problem in which an attacker is attempting to gain access to the user's account, or it could mean that the user "fat-fingers" the keys a lot. Either way, you might want to talk to this user about the problem in an effort to prevent it from reoccurring. On the other hand, user Kenneth Insco had two password resets and no account lockouts. This means he forgot his password twice during the reporting period. You should consider discussing some tips for password creation and memorization with him. Account changes all occurred about the same time on Friday, indicating they were planned and executed for off hours, as you should always attempt to do.

Help desk reports, like the other reports, should be compiled into monthly and semi-annual reports. This can help identify recurring problems, such as times when account lockouts occur, or users that have repeated difficulties. You can then take steps to remedy the situation.

Summary

Report creation is one of the most important tasks you will perform in your administration of Exchange. In this chapter we discussed the importance of creating reports for planning and evaluation purposes, as well as the mechanics of actually creating reports manually. In addition to reporting, there are a number of additional tasks you will need to perform regularly in order to keep your Exchange server running. Let's take a look at these tasks and how they facilitate proactive troubleshooting if performed periodically.

Password Security

Because you never want to use passwords that are easy to guess, I advise people to think of a sentence that can be easily remembered. This sentence should include numbers and punctuation. You can use the first letter of every word in the sentence along with the numbers and punctuation for the password. This can make your password easy to remember and difficult to guess.

11

Periodic Proactive Troubleshooting

I N ADDITION TO REPORTING AND MANAGING your intersite communications, there are a number of tasks you should perform periodically in order to implement proactive administration policies. In this chapter, we will discuss practicing your disaster recovery procedures, identifying and removing unused and unnecessary resources, performing offline defragmentation of your Information Stores, and archiving your log files.

By keeping on top of these tasks, you will be in a better position to recover from disasters.

Rehearsing Your Disaster Recovery Procedures

One of the most important things you can do to prepare for disaster recovery is to rehearse your disaster recovery procedures, which is also the most important step in backup verification. Backup verification includes the following:

- Comparing data backed up to production data on the disk. Comparison is performed by your backup software during the actual backup.
- Analyzing backup information logged to log files during the actual backup.
- Analyzing event logs each day.
- Practicing data restoration procedures periodically in the lab.

I recommend that you rehearse your restoration procedure once each quarter. As part of the rehearsal, document all problems that you encounter in addition to recording how much time it takes to fix the problems and recover the whole server. Over time, you will see your list of problems diminish and the amount of time it takes to perform the restore will be optimized. In this section, we will discuss the benefits of practice restorations, describe the ideal lab environment for such restorations, and detail the advantages of surprise rehearsals.

Benefits of Practice Restoration

Practice restorations provide three benefits. They confirm the validity of your backup set, confirm the validity of your recovery procedures, and improve the effectiveness of your disaster recovery personnel. Many companies don't bother to practice restores and inevitably the recovery from a disaster is a disaster in and of itself. Problems range from being unable to locate system CD-ROMs to personnel applying the backup tapes incorrectly. You can save yourself a lot of headaches by being well prepared for disaster recovery.

Confirmation of the Validity of Your Backup Set

Problems with the media will be detected during the practice recovery, as opposed to being discovered during an actual recovery. For example, most places rotate backup tapes such that the same tape is used over and over again. If a problem with the actual magnetic media in the tape prevents a complete, pristine backup, you will probably never know it until it becomes time to do the restore. Actual disaster recovery is not the time to find out that your tape is shot. Practice restores will allow you to detect tape problems so that you can replace the tape for use during the next backup.

Confirmation of the Validity of Your Recovery Procedures

Errors in the documentation will be discovered during the practice recovery as opposed to being discovered during a real disaster. I find that although most companies have the best intentions, updating the standard operating procedures is pretty far down the list of priority tasks. Quite often, this means that the disaster recovery SOP reflects procedures that would have worked using the previous backup software but won't work with the upgraded software. Worse yet, sometimes the use of Exchange Server has never been added to the original SOP.

If you have not yet had to restore Exchange data from backup, then you may not realize that your procedures are outdated. Outdated procedures will actually hinder your restore because your personnel will attempt to follow the directions and will fail at some point well into the restore. Subsequently, the restore will have to be restarted from the beginning, and valuable time will be lost. By practicing your restore procedures, this problem will be caught before it has an impact on your production environment, and you will have the opportunity to create a new Exchange recovery SOP.

Improving the Performance of Your Disaster Recovery Personnel

Your ability to recover in a true emergency can be greatly improved by continued practice. Your personnel will know exactly what steps to take to recover, and many snags will be ironed out during practice rather than during the true emergency. If you don't practice restores, your personnel will likely be panicking during the disaster and unable to think as clearly as they would under less stressful circumstances. Giving them the chance to practice will enable your administrators to become comfortable with the restore procedures and to therefore minimize mistakes and wasted time.

Lab Requirements

To perform practice restores, you will need a lab ideally equipped with the same hardware you use for your production server. If this is not possible, at least provide a server with enough disk space to restore the data and system files as well as perform offline defragmentation. Offline defragmentation requires free space equal to the size of the database being defragmented. If your original server occupies 8GB of space with a 5GB Private Information Store, the lab server needs at least 13GB of free space to accommodate the restore and an offline defragmentation of the Private Information Store.

By providing enough space for the offline defragmentation, you will be able not only to practice data restores, but also to rehearse any necessary recovery tasks on the non-production server prior to attempting repair on the production server. For example, if you find that your production server has a corrupt database and you need to do an ESEUTIL to actually repair the data, you should verify that the procedure will work on the lab server using production data prior to performing the procedure on the production server. Lots of available disk space will give you the most versatility with your lab server. See Chapter 14, "Disaster Recovery," for detailed information on restoring Exchange data from both online and offline backups.

Surprise Rehearsals

Although most practice restores should be scheduled, my opinion is that occasionally, disaster recovery personnel should not have prior knowledge of the rehearsal. By surprising your recovery personnel, you can provide a simulation environment most like that of a true disaster. Actual data from actual backup tapes should be used for the restore, and the effectiveness of the restore should be tested by accessing a few mailboxes and folders. Record the time it takes for restore, beginning at the time you notify your personnel to report to the office and ending at the time the server's functionality is verified. Create a report to be updated with each practice restore to see the effects of practice on response time.

Mailbox and Folder Administration

In addition to periodically practicing your data recovery procedures, there are a few tasks you should periodically perform with regard to your mailboxes and public folders. These include the following:

- Removing unused resources
- Cleaning mailboxes
- Moving mailboxes

We discussed daily management of your disk resources in Chapter 5, "Managing Disk Resources." This included tasks such as checking whether users have exceeded their storage limits and cleaning their mailboxes for them. Unfortunately, I find that although it is best to do these tasks daily, it is unlikely that the administrator of a large company will be able to perform them that often. Because disk resource management includes constant attention to the user data stored in the Private Information Store, you need to address these tasks at least weekly. Your vigilance will pay off in optimized disk space and optimized backup and restore times. Let's start by taking a look at removing unused resources.

Removing Unused Resources

You should remove unused mailboxes ideally every week, but at least every month. Unused resources are mailboxes and folders that have not been accessed in 90 days or longer. I find that many departmental managers are terribly irresponsible when it comes to notifying the IS department of personnel changes. As a result, you will be stuck with two recurring problems:

- You will constantly have to add new mailboxes during work hours (which is certainly against the recommendations in Chapter 2, "Administering Users") for new employees that you were not aware were coming in.

- You will have to figure out for yourself which mailboxes need to be removed since no one will tell you when an employee is transferred or leaves the company.

Errors in Moving Your Mailboxes

Any errors encountered while moving mailboxes will be logged to the comma-separated value (.CSV) file you identify in the Mailbox Migration dialog box. Errors are logged as they occur for each mailbox being migrated. This makes verification of migration a lot easier for you since you can quickly scan the log file for FAILURE entries.

It's my experience that in many cases, transferred employees will continue to pick their mail up at the original server, even if their new office is defined on a different server. This can become bad for your network if it happens too frequently, and there really isn't much you can do about it other than watching your network traffic like a hawk or scrutinizing the employee personnel records. On the other hand, you can easily determine which mailboxes haven't been logged in to for a long time. Long time periods between logins generally indicate that the mailboxes belong to users who have since left the company. In this case, the data contained within the former employee's mailbox needs to be analyzed and backed up for potential future use.

Before deleting a mailbox, you should be sure that no one has accessed it for a long time. This is easily accomplished if you are creating reports, as discussed in Chapter 10, "Reporting." The weekly Server Disk Usage report will identify the last time a mailbox was logged in to. If this number is higher than 90 days, the mailbox is not being used. After you have determined which mailboxes are not being used, you should verify that the mailbox owner has indeed left the company before deleting the mailbox from the server. As we discussed in Chapter 5, you wouldn't want to delete a mailbox belonging to a user on medical leave only to be confronted with this fact when the user returns to work. Prior to removing any mailbox, you should follow the recommendations in Chapter 2 for information on preserving the data contained in the mailbox.

Cleaning Mailboxes

In addition to removing unused mailboxes, you should implement a "clean mailbox" policy that removes unnecessary documents and messages from the server. We discussed the benefits and disadvantages of both manual and automatic clean mailbox procedures in Chapter 5, and procedures to clean a mailbox in Chapter 2.

Ideally, mailboxes should be cleaned nightly to prevent unwanted buildup. Unfortunately, it is my experience that many companies can't clean mailboxes each night. If you are unable to clean mailboxes each night, you need to at least clean them as part of your weekly administration. The more time you allow to pass between cleanings, the more junk will be removed as part of the clean procedures and the more space will be freed up in the database. You should attempt to minimize the amount of free space in the database so that you can optimize your hard disk resources as a whole.

If you are unable to clean user mailboxes at all, you should analyze the amount of space being used by mailboxes each week. The server disk usage report discussed in Chapter 10 will identify for you which users are taking up the most space. Analyze this report weekly so that you can personally address the issue with the offending user or that user's supervisor. There is no good reason for wasting space on the server, and I find that in companies where the administrator is reluctant to address space usage issues, the users keep every message ranging from "How was the game last night?" to the reply "Fine."

Moving Mailboxes

Aside from regular removal and cleaning of user mailboxes, you will find that periodically you will need to move a mailbox belonging to a relocated user. As your users transfer to new positions within the company, you should move their mailboxes to follow them so they continue to receive mail, and you keep your network traffic minimized. Let's take a look at the procedures for moving mailboxes within the same site as opposed to between sites.

Moving Mailboxes Within a Site

You may need to move mailboxes to other servers in the same site if your users relocate periodically to other offices that use other servers, or if you need to offload some of the existing mailboxes to another server to realize improved server performance. Fortunately, moving mailboxes within a site is really easy. Use the **Move Mailbox** command on the **Tools** menu in the Exchange Administrator Program. This tool allows you to move a mailbox to any server defined in the same site as the selected mailbox.

The best part of moving mailboxes within a site is that the Outlook and Exchange client profiles will not need to be reconfigured to locate the new server. As part of client startup, Outlook and Exchange will query the directory on the original Exchange server to locate their new mailbox server. When the directory responds with the new server name, the profile will be automatically updated.

Moving Mailboxes Between Sites

In many cases, you will need to move a mailbox to a server in another site. This will be necessary whenever a user is transferred to another branch office defined outside your local Exchange site. Unfortunately, moving mailboxes between sites is not as straightforward as moving mailboxes between servers in the same site. You have two options: moving the mailboxes manually or using the Mailbox Migration tool.

Remember, each user has an X.500 email address used for internal Exchange message routing. This X.500 address includes the name of the site on which the mailbox is defined, so moving a mailbox to a new site amounts to a new X.500 email address. This won't affect any users outside of the Exchange organization, and it won't affect any users who use the Exchange server-based address lists, but it will affect users who like to add internal recipients to their personal address books. These users will receive NDRs for messages sent to the PAB entry for recipients that have been moved to other sites. Additionally, replies sent to messages from these moved recipients sent prior to the move will also be returned as undeliverable, since the Reply-To address in the message will reflect the original X.500 address.

For example, suppose Bill sends a message to Julie, another Exchange user, on Friday. Over the weekend, Bill's mailbox is moved to another site. Julie receives the message when she gets to work on Monday and replies to it. She receives an NDR because Bill's X.500 address defined in the message she replied to is no longer valid. Julie will have to send a new message to Bill where the address is resolved using the Exchange Directory in order for the message to be delivered correctly.

Manually Moving the Mailbox

Moving mailboxes between sites can be accomplished manually by following these steps:

1. Log in to the user's mailbox.
2. Create a .PST file.
3. Download all the user's mail into the .PST file.
4. Create the user's new account in the new site.
5. Log in to the user's new mailbox. If you can't log in to it, you can email the .PST file to the new mailbox along with instructions on how the user can import his own data.
6. Add the .PST file created in step 2 to the new mailbox's profile.
7. Move all the mail from the .PST to the new mailbox.
8. Delete the user's original mailbox from the old site.

This is definitely the hard way to move a mailbox. I would recommend that you use the BackOffice Resource Kit's Mailbox Migration tool instead of performing this task manually.

Using the Mailbox Migration Tool

The Mailbox Migration tool allows you to move user data between sites and between organizations. It creates a .PST file automatically and then downloads the messages and rules from the original mailbox to the .PST file. After messages are downloaded, you can rerun the Mailbox Migration tool to import the information into a previously created, empty mailbox in the new site.

To move a mailbox to another site or organization, follow these steps:

1. Create the user's new mailbox on the correct server in the new site.
2. Create a temporary Outlook profile to be used by the Mailbox Migration tool.
3. Run the `MIGRATE.EXE` file from the BackOffice Resource Kit Second Edition.
4. Type the path and file name of the .CSV file identifying the user to be moved in the Control File dialog box. The .CSV file needs to identify the original and new server names, as well as several other parameters used for the migration.
5. Click **Start** to begin the migration.

The Mailbox Migration tool then performs the following tasks:

1. Modifies the local profile to identify the user's mailbox
2. Creates a .PST file on the local workstation to hold data from the user's mailbox
3. Logs in to the user's mailbox using the local profile
4. Copies all messages in the user's Inbox, Sent Items, Calendar, Contacts and other folders to the local .PST file

5. Logs in to the user's new mailbox using the local profile

6. Copies all data from the local .PST file to the new server

7. Updates the log file defined in the Mailbox Migration window to reflect the success or failure of the migration

8. Deletes the local .PST file

There are lots of really helpful features to the Mailbox Migration tool. For example, you can always stop the migration process before the whole .CSV file is processed by clicking the **Stop** button. The migration will stop after the current mailbox is completely processed or after an error occurs, whichever is first. Since the Mailbox Migration tool removes the corresponding entry from the .CSV file after the mailbox is successfully processed, you can restart the migration at your convenience using the same .CSV file.

Another great benefit to the Mailbox Migration tool is that you don't need network connectivity between the originating and destination servers for the move to be successful. This factor is facilitated by a field in the .CSV file allocated for defining two-part migrations. I like to do two-part migrations in most cases even if network connectivity is available because the connection between sites is almost always a WAN link. It winds up being faster to copy the .PST file to the new site and run the Mailbox Migration from a server local to the destination server, rather than generating a lot of RPC data between the original migration workstation and the destination server.

For example, Lyle Curry is defined on the SEATTLE server and is going to be moved to the HONOLULU server. There is an ISDN link between SEATTLE and HONOLULU. The Mailbox Migration tool will be run from the WKSEATTLE workstation in Seattle for stage 1 of the migration. After Lyle's data is in the .PST file, the .PST file will be transferred to the HONOLULU server. Another administrator will run the Mailbox Migration's second stage from the WKHON workstation in Honolulu. Although the migration could have been performed in a single stage from either WKSEATTLE or WKHON, the Mailbox Migration tool would have had to establish an RPC session across the ISDN link for the migration. Performance in this scenario would have been unacceptably slow.

Offline Maintenance

Now that you've cleaned, removed, and moved mailboxes and folders, you have free space being utilized by Exchange that could be released to other applications through an offline defragmentation. To perform an offline defragmentation on an Exchange version 5.5 database, use the utility ESEUTIL. Use EDBUTIL for earlier versions of Exchange.

ESEUTIL

Because Exchange 5.5 is the current version as of this writing, we will discuss ESEUTIL first. ESEUTIL.EXE is installed in the `%winnt%\system32` directory when Exchange 5.5 is installed. It is used for troubleshooting and defragmentation of any JET97 database, not just those associated with Exchange Server. You should only use ESEUTIL to defragment your database to get rid of the free space left behind by deleted user data and mailboxes as needed. You can also use ESEUTIL to make the storage used in your databases contiguous so that your drive head doesn't have to skip all around the disk to find information in the database (assuming the database itself is not fragmented). Exchange 5.5 Enterprise was improved so you shouldn't need to do an offline defragmentation as part of your regular maintenance. Because the BackOffice version still limits you to a 16GB database size, you may need to defragment it whenever considerable amounts of data are removed.

Requirements

ESEUTIL has certain requirements that must be met before defragmentation can complete, including adequate disk space and validated checksums. When you run ESEUTIL, the entire database is copied to a temporary database, which is subsequently saved in the same location as the original database at completion of the defragmentation. Because ESEUTIL creates a complete copy of the original, fragmented database, you will need to have enough disk space available on your hard drive to accommodate the temporary database. To defragment a 9GB database, you will need 9GB of free space available to the ESEUTIL utility.

Additionally, ESEUTIL will compare the checksum for each 4KB page of the database with a checksum calculated during the defragmentation. If the original and calculated checksums are not the same, ESEUTIL will stop and log an event to the Event Viewer. (see Chapter 7, "Daily Proactive Troubleshooting," for more information on common events to be on the lookout for.) ESEUTIL's checksum comparison is a nice feature for you because you will be alerted to potential database corruption problems before they become so bad that you have to restore data from a backup.

Defragmentation Process

To defragment a database, perform the following steps:

1. Stop the Exchange services. ESEUTIL is an offline utility.

2. Run ESEUTIL /d at the command prompt with the correct defragmentation switches.

Customize the operation of ESEUTIL with the command line switches described in Table 11.1

Table 11.1   **ESEUTIL Switches**

Switch	Usage
/ds	Defragment the Directory database `DIR.EDB`. The path to `DIR.EDB` is read from the Registry.
/ispriv	Defragment the Private Information Store database `PRIV.EDB`. The path to `PRIV.EDB` is read from the Registry.
/ispub	Defragment the Public Information Store database `PUB.EDB`. The path to `PUB.EDB` is read from the Registry.
/b	Identify the location for the temporary database.
/p	Preserve the original database in the original location and place the new temporary database in `\exchsrvr\bin\tempdfrg.edb`.
/t	Rename the new database.
/o	Suppress the Microsoft Exchange Server banner logo.

To defragment the Private Information Store using free space available on the `g:\` drive, use the following command:

```
ESEUTIL /d /ispriv /b g:\
```

EDBUTIL

If you run Exchange version 4.0 or 5.0 you will need to use the EDBUTIL utility to defragment your databases. EDBUTIL is almost exactly the same as ESEUTIL except that it is used exclusively for Exchange 4.0 and 5.0 databases, whereas ESEUTIL is used for any JET97 database. This means it must meet the same disk space and check-sum requirements in order to succeed.

To perform an offline defragmentation on an Exchange 4.0 or 5.0 database, follow the same procedure as for ESEUTIL except use the command `EDBUTIL` in the command line instead of `ESEUTIL`. Customize the offline defragmentation of your Exchange 4.0 and 5.0 databases using the EDBUTIL command line switches listed in Table 11.2.

> **Difficulties with Offline Defragmentation EDBUTIL /s**
>
> I've had trouble with EDBUTIL when it could not find the identified database using the Registry. In these cases, I have attempted to run the utility with the /s switch to force EDBUTIL to defragment the database. Invariably, this has led to database problems preventing Exchange from restarting, and required the /r to repair the database. See Chapter 14, for details on database repair.

Table 11.2 **EDBUTIL Switches**

Switch	Usage
/ds	Defragment the Directory database `DIR.EDB`.
/ispriv	Defragment the Private Information Store database `PRIV.EDB`.
/ispub	Defragment the Public Information Store database `PUB.EDB`.
/s	Location of the database to be defragmented.
/l	Location where the log file should be stored.
/r	Repair errors detected during defragmentation.
/b	Identify the location for the temporary database.
/t	Rename the new database.
/p	Preserve the original database in the original location and place the new temporary database in `\exchsrvr\bin\tempdfrg.edb`.
/n	Write status information to dfrginfo.txt.
/o	Suppress the Microsoft Exchange Server banner logo.

Archiving Logs

Aside from actual hands-on maintenance tasks, there are always paper tasks to address in any administrative job. As far as Exchange administration is concerned, you need to periodically archive your log files for future use. The logs you should archive are event logs and Performance Monitor logs.

Event Viewer Logs

In addition to daily perusal of your event viewer logs, you should archive them for periodic trend analysis. I would recommend weekly archives, or even more frequently if your log files fill up quickly. Periodic analysis of event log data can alert you to trends such as recurring service problems or problems that repeat at certain intervals, as shown in Table 11.3.

Table 11.3 **Event Log Archive Formats**

Format	Recommendation
Event log format	Use event log format only if you plan to review your log files using the Event Viewer or you need to retain the actual binary data associated with the event.
Text format	Archive your logs in text format only if you plan to use the data for reports created in a word processor. All binary data is lost when you archive to a text file.
CSV format	Use comma-separated value format to allow data manipulation in spreadsheets. Although the binary data is lost, I find the CSV format the most usable because of the ability to bring it into Excel for later analysis.

After your data is archived to CSV-formatted log files, you can easily open up the files in Excel or another spreadsheet. I like to manipulate the data by looking for the number of events generated by each of the Exchange services and determining if any services appear problematic. I also like to compare the logs from one day to the next to determine what events are occurring at the same time each day. You'll need to trim out the events that relate to general information such as online defragmentation events so that you can get a clear view of abnormalities in your system. Use this data to reschedule recurring events if their timing is not appropriate for your environment and to identify Exchange problems that may be related to other server or network activity.

Performance Monitor Logs

In addition to archiving your event logs, your Performance Monitor logs should also be archived. Archiving Performance Monitor logs involves identifying the samples you wish to save in addition to the actual archival.

The first step to Performance Monitor log file archiving is to identify the portions of each log's data that are of interest. I recommend opening your log data in a Performance Monitor chart to figure out what time of day was most active for that sample. After you identify the time frame, set the time window to include the interesting time period. If you find that the servers you monitor have different peak periods, I recommend archiving all data from all servers during all peak periods. For example, if the SEATTLE server has a peak from 08:30 to 09:30 but the BELLEVUE server's peak is from 09:00 to 10:30, archive data from both SEATTLE and BELLEVUE from 08:30 to 10:30 to allow the best data set for comparison.

Once you've identified what you want to monitor, create a Performance Monitor settings file (if you haven't already) to define the objects and counters you want to keep in the archive log. Archive the data using the Log Options window. Each archive will be appended to the end of the log file.

I like to use the archive files to identify long-term trends. Each quarter, create a chart showing your server performance during peak periods as defined in the archive. This will enable you to determine at what point your server may begin to have resource problems.

> **Event Viewer Sort Order Effects on Archives**
>
> The sort order defined in the current view of the Event Viewer will dictate the order the events are archived in both text and CSV formats. For consistent data, you need to be careful to sort the same way before archiving. Although it is easier to view the log in the Event Viewer with most recent events displayed at the top, archives are better if the most recent events are displayed at the bottom. Sorting oldest records to the top allows you to easily place data in consistent order in your master spreadsheet or database.

Summary

In this chapter, we discussed the tasks that you should perform regularly to keep your Exchange server running. This included rehearsal disaster recovery procedures, resource management, offline maintenance, and log archiving. Although these tasks are intended to facilitate a proactive stance to Exchange administration, there will occasionally be times when you have to react to a given situation. The next section of this book discusses troubleshooting issues such as planning, identifying, and recovering from disasters. Let's take a look now at steps you can take to prepare for disaster.

Troubleshooting and Disaster Recovery

12

Planning for Disaster

Now that you've been administering Exchange successfully following a scheduled, proactive approach, it is time to discuss a proactive approach to disaster recovery. It seems a little like creating a self-fulfilling prophecy to plan for a disaster, but if you fail to plan then you will be woefully unprepared to recover completely or quickly. In this chapter we will discuss an approach to disaster planning in addition to creating a standard operating procedure and optimizing your hardware and software configuration.

Troubleshooting Strategy

To me, a disaster is anything that causes a server malfunction. This can range from something minor, such as having to recover a user's email, to a huge disaster requiring you to rebuild your Exchange server. The first stage to preparing for any disaster is to have a tried and tested troubleshooting technique. Although sometimes it seems as though there are as many methodologies as there are administrators, ranging from very random to very structured techniques, the best solution is actually somewhere in the middle. If your strategy is too random it becomes difficult to narrow in on the problem, whereas too structured means you don't have room to try things outside of the plan. In this section we will discuss the strategy that I use when attempting to solve a problem. This strategy consists of three major steps:

1. Identifying the problem
2. Performing a solution
3. Documenting the results

Identifying the Problem

It seems as though the easiest part of solving a problem should be to identify the problem. In reality, I find that this is actually the most difficult step for many administrators. In order to identify a problem successfully, you need to obtain data from a multitude of sources, including event log files, Performance Monitor logs, server diagnostic utilities, message tracking logs, users, and other administrators. You will then need to weed through all the information you obtain to determine what is germane to the problem at hand, and finally you need to decide how to interpret the data to decide where the problem area is. You can make problem identification easier by becoming an expert in the following areas:

- Microsoft Exchange
- Microsoft Windows NT
- Your messaging clients
- Your desktop operating systems
- Your network topology

The better you understand your environment, the easier it will be to determine what the problem is. For example, as a consultant I run into a lot of difficulty identifying problems if my customers don't have a clear understanding of their environment. I had one customer call me up because his Exchange services wouldn't start. When I asked if his company had recently changed the service account password, his answer was "No." Upon further investigation, I found that they had indeed changed the password several days earlier on their mainframe server, which synchronizes with the NT PDC. The synchronization delay, coupled with the fact that Exchange had not restarted in several days, masked the problem. If the customer had been able to give me more information about his environment, I would have been able to quickly solve the problem for him over the phone instead of having to do an on-site trouble call.

Performing a Solution

After you have identified the problem, you need to plan a few solutions. Use TechNet and the Microsoft Knowledge Base as well as the Microsoft Newsgroups to obtain suggestions on potential solutions. Microsoft's support Web site is an excellent resource as well; it includes up-to-date information found on TechNet and the Knowledge Base in addition to data that has been expired from the TechNet CD Microsoft ships each month.

After you have a list of possibilities, prioritize them based on your experience with your server and your network. Once you've decided the order in which to begin applying the solutions, back your server up. *This is so important!* If you make a mistake attempting the fix, or if the fix turns out to be destructive, you will at least still have your data for restore. For example, if the fix turns out to be something scary, such as using ESEUTIL /r to repair a corrupt database, you should back up your production server and restore the data on a lab server. Apply the fix on the lab server to verify that it will work before applying the fix to your production server. If you don't have a lab server to test your fix on, you need to back up your data to prevent the possibility that you will lose your database as a result of the repair. After you have completed your Exchange backup, begin applying the solutions.

If you are the highest tier of technical support in your company but do not feel confident in your abilities as an Exchange administrator, *please* call someone for help. There are hundreds of capable Microsoft Certified Solution Providers that can help you for a lot less money than it will cost to lose an entire server. You can also call Microsoft Product Support Services for assistance, which is well worth the money in many cases.

Documenting the Results

For each solution you perform, you should document the results. The document you create should be in a table format, with the solution you tried on the left and the results of the solution on the right. Obviously either the solution will solve the problem or it won't, but what you want to keep an eye out for are any residual, detrimental effects the solution may have left on your environment. Your solutions, and whether they appeared to fix the problem at hand, should all be documented since you may experience problems at a later time and need to go through your log to figure out if anything you've done could have contributed to the problem.

For example, you may decide your Site Connector is causing network bandwidth problems across your WAN link and tweak some of the MTA Site Configuration values we discussed in Chapter 9, "Managing Intersite Communication and Replication." At first glance, the tweaks appear to solve the WAN problem, but now you are experiencing slow message transfer problems on your LAN. The fix of your original problem actually caused the secondary problem. In situations like this you need to determine whether it is better to continue with the original problem or to experience the new problem. If neither is acceptable, is there a solution that will alleviate both problems, such as using a different type of connector across the WAN link? The only way you will figure out these types of relationships is to document all of your results as thoroughly as possible.

Standard Operating Procedures

Aside from having a good troubleshooting strategy to help with small problems, it is important to prepare for disaster by having well-documented standard operating procedures (SOP) at hand before the disaster strikes. Your administrators should be well versed in the procedures, and the procedures should be periodically tested in the lab to verify their accuracy. See Chapter 11, "Periodic Proactive Troubleshooting," for information on practice restores.

Keep a copy of your backup and restore SOP in the server room along with any configuration information and repair disks that you generate. Configuration information includes your operating system and Exchange server configuration details, as well as hardware-specific data, such as RAID configuration and disk partitioning information. Every change you make to your system should be reflected in a log book and updated on your configuration sheets. Disaster recovery time is not the best time to have to go digging through your desk looking for configuration information that you meant to log but didn't get to yet. In this section, we'll discuss the two main components of the SOP: procedures for backups and procedures for restoration of all data types.

Procedures for Backups

It is important to have a standard operating procedure for your backups to ensure that they are always performed the same way. If there is any change in your backups from one night to the next, you can't validate your restoration procedures correctly. Your administrators should be very familiar with the backup SOP, and a copy of it should be available at every server to be backed up. The SOP you create might look something like the following HTS Corporation example.

HTS CORPORATION
EXCHANGE SERVER BACKUP PROCEDURE

Prerequisites

Tape Drivers. Verify that the correct NT driver is loaded on the server to be backed up by accessing **Start**, **Settings**, **Control Panel**, **Tape Devices**.

Backup Tapes. Verify that each server to be backed up has four backup tape sets. Each tape set may require multiple tapes depending on the amount of data to be backed up. The data to be backed up on each set is as follows:

- Full NT Backup (new set each year)
- Differential NT Backup (new set every six months)

- Full Exchange Backup (new set each year)
- Differential Exchange Backup (new set every six months)

NT System Settings. Verify that NT is configured for STOP errors at **Start**, **Settings**, **Control Panel**, **System, Startup/Shutdown**. Verify that the Automatically reboot check box is not selected and that the following check boxes are selected:

- Write an event to the system log
- Send an administrative alert
- Write debugging information to: **%SystemRoot%\MEMORY.DMP**
- Overwrite any existing file

Daily

Exchange Differential Backup

Perform the following steps to back up Exchange:

1. Open the NT Backup tool using **Start**, **Programs**, **Administrative Tools**, **NT Backup**.

2. Select the Exchange server to be backed up by placing an **X** in its check box.

3. Click the **Backup** button.

4. Enter a name for the tape set if no name is set.

5. Select the following options:
   - Verify after backup
   - Replace
   - Differential

6. Enter the date and description, and press **OK**.

7. After the backup is finished, look for errors in the Event Viewer and in the `c:\winnt\backup.log` file.

8. Store the backup tape set off-site.

NT Differential Backup

Perform the following steps to back up NT:

1. Stop Exchange Services at **Start**, **Settings**, **Control Panel**, **Services** by stopping the Microsoft Exchange System Attendant.

2. Open the NT Backup tool using **Start**, **Programs**, **Administrative Tools**, **NT Backup**.

3. Select drives to be backed up by placing an **X** in the check box for each drive.

4. Click the **Backup** button.

5. Enter a name for the tape set if no name is set.

6. Select the following options:

    ■ Verify after backup

    ■ Backup Local Registry

    ■ Replace

    ■ Differential

7. Enter the date and description, and click **OK**.

8. After the backup is finished, look for errors in the Event Viewer and in the `c:\winnt\backup.log` file.

9. Restart the Exchange services.

10. Store the backup tape set off-site.

Weekly

Exchange Full Backup

Perform the following steps to back up Exchange:

1. Open the NT Backup tool using **Start**, **Programs**, **Administrative Tools**, **NT Backup**.

2. Select the Exchange server to be backed up by placing an **X** in its check box.

3. Click the **Backup** button.

4. Enter a name for the tape set if no name is set.

5. Select the following options:

    ■ Verify after backup

    ■ Replace

    ■ Normal

6. Enter the date and description, and click **OK**.

7. After the backup is finished, look for errors in the Event Viewer and in the `c:\winnt\backup.log` file.

8. Store the backup tape set off-site.

NT Full Backup

Perform the following steps to back up NT:

1. Stop Exchange Services at **Start**, **Settings**, **Control Panel**, **Services** by stopping the Microsoft Exchange System Attendant.

2. Open the NT Backup tool using **Start**, **Programs**, **Administrative Tools**, **NT Backup**.

3. Select drives to be backed up by placing an **X** in the check box for each drive.

4. Click the **Backup** button.

5. Enter a name for the tape set if no name is set.

6. Select the following options:

    - Verify after backup
    - Backup Local Registry
    - Replace
    - Normal

7. Enter the date and description, and click **OK**.

8. After the backup is finished, look for errors in the Event Viewer and in the `c:\winnt\backup.log` file.

9. Restart the Exchange services.

10. Store the backup tape set off-site.

Procedures for Data Restoration

Aside from consistent backups and having an SOP for your backup personnel to follow, you should also have an SOP defined for your restores. This is even more important than having a backup SOP, since restores are not performed as often as backups and therefore won't be as comfortable as backups for your administrators to perform. To alleviate this to some extent, perform practice restores in the lab per the suggestions in Chapter 11. An SOP might look like the following HTS Corporation example.

HTS CORPORATION EXCHANGE RECOVERY STANDARD OPERATING PROCEDURE

Prerequisites

Tape Drivers. Verify that the correct NT driver is loaded on the server to be restored by accessing **Start, Settings, Control Panel, Tape Devices**.

Backup Tapes. Verify that you have the correct tape backup set. You will need the last Full Exchange Backup tape set and the last Differential Exchange Backup tape set in the event of transaction log problems. Each tape set may consist of multiple tapes, depending on the amount of data that was backed up. You will only need the Full Exchange Backup tape set unless there is a problem with the existing transaction log files, since all Exchange servers have circular logging disabled.

Recovery from Online Backup

To recover and verify Exchange databases from online backup when NT system files, Exchange system files, and Exchange transaction logs are not damaged, follow this procedure:

1. Back up Exchange transaction logs to a new tape set using NT Backup.
2. Insert the first tape of the Full Exchange Backup tape set.
3. Open NT Backup using **Start, Programs, Administrative Tools, NT Backup**.
4. Double-click **Full Backup Tape** to view the Catalog.
5. Select the Directory and Information Store objects in the catalog.
6. Click the **Restore** button.
7. Clear the **Erase All Existing Data** check box.
8. Select the **Verify After Restore** check box.
9. Select the **Start Services After Restore** check box.
10. Click **OK**.
11. After the restore is complete, click **OK**.
12. Exit NT Backup.
13. Open the Exchange Administrator Program.
14. Select the site's recipients container.
15. Verify that the Primary Windows NT Account is correct for at least five users.
16. Log in to a client computer using a valid mailbox on the restored server.

17. Verify the client's mailbox functions by sending mail to users on the same server and on other servers.

18. Verify that connections work by sending mail to users in other sites and to foreign messaging systems.

The SOP outlined in this section only illustrates one of many possible disaster recovery scenarios. You will need to customize your SOP to also include recovery from offline backups, as well as recovery using differential backups in the event your transaction log files are lost. See Chapter 14, "Disaster Recovery," for information on recovery from these scenarios.

Hardware Optimization

Having a set of established standard operating procedures is not enough when it comes to a proactive disaster recovery stance. "No disaster is a good disaster," I like to say, and as a result I am a big advocate of fault tolerance. You have a few options that ideally will find a place in your company. Let's take a look at software and hardware RAID, clustering, file placement, and SNMP.

Software RAID

In terms of fault tolerance, software RAID is the cheapest solution you can buy. Microsoft Windows NT server supports software RAID out of the box. All you have to do is buy a few hard drives. The downside is that software RAID just isn't as fast or easy to recover from as hardware RAID. As a result, I don't recommend the use of software RAID if you can afford hardware RAID.

As I'm sure you know, software RAID is Windows NT generating either a full copy of data on a secondary physical disk (mirroring/RAID1) or parity information striped across each physical disk (disk striping with parity/RAID5). Although software RAID is better than no RAID, it is slower and less robust than hardware RAID.

If you do decide to implement software RAID, put your databases on a stripe set with parity, and your operating system and transaction logs on mirror sets. By splitting your databases from your logs, you minimize the likelihood of losing both at the same time. As with either software or hardware RAID, you can lose one drive of each fault-tolerant set without having to restore data from backup.

Fault-Tolerant Floppies and ERDs

In addition to using a RAID solution, you need to create a fault-tolerant floppy disk to boot to your mirror partner in addition to keeping a current emergency repair disk (ERD). Both the fault-tolerant floppy and the ERD should be stored in the same safe location.

Hardware RAID

Hardware RAID is definitely the way to go when it comes to Exchange server fault tolerance. Hardware RAID is better than software RAID. It is unlikely that you will have to recover from backup due to hard disk crashes, but if you do lose a drive, many hardware RAID solutions are hot swappable and will allow you to simply remove the failed disk and add a new disk to replace the failed one. Software RAID, on the other hand, is not hot swappable. Unlike in software RAID, in hardware RAID all the redundancy calculations are performed by the RAID hardware, so you won't have as much of a performance hit with hardware RAID as you would with a software RAID implementation. As with software RAID, your databases should be on a stripe set with parity, and your operating system and transaction logs should be on mirror sets. Regardless of the RAID solution you choose, you need to have a good backup strategy in order to protect yourself against data loss due to database corruption.

Clustering

In addition to using RAID for fault tolerance, you could consider clustering your Exchange server. Keep in mind, however, that if you already have your data protected by a RAID array, clustering protects you from failure due only to components such as the motherboard or a network adapter failure.

A Microsoft cluster always consists of two nodes that share a set of disk drives (ideally hardware RAID5) and have the same network properties. One of the nodes is considered the active node. The active node owns all of the cluster resources and responds to all client requests until it fails. If the active node fails, the inactive node becomes the active node by taking ownership of all resources and responding to incoming client requests. Exchange Server Enterprise edition can be installed on an existing cluster as long as the nodes have the same performance settings. To be sure of this, run the Performance Optimizer with the same environment input so that Exchange will run correctly on the cluster.

The idea behind clustering Exchange is that you essentially have a "hot spare" Exchange server. This is the ultimate fault tolerance because anything can fail on the active server and be compensated for by the inactive server.

There are a few real problems with Exchange running on a cluster—one of which is that although you can cluster pretty much any Exchange service, you should not cluster the Key Management (KM) server. The KM service is configured to not restart when the active node of a cluster fails. To restart it, you need to restart the service in the Control Panel as well as bring the service online in the Cluster Administrator. This additional step is necessary because the KM service requires a startup password found on a floppy disk. The KM service is just not intended for use on a cluster, so it is best if you continue to run the Key Manager on a dedicated, physically secure Exchange server. Another problem with clustering is that the hardware configuration drives the price up considerably while not significantly improving your fault tolerance because you now have two servers maintaining the same RAID array. The most significant downfall to clustering Exchange, however, is that it generally takes a lot longer for Exchange services to fail over to the inactive node in the event of a failure than it would take to reboot a single Exchange server.

File Placement

In addition to implementing clustering and RAID solutions to protect your Exchange data, you should consider the placement of your Exchange databases and transaction log files. In Chapter 8, "Managing Server Resources," we discussed the Performance Optimizer and how it will analyze your disks for access speed to determine the optimum location for your databases and transaction logs. In addition to performance considerations, you should think about disaster recovery when it comes to file placement.

Your databases should be on a dedicated stripe set with parity. Your transaction logs should be on any other physical disk, ideally a mirror set. Keep your transaction logs on a separate disk to optimize your ability to recover from disaster. If you lose your database drive, you will still have your transaction logs from which to recover all data generated since the last backup. See Chapter 14 for information about recovering data using transaction log files.

SNMP and the MADMAN MIB

The last step in optimizing hardware is to use Simple Network Management Protocol (SNMP). Microsoft Exchange supports the SNMP Mail and Directory Management (MADMAN) Management Information Base (MIB) defined in RFC 1566. Use an SNMP management application, such as HP OpenView, to monitor your Exchange organization. Exchange will respond to SNMP requests from the MADMAN MIB if SNMP is enabled in NT on the Exchange server.

Use SNMP to track parameters related to performance, such as the number of messages queued at the MTA at a given time. Much like Performance Monitor, you can identify polling intervals at which to gather data, and thresholds that cause alerts to be generated when performance drops below the defined threshold. SNMP is such a powerful tool that I recommend implementing it in any medium to large company, whether they have Exchange server or not.

Stopping Clustered Services

Microsoft clusters have a resource manager that is in charge of starting and stopping services. As a result, you should not use the Control Panel or the net stop command to stop your NT services because the cluster may attempt to fail the service over to the inactive note. If you must take Exchange server offline, always use the Cluster Administrator to fail over all of the Exchange services first.

Server Configuration Optimization

Server configuration is just as important as hardware configuration when it comes to planning for disaster because inappropriate configuration can make complete disaster recovery impossible. Areas to consider include the following:

- Transaction Log Configuration
- Routing Calculation Server and Schedule
- Address Book Calculation Server and Schedule
- Schedule+ Free/Busy server
- Information Store Defragmentation Schedule
- Storage Warning Schedule

You can optimize the performance of your server as well as minimize problems by configuring these settings appropriately.

Transaction Log Configuration

In addition to keeping your transaction logs on a physical drive separate from your databases, you need to disable circular logging. Circular logging is disabled on a per-server basis by accessing the properties of the server in the Exchange Administrator Program. On the Advanced tab you'll find two check boxes reflecting whether or not circular logging is enabled on the local Directory database (DIR.EDB) or on the Information Store databases (PRIV.EDB and PUB.EDB). Clear the check boxes to disable circular logging for your server, and subsequently attain maximum recoverability in a disaster.

Your circular logging settings have an impact on your backup regimen. If circular logging is enabled, you will be unable to perform online differential or incremental backups because these backup types back up only transaction log files. It doesn't really make sense to back up log files that get overwritten all day long, so you will be limited to full, online backups if you leave circular logging enabled.

Circular logging is enabled by default to prevent transaction logs from taking over your hard disk. As a result, when you disable it you need to have a plan for removing the transaction logs. Fortunately, both incremental and full online backups will purge transaction log files from your server at the end of the backup. See Chapter 6, "Backing Up Your Server," for more information regarding log purging and differential backups as they relate to the circular logging settings on your server.

Routing Calculation Server and Schedule

In addition to configuring your server to disable circular logging, you should consider the server responsible for routing calculation in your site. Although reconfiguring the routing calculation server will not help with disaster recovery, it can help prevent problems that will subsequently require your attention.

The first server in every site is assigned the role Routing Calculation server. The default time for routing calculation is every day at 1:00 a.m. Because the MTA will automatically request an updated routing table when it detects a change in the routing, such as when a new connector is added in the local site, the routing calculation probably will not be too much of an issue in most companies. The only real problems you are likely to have are if you need to remove the first server in the site, or if you have a very large organization. Before removing the first server in the site, access the Site Addressing object in your site's Configuration container and change the Routing Calculation server defined on the General tab.

If you are administering a very large organization, you should be aware of a change made to the calculation algorithm that affects Exchange 5.0 SP2 and later. The original calculation caused the System Attendant (MAD.EXE) to create an empty gateway address routing table (GWART) and populate it with the address space defined on each local connector. The System Attendant would then import the GWART from other sites and add address spaces that can be accessed via connector to the remote site. It would also remove any duplicate addresses and routes that could result in looping back to the local site.

The problem with the original calculation is that in some instances it took an extended period of time for the local GWART to reflect address spaces that had been removed from a connector. To fix this, Microsoft added some extra calculations to the process. The new process causes MAD.EXE to evaluate every entry on the GWART imported from a remote site for other site entries. The process would then import the GWART for the third site and verify that the address space still existed in the third site. If you have a large organization with a lot of sites, all of this importing and verifying will take a really long time.

Although this updated algorithm was intended to fix a problem with older versions of the MTA, it can cause your server to demonstrate unacceptable processor utilization for extended periods of time. You will be alerted to this by event 5000 in the event log indicating that routing calculation is in progress. Further investigation will reveal a heavily utilized processor and will indicate one of the threads of the MAD.EXE process as being the culprit. If you are experiencing this problem, add the REG_DWORD key named RID Consistency Checking key with a value of 0 to the Registry location HKEY_LOCAL_MACHINE\System\CurrentControlSet\Services\MSExchangeMTA\Parameters. Be sure to enter the name with the correct capitalization and spaces. Stop and restart the Exchange services to incorporate the change. Adding this entry will prevent the System Attendant from performing the exhaustive checks indicated earlier in this section. As a result, you may wind up with routing tables that are not completely up to date.

Changes you make to the routing calculation server can improve routing table calculation and subsequently the ability of the Exchange MTA to route mail correctly. This pays off in reduced time tracking down problems related to an unavailable calculation server or high CPU utilization during calculation.

Address Book Calculation Server and Schedule

Now that you have your routing calculation server configured, you should take a look at your address book calculation server. The first server in the site is responsible for calculating the offline address book that will be downloaded by your Exchange and Outlook clients. Unless there have been a lot of changes to the Directory, such as you might experience during a migration, the calculation will not overly tax your system. In spite of this, it is a good idea to change the calculation schedule to reflect off-hours for your company so that your users are not unduly inconvenienced by any potential performance hits. You should also change the address book calculation server if the first server in the site does not have a high availability to your users, such as with a lab server.

Change the calculation server or the calculation schedule by accessing the DS Site Configuration object in your site's Configuration container. The server responsible for the task is defined on the Offline Address Book tab, and the schedule at which calculation occurs is on the Offline Address Book Schedule tab. The default time is every day at 3:00 am. You can also elect to replicate the Offline Address Book to other servers in the site to improve fault tolerance and provide load balancing. Replication is configured on the Offline Address Book object for each site in the System Folders section of the Exchange Administrator Program.

Changing the server that performs the address book calculation can improve your users' ability to download the offline address book if the first server in the site has availability problems. Replicating the folder containing the address book is a good idea if you have users in the same site spanning a WAN link. Additionally, if your business hours are not 9–5, you should reconfigure the schedule at which the address book is regenerated. Taking these steps can help prevent client access problems and server resource issues in some cases.

Schedule+ Free/Busy Server

In addition to the address book calculation server, you may want to optimize your Schedule+ Free/Busy server. As we discussed in Chapter 3, "Administering Public Folders" the Schedule+ Free/Busy server is the first server installed in each site. To avoid bottlenecks at this server, you may want to relocate the site's schedule data to another server, or replicate it for load balancing.

Relocate and configure replication of the Schedule+ Free/Busy public folder by accessing its properties for your site in the System Folders section of the Exchange Administrator Program. Because each client will connect to their schedule data at client startup, you can achieve considerable performance improvements by replicating the data to less heavily utilized servers. This can save you troubleshooting time as well as help desk time; in some cases the Schedule+ Free/Busy server may be too busy to respond to client RPC requests, causing the client to time out and fail to initialize.

Information Store Defragmentation Schedule

The System Attendant will perform an online defragmentation of your Public and Private Information Stores according to the schedule defined on the IS Maintenance tab of your server's property pages. This online defragmentation will check the Public Information Store public folders for items that are due to expire, and any items that have expired will be removed.

Although your users can continue to use the server while the online defragmentation is in progress, they will experience performance degradation. You should prevent this from happening by reconfiguring the schedule to be for off-hours. Optimizing this setting will prevent client trouble calls reporting slow server performance during the IS Maintenance period.

Storage Warning Schedule

We discussed storage warnings in Chapter 2, "Administering Users," as part of the user administration you should perform each day. The process of generating storage warnings will add load to your server, so you should verify that the warning messages are generated and sent after hours. Additionally, you should configure the warnings to only occur once per day at the most. I have been to customer sites where the messages are generated and sent more frequently, and this results only in irritated users. The schedule is defined on the Information Store Site Configuration property pages on the Storage Warnings tab. The default is every day at 8:00 p.m.

Summary

Planning for a disaster is the first step toward minimizing the impact of a disaster. In this chapter we talked about steps you can take to prepare yourself and your server for potential crashes. These steps included formulating a troubleshooting technique, creating standard operating procedures, and configuring your hardware and software optimally. Unfortunately, even the best-laid plans can't prevent many disasters from occurring. In the next chapter we will address the information you need to know in order to identify your problem.

13

Troubleshooting Your Exchange Server

Now that you have configured your environment to plan for disaster, it is time to talk about actually identifying the problem. As we discussed in Chapter 12, "Planning for Disaster," problem identification is frequently the most difficult part of troubleshooting. In order to recognize the symptoms that indicate a problem, you need a solid understanding of Exchange's services. Use Performance Monitor regularly to identify acceptable thresholds and Event Viewer to pinpoint problems. When you have identified the problem with your environment, use the tools discussed in this chapter to troubleshoot.

Understanding the Exchange Server Services

The key to troubleshooting any system is a rock-solid understanding of how the system works. Exchange is based entirely on services, so to troubleshoot Exchange you need to really know what the services do, what Exchange component they communicate with, and what symptoms could indicate a problem with a given service. After you have defined the general problem area, you can usually use diagnostics logging to cause additional information to be logged to the application event log or other log files. The Exchange services we are going to look at in this chapter include the following:

- System Attendant
- Directory Service
- Information Store
- Message Transfer Agent
- Internet Mail Service
- Microsoft Mail Connector

If you run third-party connectors, you will need to become familiar with how that connector communicates with Exchange in order to successfully troubleshoot it. This information can be obtained from the vendor that sold you the connector, or from resources such as Microsoft TechNet and the Microsoft Exchange newsgroups.

System Attendant

We will address the System Attendant (SA) first because it is the very root of the Exchange services. This is the first service to start and the last to shut down, so if it has problems, generally your Exchange server will not be able to start up at all.

The SA is responsible for maintaining your background processes, which include the following:

- Online defragmentation of your Information Stores
- Online garbage collection for your Directory
- Message Tracking log maintenance
- Link Monitor maintenance
- Server Monitor maintenance
- Knowledge Consistency Checking
- Gateway Address Routing Table (GWART) construction
- Communication with the Key Manager
- User proxy address generation

If you are having trouble with any of these processes, the SA could be the problem. Keep in mind, however, that the SA is either performing these processes on the databases or using the databases to do them, so the problem could be the database in question. It is my experience that database problems are more common than SA process problems. Database repair is discussed in Chapter 14, "Disaster Recovery." Because it is sometimes difficult to pinpoint the cause of a problem, it is necessary to know who the SA is communicating with and why.

System Attendant Communication

The SA communicates with administrators and with other Exchange services to perform its job. No user interaction occurs with the SA directly, although the SA is the component that receives and replies to user requests for advanced security.

For example, suppose Lisa sends the Advanced Security token she received from her administrator to the Key Management Server. The SA intercepts the message and processes the request. The confirmation Lisa receives actually is from the SA, which communicates with services as illustrated in Table 13.1.

Table 13.1 **The System Attendant's Communication Process**

Service	Purpose for Communication
Directory	Generate and store the GWART and user proxy addresses
Information Store	Send and receive Link Monitor messages and send administrative alerts
Key Manager	Enable users to get set up for advanced security
Administrator Program	Configure the number of days to retain message tracking log files

Understanding the communication process that the System Attendant participates in will help you identify problems. For example, if you are having difficulty with your user proxy address generation, the problem could be the System Attendant, the Directory service, or one of the supporting .DLLs that the SA uses to create user proxies. Understanding the communication can help narrow the troubleshooting possibilities.

Symptoms of Malfunction

Often, the only symptom you'll notice when there is a problem is that the SA will simply not start. When this happens you should check the application event log to see what error was recorded. There are two primary things I would look for before considering corrupt system files:

■ Service account password changes

■ Network problems

Service Account Password Changes

If your service account password has been changed, your Exchange services will not start. This can often be masked by the fact that the Exchange services don't have to log in every time they need to do a task—they log in when the service is started. As long as the services have not been stopped, you likely will not experience any problems. However, as soon as the services are stopped and restarted, or the server is rebooted, your Exchange services will fail to start if the password has been changed in the SAM and not within Exchange. To correct this, access the Configuration container properties for the server that won't start and change the password on the Service Account Password tab to reflect the changed password.

Network Problems

System Attendant startup problems can also be related to network issues. Before the SA can start, the following services must be started:

- EventLog
- NT LM Security Support Provider
- RPC Locator
- RPC Service
- Workstation
- Server

Because the network services depend on your NIC, it is possible that your NIC card is malfunctioning or that your network protocol support files have a problem. You will see loads of errors recorded in the event log if your network has failed to start, so you need to look at the log file and see what happened. If it turns out that you do have a network problem, obviously you will need to remedy it before determining whether or not the SA really has a problem. If the SA does have a problem, it may be that you can simply replace a corrupted system file from the installation CD. If you do attempt to correct a problem by replacing a system file, be sure to make a copy of your current file just in case that wasn't the problem and you need to revert back to it.

Directory Service

While the SA performs only system tasks, the Directory Service (DS) provides both user and system access to all of the objects and object properties defined in your Exchange organization. This access includes properties for user mailboxes, public folders, connectors, and server configuration parameters. Both users and the Information Store connect to the DS for all server-based address list queries (such as the GAL), so if the DS is not available your users will not be able to connect to the server because the IS will fail to start. Additionally, the DS provides the GWART used by the MTA for routing decisions. If the local DS is not available, the local MTA cannot function.

Since all servers in the organization need access to data defined globally, the DS is replicated to every server. This has the benefit of masking server problems from users on other servers. For example, if the DS on SEATTLE crashes, users on the BELLEVUE server will not necessarily be aware of it.

Directory Service Communication

It is not enough to know what the DS does. You must also know what it communicates with. This knowledge will help you determine an appropriate course of action in the event a process fails or malfunctions. Information on what the DS communicates with is identified in Table 13.2.

Table 13.2 **The Directory Service's Communication Process**

Service	Purpose for Communication
Information Store	Send and receive intersite replication messages.
Other Directory services	Send and receive intrasite replication updates.
Administrator Program	Administer address books; manipulate object properties; create, delete, and manage mailboxes.
MAPI and LDAP Clients	Query for address book information.
Custom Applications	Use ADSI and LDAP to manipulate objects and facilitate directory synchronization with foreign systems.

Knowledge of the DS communication patterns can help you troubleshoot intersite replication, among other things. For example, if you find that your intersite replication is not working, the problem could be the DS, the Information Store, or even an MTA or connector. To troubleshoot which of these components is causing the problem, verify that intrasite replication occurs, and that messages generated at the replication bridgehead successfully route across your connectors. If intrasite replication is successful, the problem is probably not the local DS. If messages generated at the replication bridgehead are being delivered to the remote site, the problem is not your network. Narrowing the possibilities allows you to identify a potential problem with the remote DS.

Symptoms of Malfunction

The Directory service depends on the System Attendant to start up. If the SA is not started, then your problem is not the DS but at a lower level, as discussed in the "System Attendant" section earlier in this chapter. Verify that your DS is not in a state of recovery by checking the event log. *Recovery* is when the server is not shut down cleanly and Exchange has to go through the transaction logs and apply previous transactions. This process can take up to an hour or even longer, depending on the number of transaction log files and other resource-related factors. While the DS is in recovery, you may experience performance problems related to the recovery process.

The EX Address Space

The Exchange Directory's native address type is X.500, which Exchange refers to as an EX type address space. Because the MTA natively supports X.400 as well as X.500, messages will flow between users even if there is no X.500 EX address space defined between sites. However, all system messages are sent to the X.500 EX recipient alias, not to the X.400 alias, so you absolutely need to have an EX address space defined on all connectors that you want to use to route system messages. Be sure to verify that there is an EX address space defined between the two sites on all connectors you wish to utilize for Directory Replication. Intersite replication messages are of type EX, and if the address space is not defined, the message will have no route available for delivery.

Symptoms to look for include incomplete replication within a site, incomplete replication between sites, and the existence of objects in remote sites that were previously deleted in the local site. Also look for routing table problems, errors during DIR.EDB online backups, and errors during offline defragmentation procedures. Use the event logs and Performance Monitor to identify other problems that may contribute to your DS failure. We will be discussing how to recover from tombstone problems and corrupt databases in Chapter 14.

Diagnostics Logging

Once you suspect the DS is malfunctioning, use diagnostics logging to troubleshoot the problem. I don't recommend enabling diagnostics logging as part of your daily routine because an overwhelming amount of data will be generated that you will subsequently need to go through. Only use diagnostics logging for—as its name suggests—diagnostics.

To enable this extra logging, access the properties of the problematic server in the Exchange Administrator Program and select the **Diagnostics Logging** tab. The MSExchangeDS service lists the various tasks that can be logged. Select the task that you are having difficulty with and choose the Maximum logging level. These settings are reflected in the Registry under HKEY_LOCAL_MACHINE\SYSTEM\CurrentControlSet\ Services\MSExchangeDS\Diagnostics. If you can't get into the Administrator Program to set the levels, you can edit the appropriate Registry setting. Double-click the item you want to log and enter a hexadecimal value of **1**, **3**, or **5** to correspond with Minimum, Medium, and Maximum logging levels.

After you have diagnostics logging enabled, force Exchange to perform the task that isn't working. If the service won't start, try to start it again. If replication isn't working, force it to try again. Doing so will cause events to log in the application log that should give you some insight to the cause of the problem.

Information Store

As we have discussed throughout this book, the Information Store (IS) service maintains both the Private and Public Information Stores and is a fundamental component of your Exchange server. This service is what allows users access to their mailboxes and public folders. When users send messages, the IS queries the local Directory to determine whether the recipient has a mailbox defined on the local server. If not, or if the recipient is a distribution list, the message is routed to the MTA for processing. After a message is delivered, the IS announces the delivery to the recipient if the recipient has a current MAPI session with the server. The IS also processes user-defined rules and scripts that may be associated with both private mailboxes and public folders.

Additionally, the IS is responsible for public folder replication, and, at the request of other Exchange services, it facilitates the generation of system messages such as Link Monitor and intersite replication messages. It runs a thread to identify changed documents in public folders, creates replication messages containing the changes, and sends the changes to other Public Information Stores. It also incorporates changes to public folders that originated on remote replicas and have been replicated to the local server.

The Information Store is also responsible for maintaining the public folder hierarchy, so that when a user accesses the list of available public folders, the list is provided by the Information Store service on the user's public folder server. If you are having trouble in any of these areas, the problem could be with the IS. Unfortunately, problems with the IS often boil down to database corruption.

Information Store Communication

Like the SA and DS, the IS uses other Exchange services to do its job. Communication paths for the IS are listed in Table 13.3.

Table 13.3 **The Information Store's Communication Process**

Service	Purpose of Communication
MTA	Transfer messages to users on other servers and expand distribution lists.
Directory Service	Resolve user addresses and commit public folder properties to the Directory database.
System Attendant	Generate entries in the message tracking logs.
Clients	Notify clients that they have new mail, accept client modifications to public folders, and accept client connections to download private messages.
Administrator Program	Administer mailboxes and public folders.

As with the SA and the Directory Service, knowing these communication paths helps you troubleshoot Exchange. For example, if your public folders aren't replicating correctly, the problem could be in the Information Store of either the sending or receiving server, or it could be a message transport error, such as a downed network connection or a stopped MTA.

To identify the actual problem, verify network connectivity and the ability to send user messages between the applicable servers. If user messages are deliverable, there could be a problem with the replication settings or there might not be an EX type address space defined on the functioning connection.

Symptoms of Malfunction

In order for the IS to start, the DS must first be started. You should first discover whether the IS and other Exchange services are running. If the IS is stopped but the other services are running, the problem is probably with the Information Store.

Because the IS is notoriously problematic, with intermittent, spontaneous shutdowns, often the best thing to do is create a Server Monitor to restart the IS whenever it stops.

If the IS is running but users can't connect, you may have a corrupt database or you may be experiencing network difficulties. Other things to look for are failed online backups, errors with offline defragmentation, and counters not reflecting accurate information. All of these problems indicate corruption on some level. See Chapter 14 for information on ESEUTIL, EDBUTIL, and ISINTEG that will help you repair corruption.

Diagnostics Logging

Like the DS, there are numerous diagnostics logging counters you can enable for the Information Store. To enable them, access the problematic server's Diagnostics Logging property page and view the MSExchangeIS service. You can enable counters for the Private Information Store, Public Information Store, System folders and Internet Protocols. Use your knowledge of Exchange to determine in what area a problem is being experienced, and set the logging level for that category to Maximum.

For example, if your problem is replication, log Public Information Store counters. If you can't get into the Exchange Administrator Program, access the Registry at HKEY_LOCAL_MACHINE\SYSTEM\CurrentControlSet\Services\MSExchangeIS\ Diagnostics. Select **Private**, **Public**, **System**, or **Internet Protocols** as appropriate, and set the appropriate counter to a hexadecimal value of **1**, **3**, or **5** to correspond with Minimum, Medium, and Maximum logging levels. I would personally use Maximum when troubleshooting because I believe you can never have too much information when attempting to diagnose a problem.

Message Transfer Agent

As discussed in Chapter 4, "Queue Management", the Message Transfer Agent (MTA) is responsible for routing messages between Exchange servers. It is also the component in charge of distribution list expansion. Whenever a message is destined for a remote server, the local MTA creates a two-way RPC or X.400 session with the remote server and transfers the data to the remote server based on connection properties defined on either the MTA Site Configuration object, or on the associated connector. Even in single-site environments, the MTA must expand distribution lists, so it is important to keep your MTA happy even if you don't ever send mail through connectors or to other servers. A stopped MTA will not affect your users' ability to connect to the server or send mail, but it will prevent mail from routing to remote servers or being sent to distribution lists.

Message Transfer Agent Communication

Because the MTA can't do its job without communicating with other Exchange services, you should understand the basis for the communications. Table 13.4 illustrates the services the MTA works with and the purpose for the communication.

Table 13.4 **The MTA's Communication Process**

Service	Purpose for Communication
Directory Service	Determine message routing by using the GWART.
System Attendant	Generate message tracking log entries for messages passed between servers.
Information Store	Deliver messages to local users.
MSMail Connector	Send and receive MS Mail messages.
Other MTAs	Send and receive messages from other Exchange servers and other X.400 servers.
Administrator Program	Administer MTA queues and MTA properties.

As with the System Attendant, Directory Service, Information Store, and MTA, knowing the communication paths helps you troubleshoot. For example, if users are able to send messages to each other on the same server, but messages sent to remote servers and remote connectors are bounced, your MTA might be stopped or have a problem. Alternatively, if your user messages are delivered successfully within the site, but messages for remote-site users are not delivered, the MTA at your bridgehead or one of your connectors might be malfunctioning.

Symptoms of Malfunction

The MTA depends on the Directory service to be running before it can start up. Therefore, the first thing to do is verify that the MTA service and its dependency services are running. If the MTA is not running but other services are, then your MTA is probably the problem. Corrupt messages in the MTA queue can cause the MTA to fail to start and/or function. If this is the case, you will see MTA events in the event log, so be sure to analyze the application event log to determine what the problem might be.

Diagnostics Logging

Like the IS and DS, the MTA has diagnostics logging parameters you can configure on the server's Diagnostics Logging property page from the Exchange Administrator Program. Select the **MSExchangeMTA** service and the appropriate categories for logging. Set the logging level to **Maximum** to get the most information. After logging is configured, attempt to regenerate the error. For example, if the error occurs when sending messages to users in another site, create a message for a remote user in that site and send it. Then go look at the application event log to see what was recorded.

If you can't get into the Exchange Administrator Program to configure diagnostics logging, you can enable it in the Registry at `HKEY_LOCAL_MACHINE\SYSTEM\CurrentControlSet\Services\MSExchangeMTA\Diagnostics`. Double-click the item you want to log and enter a hexadecimal value of **5** to correspond with Maximum logging levels.

Internet Mail Service

Whereas the IS, DS, and MTA provide core functionality to your Exchange users, the Internet Mail Service (IMS) provides additional connector functionality through SMTP access. This allows it to route messages out to and in from the Internet. The IMS can also be used to backbone two Exchange sites, and is necessary for any POP3 or IMAP4 clients to be able to send mail. All messages received by the IMS are transferred into the IS MTS-IN directory and converted to MDBEF content by the IMAIL process.

Internet Mail Service Communication

Because the IMS functionality is relatively limited, the communication patterns are not too complex. See Table 13.5 for information on what the IMS talks to and why.

Table 13.5   **The IMS Communication Process**

Service	Purpose of Communication
Directory Service	Resolve SMTP addresses in the FROM field of incoming messages against the local GAL.
Information Store	Queue incoming and outgoing SMTP mail. All content conversion occurs in the local IS.
POP3 and IMAP4 Clients	Send outgoing mail via SMTP, and therefore need access to the IMS.

Troubleshooting the MTA

If the MTA attempts a connection and fails, there is a default 10-minute open retry timer that must pass before the MTA will try again. To hurry this along, stop and restart the MTA service. You can permanently change the open retry counter for intrasite and Site Connector connections on the MTA Site Configuration property pages, or on the appropriate connector property pages for X.400 and DRAS connectors. See Chapter 9, "Managing Intersite Communication and Replication," for more information on MTA configuration parameters.

You should also take a look in the MTA queues to see what the message destination is. Once you know the destination, verify network connectivity to that host using the protocol used by Exchange to connect to the foreign host (ping or RPC Ping are great utilities for network verification).

Additionally, if you find that messages are stuck in your IMS outbound queue but are routed correctly in from external SMTP hosts, then you may have a DNS or HOSTS file name resolution problem.

Symptoms of Malfunction

Before the IMS can start, the Directory, Information Store, and MTA must first be started. Before looking to the IMS as the problem, you should first verify that the IMS service is started, and if not, verify that the dependency services are started. If the dependency services are started, check the following things:

- Is the IMS started? If not, start the IMS.

- Is the IMS accepting connections in the intranet by opening a port 25 TCP session using the Telnet application? If not, verify that the IMS is started and check the supporting .DLL files for corruption.

- Are SMTP sessions being accepted from outside the firewall or from the firewall itself? If not, verify that port 25 (or whatever SMTP port you have configured if you've changed this across a backbone server) is available.

- Is the domain resolvable using DNS? If not, verify the MX record using NSLOOKUP. DNS will not resolve your domain if you are not correctly registered with the InterNIC.

- Is the correct IP address configured in the IMS properties for backbone servers? If not, enter the correct IP address.

- Is the Connected Sites tab correctly filled in for backbone servers? If not, fill it in. No system messages will transfer across the IMS until this tab is filled in correctly.

- Is the IMS initiating sessions correctly with remote SMTP hosts? If not, verify the DNS MX record for the remote domain, verify your firewall settings, and verify your Internet connectivity.

- Do your Exchange users send and receive SMTP mail successfully when POP3 and IMAP4 clients cannot send mail? If so, verify that the SMTP server identified in the client properties is in fact your IMS.

- Does the routing tab of your IMS properties reflect the local site's fully qualified domain name as inbound? Verify that it does in order to prevent the IMS from rejecting POP3 and IMAP4 outbound messages from bouncing back to the sender.

Diagnostics Logging

As always, additional information can be gleaned from diagnostics logging of the IMS. Access the Diagnostics Logging tab of the server that runs the IMS in your site and select the **MSExchangeIMC** service. (The IMC part is a throwback to Exchange 4.0, when the Internet Mail Service was called the Internet Mail Connector.) Select the category you want to log and choose the **Maximum** logging level. Events will be written to the event log for all categories except for SMTP Protocol Log and Message Archival. The SMTP Protocol Log will create a text file containing the SMTP conversation between the local Exchange server and the remote SMTP host.

As with the other services, you can manually set the logging level in the Registry if you can't set it in the Administrator Program. These parameters can be found at HKEY_LOCAL_MACHINE\SYSTEM\CurrentControlSet\Services\MSExchangeIMC\ Diagnostics. Double-click the item you want to log and enter a hexadecimal value of **5** to correspond with the Maximum logging level.

Microsoft Mail Connector

Whereas the IMS allows Exchange users to send and receive mail from SMTP users, the Microsoft Mail Connector (MSMC) allows Exchange users to send and receive mail from MS Mail. The MSMC contains an MS Mail shadow post office and the MS Mail Connector Interchange in order to route mail and convert the contents to a readable format for each client. As a result, the MSMC is somewhat harder to troubleshoot because problems can actually exist in several areas internal to the MSMC. In this section we will discuss the MS Mail Connector communication process, MS Mail Directory Synchronization, Schedule+ synchronization, symptoms of a malfunctioning MS Mail Connector, and diagnostics logging.

MS Mail Connector Communication

Because the MSMC was created before the Exchange Development Kit was complete, it has a different architecture than the IMS and communicates with different components. See Table 13.6 for information on what the MSMC communicates with and why.

Table 13.6 **MS Mail Connector Communication Process**

Service	Purpose for Communication
Directory Service	Resolve MS Mail addresses to display names against the Exchange GAL. This happens for messages sent to MS Mail from Exchange and from Exchange to MS Mail. Additionally, the DS is used to embed the reply-to address for MS Mail users sending messages through the Exchange IMS.
MTA	Transfer messages to and from MS Mail recipients.

Problems with the MSMC will not only prevent user mail from flowing, but they can also prevent DirSync and Schedule+ synchronization from occurring.

Directory Synchronization

As we discussed in Chapter 9, if you have the MSMC running and are coexisting with an MS Mail network, you probably are running Directory Synchronization (DirSync) between Exchange and MS Mail. Similar to intersite replication in an Exchange organization, MS Mail DirSync uses email messages to update the directories (such as address lists) on remote MS Mail servers. Because DirSync uses email messages, the MSMC must be functioning in order for the DirSync system messages to be delivered correctly.

Troubleshooting this service is tricky; DirSync failures can result from problems in so many areas. The only place you can really go to find information on the DirSync functionality is in the DirSync log files. Go through the log files on both the DirSync Requestor and the DirSync Server to identify the problem. Also, verify that the Directory Synchronization service is running on your Exchange server.

Schedule+ Synchronization

Exchange can be configured to use MS Mail's Schedule+ Distribution utility to synchronize free and busy calendar data between MS Mail and Exchange users. (For more information about free and busy calendar data, see Chapter 3, "Administering Public Folders.") This allows Exchange users to see MS Mail users free and busy calendar data and allows MS Mail users to see Exchange users free and busy calendar data.

The MS Mail topology uses the executable SCHDIST.EXE to create email messages in each post office that reflect the current calendar data of all local users. The message is then sent to other post offices such that when users on a remote post office want to view a calendar, they actually view the data on their own post offices. Because Exchange needs to join this mix, the MSMC must be running in order for Exchange to receive the MS Mail schedule messages and send messages containing data from its Schedule+ Free/Busy system folder. To troubleshoot Schedule+ Synchronization, go through the send and receive logs on your MS Mail post offices to determine where the problem might reside. Also, verify that the Schedule+ Free/Busy service is running on your Exchange server.

Symptoms of Malfunction

As a result of there being so many pieces to the MS Mail services, symptoms are kind of all over the board. Some of these symptoms are as follows:

SMTP Message Archival

Whereas SMTP Protocol Log is useful for troubleshooting, generally Message Archival is not. Message Archival will cause Exchange to retain a copy of all incoming and outgoing mail in an archive folder on the local hard drive. Use Message Archival only if you need to keep copies of messages sent and received for security purposes.

- User mail sent from Exchange is not received by MS Mail.
- User mail sent from MS Mail is not received by Exchange.
- Exchange Directory doesn't reflect updates in the MS Mail address lists.
- MS Mail address lists don't reflect updates in the Exchange Directory.
- MS Mail users don't see Exchange calendar data, or the data is old.
- Exchange users don't see MS Mail calendar data, or the data is old.

A good indicator of where the problem lies is what server is generating the errors. By errors, I mean both event log errors and NDRs. If an Exchange user sending mail to an MS Mail user receives an NDR virtually immediately that was generated on the Exchange user's own server, the error might be in the routing table. If it takes a while for the NDR to arrive, the error could be the MTA or the MSMC. It could even be the PC MTA causing the problem, since the PC MTA must connect to the shadow post office in order for messages to transfer between MS Mail and Exchange. You can use diagnostics logging to help determine the cause of your problem.

Diagnostics Logging

As with other Exchange services, there are a number of items you can log to the event log in addition to the default critical errors. For the MSMC categories, access the properties of the server that actually runs the MS Mail Connector. The Diagnostics Logging tab has an MSExchangeMSMI service that will allow you to log the following:

- The MS Mail Connector Interchange
- The PC MTA running on the local Exchange server that delivers mail between MS Mail and the shadow post office
- The AppleTalk MTA that delivers mail between the shadow post office and your AppleTalk MS Mail post Offices

Use the Registry keys located in `HKEY_LOCAL_MACHINE\SYSTEM\CurrentControlSet\Services\MSExchangeMSMI\Diagnostics` to set this manually in the event that you can't set it from within the Administrator Program. Double-click the item you want to log and enter a hexadecimal value of **5** to correspond with the Maximum logging level.

Performance Monitor

In addition to having a good understanding of the Exchange services, you should also have a feeling for what is acceptable performance in your environment in order to troubleshoot Exchange. This requires configuration of a performance baseline. With this baseline, you can compare current data to the baseline and identify bottlenecks. You can also create alerts that send messages to you when your performance thresholds are exceeded. In this section we will be discussing the following topics:

- Creating a baseline
- Using the Exchange preconfigured charts
- Identifying and using NT counters
- Identifying and using Exchange counters

Creating a Baseline

Because the only way you will be able to identify a bottleneck is to first know what performance levels indicate acceptable server response time, let's discuss creating a baseline. A baseline should be created during production hours using actual production data. The log file should be generated from a remote workstation so that the Performance Monitor tool does not skew the data you collect. As you probably already know, log files include all counters for the objects you identify. To create a baseline, create a log file that updates no more frequently than every 15 minutes. This file should include at least the following objects:

- **Processor.** Counters for this object capture data about your processor utilization. Use to identify processor bottlenecks.
- **LogicalDisk.** Capture data about your logical disk drive performance by logging this object. Use to identify disk bottlenecks, and to see performance for the application running on the logical drive.
- **Memory.** Capture data about your paging and memory usage. Use this counter to identify memory bottlenecks.
- **Process.** Capture data about each process running on your system. Use to identify which process is using your processor the most, and determine if and when services should be relocated to another server.

Depending on the tasks your Exchange server performs, you should also log the following Exchange-specific objects:

- **MSExchange Internet Protocols.** Use to identify usage for POP3, IMAP4, NNTP and LDAP clients.
- **MSExchangeCCMC.** Use to identify traffic across the CC:Mail Connector.
- **MSExchangeDS.** Use to identify Directory replication and query statistics.
- **MSExchangeES.** Use to identify event script execution statistics.
- **MSExchangeIMC.** Use to identify traffic across the Internet Mail Service.
- **MSExchangeIS.** Use to identify total Information Store statistics and usage.
- **MSExchangeIS Private.** Use to identify usage specific to user mailbox access.
- **MSExchange Public.** Use to identify usage specific to public folder access, backfill, and replication.
- **MSExchangeMSMI.** Use to identify traffic across the MS Mail Connector.

- **MSExchangeMTA.** Use to identify message-handling statistics for the local MTA.

- **MSExchangeMTA Connections.** Use to identify association and connection data for connections between the local MTA and remote MTAs.

- **MSExchangePCMTA.** Use to determine message traffic between the MSMC and native MS Mail post offices.

- **MSExchangeWEB.** Use on the IIS to determine rendering statistics based on HTTP client requests of the Exchange server.

After you've created your log file, determine whether the logging period was an adequate window for baseline performance determination. For example, if you had a lot of user complaints during the logging period, perhaps the information you logged was not representative of acceptable performance. If you can't seem to get a log file during production hours that is indicative of acceptable performance, you will need to make an educated guess as to what the current problem is and fix it. Hopefully, you are creating your baseline early enough that you aren't already experiencing bottlenecks.

Once you have your baseline, you can use it to establish your acceptable limits. I recommend using the Load Simulator (LoadSim) to assist you with determining the load that will cause server performance to degrade unacceptably. The LoadSim utility should be run for a minimum of eight hours per test, with several tests indicative of projected growth. Each test should be configured with the most accurate representation of your environment and growth possible. This will help you identify at what point your server is likely to begin to bottleneck, and which resource will be the problem.

Preconfigured Charts

In addition to creating your own log files and charts, Microsoft has provided a few preconfigured charts for your use. If you are new to administering Exchange, these charts are a good place to start when trying to get an idea of how your server is performing. Let's take a look now at what each chart does and how you can use it. The charts we'll discuss are as follows:

- Server Health
- Server History
- IMS Queues
- IMS Statistics
- IMS Traffic
- Server Load
- Server Queues
- Server Users

Server Health

The Server Health chart is updated every second with the information listed here:

Object	Counter
System	%Total Processor Time
Process	dsamain %Processor Time
Process	emsmta %Processor Time
Process	store %Processor Time
Process	mad %Processor Time
Memory	pages/sec

Interpreted as a whole, you can use this information to identify which Exchange process is utilizing the most processor time, and determine which process may be contributing the most to your memory paging. The dsamain process is the Directory Service, emsmta is the Message Transfer Agent, store is the Information Store, and mad is the System Attendant.

If you find that your server performance is lagging during peak periods, you can open this chart and see exactly what component is using the most processor time. For example, if the problem area seems to be the store process, this may indicate that you should move some of your users to another server.

Server History

The Server History chart is updated every 60 seconds with the information in the following chart:

Object	Counter
MSExchangeIS	User Count
MSExchangeMTA	Work Queue Length
Memory	Pages/sec

Use Server History to identify memory paging as a function of the number of users connected to your Exchange server and the number of messages awaiting processing by the MTA. If you find that your Work Queue Length is increasing rapidly with small increases in User Count, and your Pages/sec is too high, you should consider moving users or adding memory.

Editing the Preconfigured Charts

When you launch the preconfigured charts, they will open in a window without the menu bar. To get to the menu bar, simply double-click on the chart.

IMS Queues

The IMS Queues chart is a histogram that updates every second. It is a great way to get a quick view of the number of messages awaiting processing by the various components of the IMS. Messages in the Queued Inbound and Queued Outbound queues are located in the file system, while messages in the MTS-IN and MTS-OUT queues are in the Information Store. You can use the information in the following chart to identify potential problems because too many messages stuck in the queue can indicate a DNS problem or other network-related problem:

Object	Counter
MSExchangeIMC	Queued Inbound
MSExchangeIMC	Queued MTS-IN
MSExchangeIMC	Queued MTS-OUT
MSExchangeIMC	Queued Outbound

IMS Statistics

The IMS Statistics chart that follows updates every 30 seconds to display the total number of messages the IMS has handled since the IMS service was started:

Object	Counter
MSExchangeIMC	Inbound Messages Total
MSExchangeIMC	Outbound Messages Total

If you see your chart flat-line, you may be experiencing routing problems or network problems to the IMS server. You should also check to see if the IMS service has stopped.

IMS Traffic

The IMS Traffic chart is updated every second with the total number of messages and connections the Exchange server has handled since the IMS service was started. It can help you determine the load on your IMS server. Watch for the number of messages and connections during peak periods to grow past your baseline threshold, since this could indicate that you should move the IMS to a dedicated connector server. These trends can be identified by using the IMS Traffic chart to track the following objects and counters:

Object	Counter
MSExchangeIMC	Messages Entering MTS-IN
MSExchangeIMC	Messages Entering MTS-OUT
MSExchangeIMC	Messages Leaving MTS-OUT
MSExchangeIMC	Connections Inbound

Server Load

Every 10 seconds the Server Load chart is updated with a variety of types of information. This chart is intended to give you an overview of the amount of work being performed by the Information Store to service message delivery. It also shows the work the Directory Service performs in order to provide address list queries and process replication messages. Because the values are rates, you should be looking for drastic changes in rates from one day to the next during peak periods, as well as rates dropping to zero or approaching the baseline threshold. Use the Server Load chart to track the following objects and counters:

Object	Counter
MSExchangeIS Priv	Message Recipients Delivered/min
MSExchangeIS Priv	Messages Submitted/min
MSExchangeIS Pub	Message Recipients Delivered/min
MSExchangeIS Pub	Message Submitted/min
MSExchangeMTA	Adjacent MTA Associations
MSExchangeIS	RPC Packets/sec
MSExchangeDS	AB Browses/sec
MSExchangeDS	AB Reads/sec
MSExchangeDS	ExDS Read/sec
MSExchangeDS	Replication Updates/sec

The Server Load chart can be used to identify service stoppages. Frequent service stoppages should be investigated with relation to other environmental factors, such as other services running or security problems.

Server Queues

The Server Queues histogram updates every 10 seconds with information about the current status of your MTA and Information Store queues. Use it to quickly see how many messages are awaiting processing. The queue lengths and sizes should be zero during off-peak hours. If the queue lengths and sizes grow too large, you probably have too many users or services running on the server. Use the Server Queues histogram to track the following data:

Object	Counter
MSExchangeMTA	Work Queue Length
MSExchangeIS Priv	Send Queue Size
MSExchangeIS Pub	Send Queue Size
MSExchangeIS Priv	Receive Queue Size
MSExchangeIS Pub	Receive Queue Size

Server Users

Every 10 seconds the Server Users histogram is updated with the MSExchangeIS User Count counter. This is a great chart to use to get a snapshot of the current server load. Watch this chart to identify peak periods of user activity during the day.

Useful Windows NT Counters

In addition to the Exchange preconfigured charts, there are a number of NT counters in the Performance Monitor you should be keeping an eye on in order to identify problems with your Exchange server. Whereas the Exchange counters can tell you what service is running high or low, the NT counters can tell you the effect that service is having on the server resources. Under normal conditions, you should be logging the NT counters no more frequently than every 15 minutes. During troubleshooting, update the frequency to every minute or less if necessary.

While troubleshooting, consider focusing on the following counters:

Object	Counter	Instance
Processor	%Processor Time	All instances
Process	%Processor Time	DSAMAIN
Process	%Processor Time	EMSMTA
Process	%Processor Time	MAD
Process	%Processor Time	STORE
Process	%Processor Time	MSEXCIMC

Useful Exchange Counters

In addition to tracking NT counters while troubleshooting, you should also be watching some of the Exchange counters. Consider tracking the following counters as applicable to your server at a frequency of one minute or less:

Object	Counter
MSExchangeMTA	Work Queue Length
MSExchangeIS Private	Messages Delivered/Minute
	Messages Sent/Minute
MSExchangeDS	Pending Replication Synchronizations
	Remaining Replication Updates
MSExchangeMTA	Messages/Second

Object	Counter
MSExchangeIMC	Queued Inbound
	Queued Outbound
	Queued MTS-IN
	Queued MTS-OUT
MSExchangeMTA Connections	Queue Length (IMS)

Event Viewer

In addition to using Performance Monitor to identify bottlenecks and hardware problems, you should use your event logs to determine service problems. Any time a service fails to start or fails to perform an assigned task, information will be logged to the Event Viewer. As discussed in Chapter 7, "Daily Proactive Troubleshooting," you should be analyzing your event logs daily to identify problems before they become disastrous. Refer to Chapter 7 for some specific events to be on the look out for.

Troubleshooting Utilities

There are a few really useful troubleshooting utilities that you should be aware of. Some of them come with Exchange, whereas others are available on the Resource Kits. In addition to familiarizing yourself with the various tools, you should also take advantage of resources such as TechNet, the Microsoft Knowledge Base, and the Microsoft Newsgroups available at nntp://msnews.microsoft.com. In this section we will be discussing both the tools that come with Exchange as well as the tools on the Resource Kit. The Exchange and Resource Kit tools include the following:

- RPC Ping
- Message Tracking
- CleanSweep
- GAL Modify
- PAB–GAL
- Crystal Reports
- Mailbox Cleanup Agent
- Administrative Mailbox Agent
- InterOrg
- ONDL

RPC Ping

If you suspect a network problem, or a problem with RPCs on your clients or server, you can use the RPC Ping tool to troubleshoot. The RPC Ping tool is just like a regular IP Ping in that it sends out a series of requests and expects a response back to indicate that the service is alive and functioning. But because RPC is a higher level protocol than IP, you need to tell the utility which protocol you want to test and what the service endpoint is that you are interested in verifying.

Install RPC Ping on the client and the server. For 16-bit clients, use `RPINGC16.EXE`. Use `RPINGC32.EXE` for your 32-bit clients. Start the `RPINGS.EXE` on the server to force it to wait for the RPC Ping request from the client, and then start the client RPC Ping announcement.

Message Tracking

In addition to using RPC Ping to identify potential network and RPC problems, you can use message tracking to determine at what point a message has failed to transfer. I love message tracking because it is so useful for figuring out what component of message transfer had a problem. For example, message tracking will tell you exactly what service a message was returned by so that you can go to the server that returned the message and determine the problem. Before you can track messages, you must enable message tracking—by default it is disabled.

Enabling Message Tracking

To track messages completely, you need to enable message tracking at the following three levels:

- **Information Store Site Configuration**. Enable message tracking at the Information Store level to cause all servers in the site to record transfer information about messages originating with or received by users on the local server. This includes messages handled by the IS that originated with foreign connectors if the connector is installed on the local server.

- **MTA Site Configuration**. Enable message tracking at the MTA level to cause all servers in the local site to record transfer information regarding messages handled by the MTA. This includes messages routed through bridgeheads, and messages that originated or were received by users on the local server.

- **Connector Properties**. Enable message tracking for each connector to cause the System Attendant to record the fact that a message was successfully processed by the connector service. Exchange cannot track messages once they have left the connector's queue, so any delivery issues encountered in the foreign system will be unacknowledged by your Exchange server.

There is a check box located in the bottom-left corner of the default property page for each of these objects. Check the box in all locations to cause the System Attendant to record all stages of message transit. Records of each item to be tracked will appear in a single file named for the day the entry was logged.

For example, suppose Lyle is a user on the SEATTLE server and he sends a message to Mark on the SPOKANE server on January 16, 1999. Both SEATTLE and SPOKANE are in the same site, and message tracking is enabled at all levels. There will be entries in the SEATTLE server's `exchsrvr\TRACKING.LOG\011699.log` file indicating the local IS passed the message to the local MTA and that the MTA passed the message to SPOKANE's MTA. SPOKANE's `exchsrvr\tracking.log\011699.log` file will reflect that the local MTA received the message from SEATTLE's MTA and delivered the message to the Information Store, which delivered the message to Mark's mailbox. As you can see, to view all information about the message's transfer, you have to go through the log files on each server that handled the message.

By default, message tracking logs are retained for seven days. If you need to customize this value, edit the System Attendant properties for each server in your site. While enabling message tracking is a site-wide task, configuring tracking log retention is done per server.

Tracking a Message

After you have message tracking enabled, you need to know how to track the message. Because the actual log files are just text, you could go through them manually if you wanted to. Fortunately, you don't have to; there is a Track Message tool available on the Tools menu in the Administrator Program. Open the **Track Message** dialog box and select the server on which you want to begin your search and enter your search criteria. Criteria could be the message originator, message recipient, or parameters such as message ID and whether the message was transferred into the site.

You can also track system messages, which I really use a lot when troubleshooting replication problems. After the search has yielded a selection of messages meeting your criteria, select the message you want to track to highlight it and click the **Track** button. The window will display the conversation between the local MTA and the remote MTA as perceived by the log file.

The best part is that your search will automatically parse the tracking logs on all of the servers that are identified in the local log file. For example, if the local log file says that the MTA passed the message to the SPOKANE MTA, your search window will then display information it reads from the SPOKANE log file. You'll be able to tell what log file is being read because the search window indents the receiving server's conversation. When you query a message transferred from SEATTLE to SPOKANE, the SEATTLE information will be left justified and the SPOKANE information will be indented. Use this information to determine at what point message delivery was halted.

Resource Kit

The best set of tools available to help you save time and gain additional administrative functionality with your Exchange server is the BackOffice Resource Kit, Second Edition. There is an ever-changing number of utilities, ranging from client to administrator functions. Details on their installation and configuration can be found on TechNet. See Table 13.7 for a list of some of my favorite tools and a summary of what they do.

Table 13.7 **Resource Kit Utilities Available from Microsoft**

Tool	Usage
CleanSweep	Use this tool if your Inbox Assistant or Out of Office Assistant are not functioning to delete permissions, views, forms, rules, and templates from a mailbox.
GAL Modify	Allow users to make changes to their own user properties from the Outlook client.
PAB-GAL	Synchronize personal address books with the Global Address List.
Crystal Reports	Create custom reports for Exchange.
Mailbox Cleanup Agent	Automatically clean user mailboxes. Be sure to install the Exchange service pack before you use this.
Administrative Mailbox Agent	Create and delete mailboxes and NT accounts via email.
InterOrg	Use SMTP to synchronize the Directories of two different Exchange organizations.
ONDL	Display members of distribution lists either on screen or in an output file.

Summary

In this chapter we discussed a variety of methods you can use to identify, and in some cases resolve, problems with your Exchange server. This included gaining a good understanding of what the services do in addition to using Performance Monitor and Event Viewer to identify problem areas. We ended with a discussion on some of the tools available to you for troubleshooting and fixing problems. Let's now move on to discuss some problem scenarios and what steps you need to take to resolve them.

14

Disaster Recovery

IN CHAPTER 13 WE DISCUSSED HOW TO identify common problems. Now let's discuss possible solutions to such problems. The problems range from small disasters that will affect a limited number of users—such as recovery of user mail and public folder contents—to large disasters that will impact all users on a server. The solutions can be as simple as running a utility to repair a corrupt .PST file or as difficult as restoring an entire server. Keep in mind that many problems are easily resolved by applying the latest service pack, so be sure to check out the list of service pack fixes before bending over backwards trying to solve a problem yourself. Let's start by looking at solving what I would consider to be small disasters.

Recovering from "Small" Disasters

To me, a *small* disaster is a disaster that is limited in scope. Although there are small disasters that require you to restore an entire backup tape to an offline server, none of them will require the restoration to actually occur on the production server. Small disasters we will address in this section include the following:

- Recovery of individual user mailboxes and messages
- Recovery of public folder contents
- Recovery of deleted Directory objects

- Recovery from deleted Replication Connectors
- Resolution of replication conflicts
- Repair of corrupt databases
- Repair of corrupt MTA queues
- Repair of corrupt .PST and .OST files
- Resolution of client permissions problems

Let's begin by discussing the recovery of individual user mailboxes and messages.

Recovering User Mail

Recovery of user mail can involve recovery of individual messages or an entire mailbox recovery. Both scenarios can require either a full server restore (if you don't have a bricks-level backup) or recovery from .OST files.

Recovering from Server Backups

To recover user mail from a regular backup (not bricks-level) you will need to restore the entire production server's Information Store backup to an offline server. This includes setting up a lab server, installing NT and Exchange Server, restoring the Private Information Store, logging in to the lab server, and retrieving the user's data into a .PST file. The lab server cannot be connected to your corporate network. The server should be configured to be in the same organization and site as the user's server (although the server name can be different). Following are the steps to take to restore user data from an online backup set:

1. Install Windows NT Server on the lab server.
2. Install any NT service packs that were running on the user's mailbox server when the backup you are restoring was created.
3. Install Exchange Server on the lab server. Be sure to create a new site with the same organization and site directory names as the user's server.
4. Install any Exchange server service packs that were running on the user's mailbox server when the backup you are restoring was created.
5. Insert the backup tape and open **NT Backup** from the **Start**, **Programs**, **Administrative Tools** group.
6. Select **Operations, Microsoft Exchange**.
7. Click the **Tapes** button and open the tape catalog by double-clicking the backup set name.
8. Select the correct Information Store in the Tapes window.
9. Click the **Restore** button.
10. Type the name of the lab server in the Restore Information dialog box.

11. Select the following options:

    - **Erase all existing data**
    - **Private**
    - **Public**
    - **Verify after Restore**
    - **Start Service after Restore**

12. Click **OK**.

13. After the restore is finished, verify that the services are running in **Control Panel**, **Services**.

14. Run the Consistency Adjuster found on the Advanced tab of the server property pages. Adjust all consistencies for the Private and Public Information Stores.

15. Assign the local Administrator account as the Primary Windows NT Account for the user mailbox on the mailbox's General property page. If you are recovering public folder contents, assign the local Administrator account as the folder owner in the folder's Client Permissions dialog box.

16. Install Outlook (or the appropriate client) on the recovery server.

17. Create a client profile to connect to the lab server using the **Control Panel**, **Mail and Fax** icon. Add a .PST file to the new profile.

18. Open Outlook (or whatever client you installed in step 16).

19. Either copy individual items to the Personal Folder object, or export all data to the .PST file by using Outlook's **File**, **Export** option.

20. Give the .PST to the user to add to his production profile. The user should restore his own data to the production server and remove the .PST file from his profile. If you are recovering public folder data, give the .PST to the folder's owner to recover data.

21. To recover Schedule+ data for users that use the Schedule+ client (as opposed to the Outlook client), log in to Schedule+ as the user and create a local .SCD file. Give the .SCD to the user.

Installing a New Copy of NT on the Lab Server

Bear in mind that each computer in an NT domain registers both its computer name and SID with the domain. This means that if you wish to install a lab server with the same name as the production server, the lab server will have to be removed from the network to prevent NetBIOS naming conflicts. In addition, the production server will have to be removed from the domain so that the same computer name is associated with the lab server's new SID. This SID problem occurs only if you install NT on the lab server as opposed to recovering NT from backup or an emergency repair disk. Recovery from backup or emergency repair will replace the newly installed SID with that of the originally backed up production server, although you will still have to remove the lab server from the LAN after restore to prevent NetBIOS conflicts with the production server.

If you don't have an online backup, but you do have an offline backup of your Information Store, replace steps 5–12 in the previous list with the following seven steps:

5. Stop the Exchange services.

6. Delete the contents of the `\exchsrvr\mdbdata` directory on all drives on the lab server.

7. Restore `PRIV.EDB` and `PUB.EDB` to the `\exchsrvr\mdbdata` directory on the database drive.

8. Restore the Information Store `*.LOG` files to the `\exchsrvr\mdbdata` directory on the transaction log drive.

9. Start the Microsoft Exchange Directory Service using **Control Panel**, **Services**.

10. Run `isinteg -patch` from the command prompt to resynchronize the database GUIDs.

11. Start the Microsoft Exchange Information Store service using **Control Panel**, **Services**.

If individual item recovery is a real problem in your environment, you should consider implementing the deleted item recovery option in Exchange 5.5. Deleted item recovery configuration is discussed in Chapter 2, "Administering Users."

Recovering from .OST Files

In addition to recovering mailboxes from server backups, you may be able to recover data from user .OST files. As we discussed in Chapter 6, "Backing Up Your Server," an *.OST* file is the offline folder store used for users who travel and therefore need access to data offline. Because the .OST synchronizes with the server, it is possible that information a user wants to recover exists in the local .OST file. To recover data from the offline store, perform the following steps:

1. Configure the Exchange properties in the user's profile to work offline. Add a .PST to the user's profile.

2. Open the user's Outlook client. Because you are working offline, the information you see will be obtained from the .OST file.

3. Select the documents you want to recover and move them to the .PST file.

4. Configure the Exchange properties in the user's profile to work online.

5. Close Outlook and reopen it.

6. Move the recovered data out of the .PST and into server-based storage, such as the Inbox.

There are a few things to watch out for when recovering from offline storage. The first is that the .OST file is linked to the user's profile. *Never* delete the user's profile as part of mailbox recovery. Although the .OST file will remain on the user's hard drive, it will be inaccessible without the original profile. The second issue is to be careful not to synchronize the .OST with the server before recovering data from the .OST. Many users, myself included, have the .OST configured to synchronize while online and while exiting so that manually electing to synchronize the folders is never necessary and therefore never forgotten. If these settings are configured, you may not be able to recover from the .OST because the deletion will synchronize to the local file.

Recovering Public Folder Contents

In addition to recovering user messages and mailboxes, you may find that you have to periodically recover documents stored in public folders, or even entire public folders. The recovery steps are almost the same as for individual message recovery. You will need to create the lab server and install the Exchange client as described in the earlier "Recovering User Mail" section. The client you use to recover the contents must have access permissions on the folder, so you should verify this using the Exchange Administrator Program. After you have the server recovered and permissions config-ured correctly, open the public folder and move the documents that you need into the local .PST file. You can then recover the public folder data from the .PST file much like you would recover individual messages from a user's .PST file.

If the problem you experience requires you to actually restore the Public Information Store on a production server to recover lost items, you may find yourself in a weird predicament because of the way Exchange replicates.

Suppose you accidentally delete a large amount of important information out of a public folder configured for replication. The information is immediately removed from your local Information Store and shortly thereafter the delete instructions are replicat-ed to other servers. You restore the Public Information Store on the server from which you deleted information, but the delete command is replicated back to your server and the information is again deleted! This is a frustrating scenario that can be resolved using the Authoritative Restore (AUTHREST.EXE) utility located on the Exchange server installation CD-ROM.

Use Authoritative Restore to identify the newly restored Public Information Store as the master so that deleted information cannot be replicated back to the server. This will force the newly restored documents to have more recent change numbers than that of the originally deleted items so that the restored server can replicate the restored information back to the servers that receive replicas.

Recovering Deleted Directory Objects

Just as accidental deletion of public folder contents can cause strange replication problems, deletion of Directory objects can also result in problems. Consider the following scenario.

You are the administrator of the SEATTLE server in the North America site and your site's tombstone lifetime is set to 3 days. You delete the LWILLIAMS mailbox from the SEATTLE server. Meanwhile, your WAN link to Canada is currently down. The WAN link does not come back up for 5 days. Canada's directory fails to reflect the mailbox deletion. You need to force Canada to remove the LWILLIAMS mailbox from the Canada site but you can't delete the mailbox from Canada since it was actually created in North America. What do you do?

Although there are a few things you can do, the least invasive method is to trick Exchange into thinking that a new mailbox is the same as the original mailbox. To do this, perform the following steps:

1. Record the `Obj-Dist-Name` and `Object-Version` values found on the General tab of the original mailbox in the site that you want the mailbox removed from. In our scenario, you would view the Raw Properties of LWILLIAMS from a server in Canada.

2. Re-create the mailbox with the same X.500 distinguished name as the deleted mailbox in the same site the deleted mailbox is in. In our scenario, re-create the LWILLIAMS mailbox on the SEATTLE server in North America. The X.500 distinguished name is the `Obj-Dist-Name` value recorded in step 1.

3. Change properties of the new mailbox on the server until the `Object-Version` value is a higher number than the one recorded in step 1. In our scenario, we would modify LWILLIAMS on the SEATTLE server. If the value in step 1 was a 6, then alter the new mailbox until the `Object-Version` is a 7.

Tombstone Lifetime

The default tombstone lifetime is 30 days, which is plenty long enough. After all, if your network is down for that long you have bigger problems to worry about. Still, I wouldn't change this value because you don't want to find yourself living out the example scenario described in the earlier "Recovery of Deleted Directory Objects" section.

Deleting Directory Replication Connectors

To correct the tombstone problem you could delete and re-create your Directory Replication connectors. Don't do this because it will cause *all* objects to be removed from both Directories, and all objects will have to be re-sent. This is a huge inconvenience for users, and a huge resource problem with both the replication bridgehead servers and the network.

4. Wait for the re-created mailbox to replicate to the remote site (wait for LWILLIAMS to appear in Canada). You will know this has occurred by checking the `Object-Version` value in Canada. If the value reflects the increased number generated by altering the mailbox properties in the original site, then replication has occurred.

5. Delete the re-created mailbox from the original site—delete LWILLIAMS from the North America site.

Recovering from Deleted Replication Connectors

In addition to recovering tombstones, you may find yourself receiving an entire replicated Directory if some unknowing administrator unwittingly deletes your Directory Replication connector. Not only is this a terrible thing to do, but it can result in a problem with your public folder replication scenario.

One of two things will happen to your public folders when the Directory Replication connector between the sites that contain the replicas is removed:

- Public Folders are removed.
- Public Folders are rehomed.

Both situations are undesirable, although at least rehoming won't eat up your network resources.

Public Folder Removal

When a Directory Replication connector is removed between sites that replicate public folders, the original public folder will be preserved in the originating site, but the copies that replicated to other sites will be deleted.

For example, suppose the Sales public folder is created on the SEATTLE server in North America and replicated to the OTTAWA server in Canada and the Directory Replication connector between North America and Canada is deleted. The SEATTLE server will then retain the Sales folder, but the OTTAWA server will delete the local copy. This happens if the **Limit administrative access to home site** check box is selected (it is selected by default) on the public folder's property pages. To recover from the deleted connector, you will have to re-create the connector and reconfigure public folder replication.

Public Folder Rehoming

In Exchange version 4.0, public folders are always rehomed when a Directory Replication connector is deleted and the DS/IS Consistency Adjuster is run. The Administrator Program will instruct you to run the Consistency Adjuster unless you have Service Pack 3 installed. *Rehoming* means that instead of everybody deleting the local copy of the public folder, the public folder properties are modified such that the folder is now local to the replica server. Going back to our previous example, the OTTAWA server would retain a copy of Sales that is no longer associated with the folder on SEATTLE. The problem here is that when the Directory Replication connector is reestablished, the folders are not able to replicate because they are no longer considered copies of the same folder.

To recover from public folder rehoming, you will need to use a tool called PFADMIN (version 3.0) found on the BackOffice Resource Kit. To force the rehomed folders to be reassociated with the original folder, follow these steps:

1. Create a profile on the replica server that has Service Account Admin rights on the original and replica server. To do this in our example, I would log into the OTTAWA server as the actual service account in OTTAWA. If this account is not the same as the service account in North America, assign it Service Account Admin permissions in North America temporarily. I would create a profile named `pfrehome` to connect to the OTTAWA server.

2. Access the Public Information Store properties on the server from which you want to rehome folders and add the original folder from the original server to the local Information Store. In our example, we would access OTTAWA's Public Information Store Instances property page and add the Sales folder defined on the SEATTLE server to the OTTAWA server.

3. Run the PFADMIN tool at the command prompt for the folder you want rehomed with the following format:
   ```
   Pfadmin /e5 profile_name rehome folder_name
   original_home_site\original_home_server yes/no subfolders
   ```
   To rehome Sales and all subfolders to SEATTLE, we would go to a command prompt at OTTAWA and type the following:
   ```
   Pfadmin /e5 pfrehome rehome Sales North America\SEATTLE yes
   ```

4. After replication has occurred, run the DS/IS Consistency Adjuster found on the server's Advances property page on all servers involved with the rehoming. We would run it on the SEATTLE and OTTAWA servers in this example.

Resolving Replication Conflicts

Now that replication is reestablished between your sites, you will need to periodically address replication conflicts. Fortunately, this is really easy. There are two conflicts you can run into:

- Content conflicts
- Administrative conflicts

Content conflicts occur when two people edit the same document during the same replication cycle. To minimize this problem, your replication schedule should be tuned.

In addition, the need to allow multiple users to edit existing data should be considered. If you have already optimized your replication schedule and client permissions and still receive a conflict, the resolution is to select which document should receive priority.

The users that created the conflict will receive a conflict message identified by a crossed swords icon. Opening the message gives them the opportunity to select which of the document versions should be retained. Unfortunately, Exchange can't merge the changes even if the changes are in different parts of the document. Additionally, changes to attachments are considered changes to the document as a whole, so if two users edit different attachments, they will be asked to select which modification to retain. If each user selects a different version, the conflict will be regenerated. You should educate your users about conflict resolution so that they understand the need to work together to decide how the conflict will be resolved.

You may also run into *administrative* conflicts, also known as *folder design* conflicts. The most recent change made will be retained, so if two administrators make a change to the same property of the same folder during the same replication cycle, the last change made will be retained. See Chapter 3, "Administering Public Folders," for more information on public folder conflicts.

Repairing Database Corruption (ESEUTIL, EDBUTIL and ISINTEG)

Although public folder conflicts can be easily resolved, database corruption cannot. There are three utilities that can be used to resolve database problems: ESEUTIL, EDBUTIL, and ISINTEG.

ESEUTIL and EDBUTIL

ESEUTIL and EDBUTIL can be used to detect and repair low-level database problems while your Exchange server is offline. We discussed in Chapter 11, "Periodic Proactive Troubleshooting," when and how to use ESEUTIL and EDBUTIL for offline defragmentation of your databases should it become necessary. We will now discuss their use for repairs.

For Exchange 5.5, if you suspect database corruption and want to verify your suspicions, stop the Exchange services and use the command ESEUTIL with the /g switch at the command prompt (Refer to Chapter 11 for information on ESEUTIL switches). The /g switch will cause ESEUTIL to search for damaged pages in the database and will report any errors to you, but will not attempt to repair the database. For example, to check the Private Information Store, type **eseutil /g /ispriv** at the command line on the Exchange server to be checked. If you receive confirmation of database corruption you can then decide whether you wish to do a database repair.

To repair an Exchange 5.5 database use the /p switch at the command line. For example, to repair the Private Information Store, type **eseutil /p /ispriv** at the command line. You should *never* do this on the production server. Always back up your data and re-create the production environment in the lab. You will *always* lose data when repairing a database with ESEUTIL, so this utility should be used only as the very last resort. At the end of database repair, run the ISINTEG tool discussed in the next section.

If you are using Exchange version 4.0 or 5.0, use `edbutil /c` to check for consistency problems. If your database is found to be in an inconsistent state, EDBUTIL will return errors indicating you should attempt a repair. To repair using EDBUTIL, use the `/r` switch.

ISINTEG

Whereas ESEUTIL and EDBUTIL will identify and repair low-level database corruption in all Exchange databases, ISINTEG is used to repair data problems such as unsynchronized counters only in the Information Stores. For example, if your users complain that their unread message counter says they have unread messages when they don't, you probably have a data problem in your Private Information Store that could be repaired with ISINTEG. It is also used to resynchronize your GUIDs after an offline restore.

As with ESEUTIL and EDBUTIL, you should never run ISINTEG on your production server. You should always restore a backup of your production data on a lab server and run ISINTEG on the lab server. ISINTEG has two modes: Test and Fix. *Test mode* causes ISINTEG to identify database errors but not repair them. *Fix mode* allows ISINTEG to actually repair the database.

To check for database problems, stop the Exchange services and type **isinteg -test** *switches* at the command line. As you can see in Table 14.1, you can customize the use of ISINTEG when repairing data problems in the Private and Public Information Stores.

Table 14.1   **Switches Supported by ISINTEG**

Switch	Usage
-?	Provides onscreen help
-pri	Identifies the Private Information Store
-pub	Identifies the Public Information Store
-fix	Repairs problems
-detailed	Performs optional tests
-verbose	Reports all problems
-l	Logs to a log file
-t	Indicates the location of the temporary database
-test	Performs identified tests

There are a number of tests that can be performed against the Private and Public Information Stores. See Table 14.2 for a few of the most useful options.

Table 14.2 **Tests Run by *ISINTEG* to Optimize the Test Environment**

Test	Usage
`attach`	Verifies attachment properties
`attachref`	Verifies attachment references
`fldrcv` (private store only)	Verifies counters for mailbox folders such as the Inbox, Sent Mail, and Deleted Items folders
`mailbox` (private store only)	Inspects mailbox folders for problems
`peruser`	Verifies each user's unread message counter

Repairing Corrupted Queues (MTACHECK)

In addition to corruption in the Private and Public Information Stores, you may occasionally experience corrupt MTA queues. For this reason, Microsoft provides the MTACHECK utility, which runs automatically after any hard reset of the Exchange server. If you suspect that you have a corrupt MTA queue, use MTACHECK to fix the problem.

Results of running MTACHECK will be logged to the `exchsrvr\mtadata\mtacheck.out\MTACHECK.LOG` file located on the same drive as your `DB*.DAT` files. If MTACHECK finds a problematic message in the queue, it moves the message to the `exchsrvr\mtadata\mtacheck.out` directory so that you can look at it later. The MTACHECK utility will summarize the results of the test in the log file by reporting whether the database is clean or whether repairs were made.

Type **MTACHECK** at the command prompt to run it manually. You can run MTACHECK without switches for normal operation, or customize it by adding one of the optional switches listed in Table 14.3.

> **`edbutil /d /r`**
> Never run EDBUTIL with both `/d` and `/r` switches at the same time, such as `edbutil /d / r /ispriv`. This can cause terrible problems because the utility will attempt to repair while it is defragmenting, and you may not be able to recover without restoring from backup.

> **Additional `ISINTEG` Tests**
> There are actually quite a lot more tests that ISINTEG can be used to perform. For a list of all tests, type **`ISINTEG -?`** at a command prompt or view the `ISINTEG.DOC` file on the Exchange server installation CD-ROM.

Table 14.3 **Switches That Customize MTACHECK Performance**

Switch	Recommendation
/v	Use this switch to obtain the maximum amount of information in the log file about the operation of MTACHECK. v stands for Verbose.
/f *filename*	Identify another filename for the log file.
/rd	Remove queued directory replication messages. This is helpful if your network connection has been down and you don't want a flood of replication messages tying up the network.
/rp	Remove queued public folder replication messages. Although this can alleviate some of the initial traffic across a recently repaired network connection, it can result in excessive creation of public folder status messages. Refer to Chapter 3, "Administering Public Folders," for more information on status messages.
/rl	Remove queued Link Monitor messages to prevent them from being processed across recently repaired network connections.

Repairing Corrupted Personal Folder Stores and Offline Folder Stores

While MTACHECK can be used to repair corrupt MTA queues, the Inbox Repair Tool (SCANPST) can be used to repair corrupt personal folder stores (.PST files) and offline folder stores (.OST files). The Inbox Repair Tool can be found in the Exchange client directory on your user workstations.

After you run SCANPST, you will see a folder named Lost and Found in the repaired personal folder. Inside Lost and Found are the items that the Inbox Repair Tool was able to save. Remove the recovered items from the Lost and Found folder and place them into a newly created .PST file to prevent the original, corrupt .PST file from damaging the recovered messages.

Resolving Client Group Permissions

In addition to problems you might have with database and data corruption, you might also have problems with client access to your server resources. Although issues with permissions aren't exactly on the same disaster level as corrupt files and databases, they can be quite troublesome and time consuming. This is because the way Exchange processes resource access permissions is not the same as the way Windows NT processes permissions.

In Windows NT, clients are given the least restrictive permission of all assigned permissions unless there is a No Access permission defined for a SID associated with the user or a group the user belongs to. In Exchange, client permissions are given the least restrictive permission of all group permissions, but if the user is identified explicitly on an access control list, the explicit permissions override the group permissions.

For example, suppose April is a member of the Managers and Sales groups. The NT folder named Data has NTFS permissions assigned as follows:

SID Owner	Permission
April	Read
Managers	Full Control
Sales	Read

As a result, April has full control over data in the Data folder because she has the least restrictive of all combined permissions, and none of her SIDs has a No Access permission assigned. On the other hand, there is a public folder in Exchange named Data with the same permissions as the NTFS Data folder. April has Read access to the Exchange Data public folder because although her group membership will give her full control, her mailbox is identified explicitly and explicit permissions assignments override group assignments in Exchange.

This public folder access problem leads to some sticky troubleshooting in which the only solution is to go into the Client Permissions dialog box of your public folders and assign permissions appropriately for Exchange.

Recovering from "Big" Disasters

Now that we've discussed some of the smaller disasters you will likely encounter and how to resolve them, let's take a look at what I would consider a *big* disaster. To me, a big disaster requires substantial restoration from tape backup onto the production server. Big disasters, in order of magnitude, include the following:

- Database restores
- Complete server restores

We'll start by restoring individual databases.

Restoring the Database

A database restore is the mildest of big disasters because it means that your Exchange system files, NT files, and transaction logs are available. You will need to restore a database if your production database becomes so corrupt that the services won't start, or if your hard disk crashes and you don't have fault tolerance configured. In either of these scenarios, all that needs to be restored are the Information Stores and/or the Directory.

To perform an Information Store restore, follow these steps:

1. Back up existing transaction log files to tape.

2. For the Private Information Store, restore the `PRIV.EDB`, `PRIV.PAT`, `EDB.CHK`, and `EDB*.LOG` files from the tape to the correct locations on the server.

For the Public Information Store, restore `PUB.EDB`, `PUB.PAT`, `EDB.CHK`, and `EDB*.LOG` files from the tape to the correct locations on the server.

If you have incremental backups, you need to apply each incremental backup set to the full backup in order. For example, if your backup was performed on Saturday and you crashed on Tuesday after having done incremental backups on Sunday and Monday, apply the full backup to restore the databases and log files first. Then apply Sunday's tape to restore Sunday's log files, and last apply Monday's tape to restore Monday's log files.

If you have differential backups, apply the full backup and then the latest differential backup.

3. Start the Information Store service. If you have trouble starting the IS, run `ISINTEG -patch` to resynchronize the database GUIDs.

In some cases, you may need to restore more than just the databases from tape. In this event you will need to perform a full server restore. Depending on whether your backup was online or offline, there are different procedures you must follow to get your server back online. Let's take a look at data restoration from online and offline backups.

Restoring the Complete Server

A complete server restore involves reinstalling or recovering NT, reinstalling or recovering Exchange, and recovering your Exchange databases. This is useful if you want to move your Exchange functionality to a new, upgraded server. If so, you will need the following:

- NT and Exchange installation CD-ROMs
- Exchange and NT service packs (if they were applied to the production server)
- NT and Exchange configuration information from your production Exchange server
- A full backup of your production databases
- Access to the NT SAM

The new server must have the same computer name as the original production server. You will have to delete the original server from the SAM using Server Manager in order for the new server to be added to the domain. To restore the server databases to a new server from an online backup, perform the following steps:

1. Perform a full online backup of the original server.
2. Delete the original server from the domain SAM using Server Manager.
3. Install NT on the new server with the same computer name and NT role as the original server (BDC, member server) and in the same domain as the original server.

4. Install the same NT service packs on the new server as the original server had at the time you created the backup set.

5. Log on as an NT and Exchange administrator, or as the Exchange service account.

6. Install Exchange as a new site, using the same site and organization directory names as the original server. (If you are running Exchange 5.0 or 5.5, use `setup /r` instead of `setup` to recover data.)

   If you are unsure of the directory names, verify them by accessing the site and organization properties on an existing Exchange server in the same site. This is important because the display name can be easily changed, leading you to believe that your organization and site names are one thing, while the directory name is something else.

7. Identify the site's original service account.

8. Install any Exchange service packs that were installed on the original server at the time the backup set was created. (For Exchange 5.0 and 5.5, use `update /r` instead of `update` for recovery.)

9. Configure the MS Mail Connector and any third-party connectors that were running on the original server manually to get their settings stored in the Registry before restoring the server data.

10. Install Key Manager server if you had it running on the original server.

11. Insert the backup tape and open NT Backup.

12. Double-click **Tapes** and **Full Backup Tape** to load the tape set's catalog.

13. If you have transaction logs from the original server that are not on the backup tape that you want applied to the new server, restore the Directory and Information Store `EDB*.LOG` files to the `MDBDATA` and `DSADATA` directories on the new server before continuing. Do *not* select to **Erase all Existing Data**.

14. Select to restore the Directory and Information Store.

15. Click **Restore**.

16. Select the following restore options:

   ■ **Erase all Existing Data** (only if you have not restored transaction logs already)

   ■ **Private**

   ■ **Public**

   ■ **Start Services After Restore** (after both the Information Store and Directory have been restored—*don't* select if the databases are on separate tape sets)

   ■ **Verify after Restore**

17. Click **OK** to close the window, and click **OK** to start the restore.

18. If you were running Key Manager on the original server, restore the Key Manager data from either `exchsrvr\security\mgrent` or `exchsrvr\kmsdata` directory, depending on the version of Exchange you are running.

19. Exit **NT Backup**.

20. Verify that your services are running. If not, run `ISINTEG -patch` to resynchronize your database GUIDs.

21. Verify that your connectors and server settings are all correct according to your Exchange configuration sheets.

22. Verify that the Primary NT account associated with your mailboxes is correct.

23. Install Outlook on the new server.

24. Verify that you can access the Private and Public Information Stores from the client.

25. Verify that you can send messages via connectors from the client.

If you don't do online backups on your Exchange server, or if you must do the restore from an offline backup, the procedure is a little different. Add steps 10a and 10b immediately after step 10:

10a. Stop the Exchange services (stopping the System Attendant will stop everything else).

10b. Use the Registry to locate the correct restore path for your databases and log files.

Replace steps 13–14 as follows:

13. Restore `DIR.EDB`, `PRIV.EDB`, and `PUB.EDB` to the correct restore paths.

14. Restore all the associated transaction logs to the correct restore paths.

Replace steps 19 and 20 with the following step:

20. Start the Directory Services.

Finally, add these two steps immediately before step 21:

20a. Type `isinteg -patch` at the command prompt to resynchronize your GUIDs.

20b. Start the Information Store service.

Summary

In this chapter we addressed how to resolve some of the most common issues that you are likely to run into. Unfortunately, there is no way to include everything you will ever need into a single book. As a result, I recommend you purchase a subscription to

Microsoft's *TechNet* technical support CD-ROM set in addition to utilizing the Microsoft support Web site and the Microsoft newsgroups to obtain answers to questions. If these resources do not have the answers you need, purchase a support incident with Microsoft's Product Support Services. The dollars you spend on these resources will be well worth the time you save attempting to fix Exchange server problems by yourself.

IV

Appendixes

A

Maintenance Schedule

Table A.1 provides a list of the many maintenance tasks you will need to perform when administering Exchange, along with my recommendations on how often you should do them. For more information, please see the referenced chapter of the book.

Table A.1 **Maintenance Schedule**

Task	Chapter	Daily	Weekly	Monthly	Quarterly	Semi-annually	As Needed
Add Recipients	2	✔					✔
Remove Recipients	2	✔					✔
Edit Recipients	2	✔					✔
Add Public Folders	3	✔					✔
Remove Public Folders	3	✔					✔
Edit Public Folders	3	✔					✔
PF Replication Verification	3	✔					
PF Conflict Management	3						✔
Queue Management	4	✔					
Check Available Disk Space	5	✔					

continues

Table A.1 **Continued**

Task	Chapter	Daily	Weekly	Monthly	Quarterly	Semi-annually	As Needed
Perform Server Backup	6	✔					
Analyze Event Logs	7	✔					
Analyze Backup Logs	7	✔					
Analyze Server and Link Monitors	7	✔					
Analyze Performance Monitor Logs	7	✔					
Upgrade Server Hardware	8						✔
Run Performance Optimizer	8						✔
Optimize Connectors	9						✔
Create and Review Server Disk Usage Report	10		✔	✔		✔	
Create and Review Server Downtime Summary Report	10		✔	✔		✔	
Create and Review Server Backup Status Report	10		✔	✔		✔	
Create and Review Server User Population Report	10		✔	✔		✔	
Create and Review Server Connector Throughput Statistics Report	10		✔	✔		✔	
Practice Restore in Lab	11				✔		
Offline Defragmentation (versions 4.0 and 5.0)	11				✔		
Offline Defragmentation (version 5.5)	11						✔
Remove Unused Mailboxes	11		✔				
Clean Mailboxes	11	✔	✔				
Move Mailboxes	11						✔
Archive Event, Backup, and Performance Monitor Logs	11		✔				

B

Exchange Registry Tuning

YOU CAN DO A LOT OF REALLY GREAT THINGS with the Registry to tune your Exchange server. As always, you should not take Registry editing lightly. Always back it up before you change anything, and don't change anything without first considering the ramifications. Most Registry edits are not supported; always test your changes in a lab to be sure they won't have unpredicted affects on your environment before actually implementing the change on a production server. That being said, some of the things you can do with the Registry are to tune the following areas of Exchange:

- Information Store
- Message Transfer Agent
- Directory Service
- Internet Mail Service
- TCP/IP Settings
- Message Journaling Settings

Information Store Registry Settings

Settings that tune the Public and Private Information Stores are located in HKEY_LOCAL_MACHINE/System/CurrentControlSet/Services/MSExchangeIS/. Table B.1 gives some recommendations for tuning the Information Store.

Table B.1 **Information Store Registry Tuning Settings**

Setting	Recommendation
ParametersPublic\ Replication Send Status Timeout	If there are more than 50 sites in the organization with slow links involved, you may wish to adjust this parameter on each Public Store Server to change the minimum amount of time Exchange waits before sending public folder status messages. Increasing this value lowers the total amount of system traffic generated, although it increases the time required to resolve inconsistencies in the public folder hierarchy. The default is 23.5 hours, which is represented in the Registry as 84,600 seconds.
ParametersPublic\ Replication Send Status Alignment Skew	By default, the public folder status thread runs at 12:15 AM and 12:15 PM. This may conflict with busy periods in your work environment, so adjust the skew to the number of seconds past the default time you wish the thread to run. The default value is 0 seconds.
ParametersPublic\ Disable Replication Messages at Startup	This setting instructs your public folder servers to generate status messages when the IS service is started. If you have to restart the service a lot, this can cause overhead that you can avoid by setting the value to 1. (The default is 0.) You must have Exchange version 4.0/SP5, Exchange 5.0/SP2, or Exchange 5.5/SP1 to configure this setting.
ParametersPublic\ Log Downloads	Add this REG_DWORD value to log downloads from public folders to the application log.
ParametersPrivate\ Log Downloads	Add this REG_DWORD value to log downloads from mailboxes to the application log. The data to enter in the Log Downloads value corresponds with the following decimal numbers:

Data	Number
Attachments	1
Messages	2
Attachments and messages	3
Folders	4
Attachments and folders	5
Messages and folders	6
All	7

Max Recipients on Submit	Add this `REG_DWORD` value with data representing the maximum number of recipients you want a message to have. The client will receive an error message when attempting to send a message with more than the indicated number of recipients.
ParametersSystem\ POP3 Protocol Logging Level	Add this `REG_DWORD` setting with a value between 0 (no logging) and 5 (maximum logging) to start logging the conversation that occurs using the POP3 protocol on the local server. The conversation will be recorded in the `L0000001.log` file.
ParametersSystem\ POP3 Protocol Log Path	Add this `REG_SZ` setting with a value representing the path to log POP3 data. The default location is `c:\exchsrvr\ mdbdata`.
ParametersSystem\ IMAP Protocol Logging Level	Add this `REG_DWORD` setting with a value between 0 (no logging) and 5 (maximum logging) to start logging the conversation that occurs using the IMAP4 protocol on the local server to the `L0000001.log` file.
ParametersSystem\ IMAP Protocol Log Path	Add this `REG_SZ` setting with a value representing the path to log IMAP4 data. The default location is `c:\exchsrvr\ mdbdata`.

Message Transfer Agent Registry Settings

Settings that tune the Message Transfer Agent are located in `HKEY_LOCAL_MACHINE/ System/CurrentControlSet/Services/MSExchangeMTA/Parameters`. Recommendations on tuning these settings are listed in Table B.2.

Table B.2 **MTA Registry Settings**

Setting	Recommendation
Message timeout (urgent), minutes	Add this `REG_DWORD` value to specify the amount of time urgent, non-system messages are allowed to wait in the MTA queue in Exchange 5.5 prior to being returned to the sender as non-deliverable. A value of 0 indicates that urgent messages will not be processed by the MTA.
Message timeout (normal), minutes	Add this `REG_DWORD` value to specify the amount of time normal, non-system messages are allowed to wait in the MTA queue in Exchange 5.5 prior to being returned to the sender as non-deliverable. A value of 0 indicates that normal messages will not be processed by the MTA.
Message timeout (non-urgent), minutes	Add this `REG_DWORD` value to specify the amount of time non-urgent, non-system messages are allowed to wait in the MTA queue in Exchange 5.5 prior to being returned to the

continues

Table B.2 **Continued**

Setting	Recommendation
	sender as non-deliverable. A value of 0 indicates that non-urgent messages will not be processed by the MTA.
`<server/connection>\` `Content Length Threshold`	Add this `REG_DWORD` value to instruct the MTA to wait until the queue holds the specified amount of data before creating a connection to the indicated server or connection.
`<server/connection>\` `Queue Length Threshold`	Add this `REG_DWORD` value to instruct the MTA to wait until the outbound queue holds the specified number of messages before creating a connection to the indicated server or connection. If you set both this value and the `Content Length Threshold` value, the MTA creates a connection at the earliest threshold. (For example, if your `Content Length Threshold` is 1MB and your `Queue Length Threshold` is 10, the MTA will connect when the queue is at 1MB regardless of the number of messages queued, or when the number of messages reaches 10 regardless of the total size of the data queued.)
`<server/connection>\` `Urgent Overrides Thresholds`	Add this `REG_DWORD` with a value of 1 to force the MTA to send urgent messages immediately without waiting for the content or queue length thresholds to be reached. A value of 0 causes urgent messages to be subjected to the same thresholds as other messages.
`Work queue alarm on`	Add this `REG_DWORD` setting to force the MTA version 1459.39 and later to log events to the application event log when the local inbound queue has exceeded the indicated number of messages awaiting processing.
`Work queue alarm off`	Add this `REG_DWORD` setting to force MTA version 1459.39 and later to log events to the application event log when the local inbound queue has dropped below the indicated number of messages awaiting processing. If this setting is not configured, the MTA will log events when half the `Work queue alarm on` value is reached.
`Outbound queue alarm on`	Add this `REG_DWORD` setting to force the MTA version 1459.39 and later to log events to the application event log when the local outbound queue has exceeded the indicated number of messages awaiting processing.
`Outbound queue alarm off`	Add this `REG_DWORD` setting to force the MTA version 1459.39 and later to log events to the application event log when the local outbound queue has dropped below the indicated number of messages awaiting processing. If this setting is not configured, the MTA will log events when half the `Outbound queue alarm on` value is reached.

`Text Event Log`	Set this value to 1 to enable additional events to be logged to the application event log.
`Unbounded Event Log`	Add this `DWORD` value to allow configuration of this parameter to write events to the `Ev0.log` file. All data that is logged to the application log will also be written to this file. After this key is added, use the Diagnostics Logging tab on the server object in the Administrator Program to enable maximum logging, or set the Registry value to 1.
`Unbounded APDU`	Add this `DWORD` value to allow configuration of this parameter to write events to the `Bf0.log` file. All binary information will be logged to the file, and can be viewed with the Aspirin viewer found on the BORK 2 CD. After this key is added, use the Diagnostics Logging tab on the server object in the Administrator Program to enable maximum logging.
`Unbounded Interop Log`	Add this `DWORD` value to allow configuration of this parameter to write events to the `Ap0.log` file. All text transferred in or out of the MTA will be recorded in the log file. After this key is added, use the Diagnostics Logging tab on the server object in the Administrator Program to enable maximum logging.

Directory Service Registry Settings

Tune Directory Replication performance by editing keys found in `HKEY_LOCAL_MACHINE/System/CurrentControlSet/Services/MSExchangeDS/Parameters`. See Table B.3 for recommendations on tuning these keys.

Table B.3   **Directory Service Registry Settings**

Setting	Recommendation
`Replicator notify pause after modification`	Configure this `REG_DWORD` value to delay the time lapse between directory changes and the directory change announcement Exchange sends out to servers in the same site. The default is 300 seconds (five minutes), but I find that most companies with sites spanning a WAN link can tolerate a delay of 1800 seconds (30 minutes) or longer.
`Replicator notify pause between DSAs`	After the `Replicator notify pause after modification` time expires, the local Directory will

continues

Table B.3 **Continued**

Setting	Recommendation
	make an announcement to each server listed in its REPS-TO list one at a time, with a pause defined by this parameter between notifications. The default is 30 seconds, but you can increase this value if your Directories are becoming overloaded servicing change requests.
Replicator inter site sync at Startup	Configure this value to prevent the directory replication bridgehead server from triggering a full inter-site replication with all of its replication partners every time it is restarted. If your replication bridgehead's Directory Service is restarted frequently, you may want to change this value to 0.

Internet Mail Service Registry Settings

Run the IMS/IMC in a console window to view all transfer statistics in real time. This can help you troubleshoot problems and get a good feel for the IMS performance on your server. IMS settings are found in HKEY_LOCAL_MACHINE\SYSTEM\CurrentControlSet\Services\MSExchangeIMC\ Parameters. Table B.4 gives my recommendations for tuning the IMS.

Table B.4 **IMS Registry Settings**

Setting	Recommendation
DisplayErrsOnConsole	Stop the IMS and add this REG_DWORD value with HEX data of 100 to cause the IMS to run in a console window. From a command prompt, type **MSEXCIMS -console** when in the \Connect\Msexcimc\Bin directory.
ConsoleStatFrequency	Decrease this value to increase the rate at which updates are written to the console window.
TurfDir	Add this REG_SZ value with data of c:\exchsrvr\imcdata\turfdir to cause messages from certain individuals or domains to be routed to the Turf Directory for future perusal.

Setting	Recommendation
TurfTable	Add this REG_MULTI_SZ value with data identifying the user email addresses and/or email domains that you wish to prevent from sending mail into your organization. Enter one address on each line without delimiters. The FROM field of incoming messages will be compared to this list. If a match is found, the message will be routed to the TurfDir. Restart the IMS to enable the change.

TCP/IP Registry Settings

You can change the port allocation for RPC sessions by editing the following keys for the Directory Service and Information Store:

```
HKEY_LOCAL_MACHINE\SYSTEM\CurrentControlSet\Services\MSExchangeDS\
Parameters\TCP/IP port
```

```
HKEY_LOCAL_MACHINE\SYSTEM\CurrentControlSet\Services\MSExchangeIS\
ParametersSystem\TCP/IP port
```

Edit these values to include the port you want your MAPI clients and Site Connectors to connect through after having been accepted through port 135.

Message Journaling Registry Settings

As we discussed in Chapter 5, "Managing Disk Resources," message journaling can be enabled to allow Exchange to keep a copy of all incoming and outgoing messages. The messages retained will be routed to a dedicated journaling recipient. To enable message journaling on your Exchange 5.5 service pack 1 servers, edit the Registry keys listed in Table B.5.

Table B.5 **Message Journaling Registry Settings**

Setting	Recommendation
HKEY_LOCAL_MACHINE\SYSTEM\ CurrentControlSet\ Services\MSExchangeMTA\ Parameters	Add a string named **Journal Recipient Name** with the value set to the Obj-Dist-Name value found on the recipient mailbox when viewing its raw properties.
HKEY_LOCAL_MACHINE\SYSTEM\ CurrentControlSet\ Services\MSExchangeMTA\ Parameters	Add a DWORD value named **Per-Site Journal Required** with a value of 0 for organization-wide journaling, a value of 1 for site-wide journaling, or a value of 2 for per-server journaling.

continues

Table B.5   **Continued**

Setting	Recommendation
HKEY_LOCAL_MACHINE\SYSTEM\ CurrentControlSet\ Services\MSExchangeIMC\ Parameters	Add a DWORD value named **RerouteViaStore** with a value of 1 to force the IMS to route all incoming messages through the Private Information Store.
HKEY_LOCAL_MACHINE\SYSTEM\ CurrentControlSet\ Services\MSExchangeIS\ ParametersSystem	Add a DWORD value named **No Local Delivery** with a value of 1 to force the IS to route all messages to the MTA, even if the recipient is on the same server as the originator.

C

Raw Mode

THE EXCHANGE ADMINISTRATOR PROGRAM can be run in Raw Mode, which exposes the X.500 directory to you. From Raw Mode you have access to attributes that are not available when running the Administrator Program normally. Be *very* careful when running the Administrator Program in Raw Mode—it is analogous to editing the Registry and you can do a lot of damage if you don't know what you are doing. The tasks you can perform with Raw Mode include the following:

- Hiding the Microsoft Schedule+ Free/Busy Connector
- Resetting Exchange's MS Mail DirSync Numbers
- Verifying intrasite directory replication
- Identifying the administrator making unauthorized changes
- Moving Exchange to another NT Domain
- Searching the GAL by first name

Hiding the Microsoft Schedule+ Free/Busy Connector

Using Raw Mode, you can hide the Schedule+ Free/Busy Connector mailbox agent so that it doesn't show up in the global address list (GAL). You may need to do this on more than one server to prevent it from replicating to other servers in the organization and showing up in their GAL as well. The Free/Busy Connector allows you to synchronize free and busy information between the Exchange Schedule+ Free & Busy system folder and MS Mail post offices using the MS Mail Schedule Distribution (SchDist) program. Because the SchDist program uses a mailbox called Adminsch on each MS Mail post office, each Exchange server must have an Adminsch recipient that can be addressed by SchDist. To hide the Exchange Adminsch mailbox agent, perform the following steps:

1. Run **Admin.exe /r**.
2. Select the **Microsoft Schedule+ Free/Busy Connector**.
3. Select **File, Raw Properties**.
4. Select **Hide from AB** in the Object Attributes windows.
5. Change the Edit value to **1** and click **Set**.
6. Click **OK**.

Resetting Exchange's MS Mail DirSync Numbers

You can use Raw Mode to reset Exchange's DirSync numbers as well. You may need to do this occasionally because unfortunately, sometimes directory synchronization with MS Mail fails to the point where you have no other choice. If this happens to you and you determine that resetting them is the best solution, follow one of these two sets of steps, depending on whether Exchange is the DirSync Server or a DirSync Requestor.

If Exchange is the DirSync Server, do the following:

1. Open **Admin /r**.
2. Select your Exchange server's DirSync Server object.
3. Select the remote DirSync requestor that you want to reset.
4. Select **File, Raw Properties**.
5. Change the List Attributes to **ALL**.
6. Set the following values:
   ```
   DXA-Conf-Seq=0

   DXA-Imp-Seq=0
   ```

```
DXA-Req-Seq=0
DXA-Svr-Seq=0
```

7. Stop and start the **Microsoft Exchange Directory Synchronization** service.

8. Run **LISTDS.EXE** on the MS Mail post office that you reset to change the local DirSync numbers.

If Exchange is a DirSync Requestor, perform the following steps instead:

1. Open **Admin /r**.

2. Select your Exchange server's DirSync Requestor object.

3. Select **File**, **Raw Properties**.

4. Change the List Attributes to **ALL**.

5. Set the following values:
```
DXA-Conf-Seq=0
DXA-Imp-Seq=0
DXA-Req-Seq=0
DXA-Svr-Seq=0
```

6. Stop and start the Microsoft Exchange Directory Synchronization service.

7. Delete and re-create the **Exchange Shadow Post Office** in MS Mail Admin on the MS Mail DirSync server.

Verifying Intrasite Directory Replication

You can use Raw Mode to compare the USN of an object in one Exchange server's Directory with the same object in another Exchange server's Directory to verify that the object is replicating correctly. The USN should be the same in both Directories if replication has occurred. You may want to do this if your WAN link has gone down for an extended period of time, or if you have reason to suspect that replication is not succeeding. To verify replication between SEATTLE and OTTAWA servers, perform these steps:

1. From both SEATTLE and OTTAWA, open **Admin /r**.

2. From both SEATTLE and OTTAWA, select the object you are concerned about and choose **File**, **Raw Properties**.

3. Record the USN-Changed and USN-Source values.

4. From SEATTLE, record Reps-From for OTTAWA.

5. From OTTAWA, record `Reps-From` for SEATTLE.

6. Change the object's properties on SEATTLE.

7. Force replication with OTTAWA.

8. Verify that the USN on OTTAWA has increased to a number larger than what you recorded.

Identifying the Administrator Making Unauthorized Changes

If you are experiencing administration problems due to an unidentified administrator making unauthorized changes, you can use Raw Mode to determine who is doing it. You first determine which server the administrator is connected to when making changes, and then determine which user is making the changes. You can do this for any type of change, including ADSI changes and Import/Export changes. Simply perform the following steps:

1. Open **Admin /r**.

2. Select the object that was changed by the mystery administrator and select **File**, **Raw Properties**.

3. Record the 32-character DSA-Signature value.

4. Close the object's properties and select your site name from the Administrator Program.

5. Select **File**, **Raw Properties**.

6. Record the `Reps-From` value. The `Reps-From` value is made up of six values separated by commas. The fifth value is your server's Invocation-ID and the sixth value is your server's computer name. Scroll through the list until you find an Invocation-ID that matches the object's `DSA-Signature` value. The server name in the sixth field of that line is the server from which changes are being made.

7. To determine who is making changes, you will need to enable Security logging. To do this, select the server from which changes are being made and get the regular (not Raw) properties.

8. On the Diagnostics Logging tab, select **MSExchangeDS** and turn on **Maximum logging** for the Security object.

Changes administrators make to the server will log to the Application event log as Event 1053.

Moving Exchange to Another NT Domain

You can use Raw Mode to move an Exchange server to another NT domain if you are running a single server, single site environment and the Exchange server is installed as an NT member server. This is not supported by Microsoft. If you have more than one Exchange server in your organization, you will have to reinstall it to move it to the new domain. You will need to have a service account created in the new domain that is given permissions to the organization, site, and Configuration containers first. After you do, perform the following steps:

1. Back up the DSADATA directory on the server.

2. Establish a trust in which the Exchange server is the trusting domain and the new domain is trusted.

3. Create a new service account in the new domain with the same username and password as the old account. Give it **Act as Part of the Operating System**, **Backup**, **Restore**, and **Logon** as a Service rights (you'll have to show Advanced user rights).

4. Open **Admin /r**.

5. Add the new service account to the organization, site, and Configuration containers with Service Account Admin rights.

6. Select **View**, **Raw Directory**.

7. Select **Schema and File**, **Raw Properties**.

8. Select the NT-Security-Descriptor and add the new service account with Service Account Admin rights.

9. Click **OK** and click **Set**.

10. Stop the Exchange services and change the startup account to the new service account.

11. Have the Exchange server join a new domain from the Network Properties dialog box.

12. Reboot the server and break the trust relationship.

13. Open **Admin /r** and remove the old service account from the Organization, Site, Configuration, and Schema levels.

14. Assign new Primary NT Accounts to the user mailboxes.

Searching the GAL by First Name

You can use Raw Mode to add attributes that can be searched for in the GAL, such as users' first names. Generally, GAL searches are by user mailbox ID or user display name. If you want Exchange to allow searches by first name, you can assign additional attributes to allow that in each site, as follows:

1. Open **Admin /r**.
2. Select **View**, **Raw Directory**.
3. Double-click **Schema**.
4. Select the **First Name** object and click **File**, **Raw Properties**.
5. Select the **Search-Flags** attribute.
6. Enter the value **2** in the Edit box and click **Set**.
7. Click **OK**.
8. Reboot the server.

D

Exchange 5.5 Versus Platinum

PLATINUM IS TO BE THE NEXT MAJOR release of Exchange Server. It will run exclusively on Windows 2000, and upgrade exclusively from Exchange version 5.5. As a result, there will likely be a slow move in the industry from their current Exchange implementation to Platinum. That being said, there are many major improvements to Exchange Server 5.5 implemented in Platinum, including the ability to have multiple Information Stores on the same server, and the incorporation of the Exchange Active Directory into the NT Domain database. Some of the most significant improvements are listed here:

- Platinum utilizes the Windows 2000 Active Directory exclusively.
- Platinum is fully compliant with older versions of Exchange clients.
- With Platinum, more than 10 million objects per Information Store are supported.
- Multiple Information Stores per server are supported.
- In the Platinum version, the Windows 2000 multiple-master directory model is used for both Windows 2000 and Platinum/Exchange rather than there being a separate Windows NT PDC single-master domain model and a separate Exchange X.500 multiple-master directory.

- Now you can administer both Windows 2000 and Platinum/Exchange through MMC snap-ins.

- Permissions can be assigned to each property of an object rather than to an entire object.

- Global administration is managed; you don't have to be connected to the site on which the object was defined in order to administer the object.

- Platinum supports ADSI in order to provide a programming interface that can be queried and manipulated by custom programs and scripts.

- Replication occurs at the property level in the Windows 2000 Active Directory instead of at the object level, and therefore is much faster and produces much less network traffic.

- User mailboxes are defined by "mail-enabling" a Windows 2000 Active Directory user account.

- Windows 2000 groups will be "mail-enabled." The ability to create Exchange/Platinum distribution lists is retained.

- The concept of Exchange sites is gone, eliminating the issues associated with moving users between sites. Users are mapped to a physical, geographical location in the Active Directory. Organizational directory replication will be configured automatically based on the site topology.

- Public Folder permissions will be based on the Windows 2000 security model and will use Windows 2000 access control lists.

E

Importing and Exporting

THE IMPORT AND EXPORT ABILITIES OF THE Exchange Directory allow you to do a lot of really useful things. You can either manually import or export to a .CSV file, or you can write a script that automatically imports or exports at a more appropriate time. In many cases, combining import/export with the Performance Optimizer can get you the best results, although this does require that you stop your Exchange services. Either way, you can use the Import/Export tool to complete the following tasks:

- Perform Directory Synchronization between Exchange and a foreign database
- Modify mailbox properties, such as storage limits and protocol settings
- Delete object property data
- Change object permissions
- Delete users from the Directory
- Add users to distribution lists
- Create custom recipients

Before you can begin to complete these tasks, you must do two things: Create a header file and determine how you will run the import/export file.

Creating a Header File

The first step toward completing the tasks listed at the start of the chapter is to create a header file containing the property names of the data you want to import or export. You can either create the file manually, or you can use the HEADER.EXE tool found on the BackOffice Resource Kit. I recommend using HEADER.EXE because it is a lot easier than typing in all of the property names manually. The file you will ultimately use is a comma-separated value file, in which the first line is the comma-delimited list of the properties you want to import or export.

To create a header file, open the HEADER.EXE tool and choose the object class you want to modify from the Object Class drop-down list. Each object class has certain attributes that must always be present in every header file you use to modify objects in the class. These are listed in the Available Attributes window in boldface. Click the **Add Required** button to bring the required attributes to the Selected Attributes window. Verify that your Directory Mode is correct (Export is default and is generally the mode you will need to use first because you will have to export data from the Directory prior to modifying and re-importing) and identify the filename you want to create. Additional attributes will be required to perform specific functions, as listed earlier in this section.

Running Import/Export in Batch Mode

After you've created a header file, you should choose how you're going to run the Import/Export tool. Fortunately, the import/export process can be run from a command line or from a batch file using WinAT or AT at a later time. This is great because some times of day are simply not convenient or appropriate for making large numbers of Directory changes. For example, you shouldn't be doing any large changes during peak work hours because you want to avoid adding to the server's workload and contributing to network congestion. The following sample batch file could be used to run the Import/Export tool:

```
perfwiz -f d:\datafile\exchange\imprtopt.inf
admin /i import.csv /d ORLANDO /n /o import.inf
perfwiz -f d:\datafile\exchange\prodopt.inf
```

This sample will perform the following steps:

1. Run the Performance Optimizer in Silent mode using settings defined in the `imprtopt.inf` file to configure the server for best import performance.

2. Import data from the `import.csv` file to the ORLANDO server with settings defined in the `imprtopt.inf` file without displaying the status bar.

3. Re-run the Performance Optimizer in Silent mode using the `prodopt.inf` file to return the settings back to the correct configuration for the production environment.

See Chapter 8, "Managing Server Resources," for more information about the Performance Optimizer, and Chapter 1, "Understanding the Exchange Administrator Console," for more information about using `admin /i`. For tips on creating the `import.inf` file, see the Microsoft Exchange Administrator Help.

Performing Directory Synchronization with a Foreign Database

You're now ready to perform the tasks Import/Export can help you complete. Import/Export can be used to synchronize user properties between Exchange and a foreign database. Many companies already use Import/Export to populate the Exchange GAL with custom recipients imported from a foreign messaging system. In addition to this fairly standard application of Import/Export, you can use it to import user properties into your existing user mailboxes. Almost every company has a personnel database that is kept up-to-date with current information, such as phone numbers and addresses. If you can extract this data into a file and then format the file into a .CSV that is understood by Exchange's Import/Export tool, you can bring in all of that data into the Exchange Directory.

If you are administering a large company, this particular import feature can be extremely useful because the properties of your user mailboxes will suddenly contain information previously available only by querying your company phone book or other disassociated resources. Bear in mind that the more data you import, the more resources Exchange will require to perform the import (although you can alleviate this to some extent by using the Performance Optimizer prior to and after the import, as discussed in the "Running Import/Export in Batch Mode" section earlier in this appendix). Although changes to existing mailboxes must be imported into the same site as the mailbox, imports of custom recipients can be performed anywhere. To optimize custom recipient imports, perform the import on one of the servers in your company's hub site.

A sample header file that could be populated and used to import mailbox properties might look something like this:

```
Object-Class,Delivery-Mechanism,Directory Name,Address,
Address-Home,Business phone number 2,
City,Company,Country,Department,Display Name,Fax number,
Forwarding-Address,Home phone number,Home phone number 2,
Last name,Mobile number,Office,Pager number,Personal-Title,
Phone number,Postal code,State,Street-Address,Telephone-Home-Fax,
Telephone-Number,Telephone-Personal-Mobile,Telephone-Personal-Pager,Title
```

The data you extract from your personnel database needs to be manipulated to get it into a text file with this header as the first line. Extract personnel data weekly to this file and import it into Exchange using a batch file, as described earlier in this appendix.

Modifying Mailbox Properties

With the Import/Export tool, you can also reconfigure several mailboxes at one time. You may need to do this for a multitude of reasons, such as if you decide to change the storage limits on your mailboxes, or if a new manager is brought in and you want the Direct Reports fields to be correct for this new manager's department.

To modify mailbox properties, perform the following steps:

1. Create a header file, as discussed in "Creating a Header File."

2. Export the recipients container that holds the users you want to reconfigure to the header file.

3. Open the now populated header file in Excel and delete the records corresponding to users you don't want to modify.

4. Change the appropriate data for the remaining users.

5. Save the .CSV file.

6. Import the .CSV file either manually or using a batch file into the Exchange Directory.

7. Verify that the information you changed through the import has been successfully applied by opening a few of the mailboxes.

This procedure can be used to modify almost any mailbox attribute, including custom attributes, proxy addresses, and manager information. The .CSV file you export to just needs to identify the appropriate attributes in the header.

Modifying Custom Attributes

Many companies use custom attributes to reflect employee IDs, Social Security numbers, and other information. If you would like to include this information in your Directory, it is much easier to import it in bulk than to go through each individual mailbox and enter it manually. Create a header file as discussed in "Creating a Header File" and populate the appropriate Custom Attribute field with the correct information. If your company has changed the name of your Custom Attribute fields, you will need to select the new name from the Available Attributes list in the HEADER.EXE program. The following sample header file could be used to modify custom attributes:

```
Object-Class,Delivery-Mechanism,Directory Name,Custom Attribute 1,
Custom Attribute 10,Custom Attribute 11,Custom Attribute 12,
Custom Attribute 13,Custom Attribute 14,Custom Attribute 15,
Custom Attribute 2,Custom Attribute 3,Custom Attribute 4,
Custom Attribute 5,Custom Attribute 6,Custom Attribute 7,
Custom Attribute 8,Custom Attribute 9
```

Reconfiguring Recipient Proxy Addresses

If you are migrating to Exchange from an older messaging system, or if you have merged with another company, you might need to reconfigure the recipient proxy addresses defined within Exchange. Although you can change all proxy information for a site at the Site Addressing object in the Exchange Administrator Program, you cannot change proxy information for specific groups of users defined in the site. For example, within a site you may have three groups of people that need different recipient proxy addresses. To change these addresses you could edit each user's mailbox manually, or you can use an import file to change them all at once. Edit the E-Mail Addresses column for your users to configure the correct primary email addresses. A sample export header file to modify primary proxy addresses might look like this:

```
Object-Class,Delivery-Mechanism,Directory Name,E-mail Addresses
```

Most large companies have a primary incoming domain name and several internal domain names used for routing purposes. In order for an Exchange recipient to receive mail at the internal domain name, a secondary proxy address needs to be added to reflect the secondary address. Edit the Secondary-Proxy-Addresses column to include additional email addresses for your users. A sample export header file to add or modify secondary proxy addresses might look like this:

```
Object-Class,Delivery-Mechanism,Directory Name,E-mail Addresses,
Secondary-Proxy-Addresses
```

Modifying Manager Information

You can modify the Manager field of several user mailboxes at a time using Import/Export. You might want to do this when a manager is transferred, or an employee promoted to a new management position. To do this, export the affected employees to a .CSV file, as displayed below, and enter the Exchange alias of the new manager into the Manager column. This will automatically update the new manager's Direct Reports field to reflect the new subordinate employees. A sample export header file to change a recipient's manager might look like this:

```
Object-Class,Delivery-Mechanism,Directory Name,Manager
```

Deleting Object Property Data

Sometimes the edit you want to make to your Directory is to remove data altogether, not simply to change it to a new value. To use the Import tool to delete data, create a header file that includes the field you want removed and use the **~DEL** key to cause the field to be deleted. Importing blank values will not cause the associated attribute to be cleared from the mailbox properties. A sample file to remove Julie Rice's assistant's name from her mailbox properties might look like this:

```
Obj-Class,Delivery-Mechanism,Directory Name,Assistant
Mailbox,0,Julie Rice,~DEL
```

Changing Object Permissions

It can be useful to be able to change access permissions on your recipients using the bulk Import/Export tool. You can modify the Permissions page for mailboxes, distribution lists, and custom recipients by importing a header file defining the Obj-Admins, Obj-Perm-Admins, and Obj-Users fields.

Use Obj-Admins to define the NT accounts that have Administrator permissions on the recipient, Obj-Perm-Admins to define the NT accounts that have Permissions Admin rights to the recipient, and Obj-User to define the NT accounts that have User permission to access the recipient.

1. Export the users you want modified to the header file.

2. Enter the Exchange Alias of the users you want to add to the Permissions Page in the correct column as discussed above.

   Or, enter **~DEL** in the correct column to delete accounts with the associated right from the recipient.

You cannot use Import/Export to modify any custom permissions, and you can't use it to delete the primary NT account or the owner of a distribution list.

A sample header file that can be used to modify the Permissions fields might look like this:

```
Object-Class,Delivery-Mechanism,Directory Name,Obj-Admins,Obj-Perm Admins,
Obj-Users
```

Deleting Users from the Directory

Rather than deleting just individual fields, you may want to delete groups of users from the Exchange Directory. To do this, you will need to add a field called Mode to the header file. A sample file to delete the user Julie Rice from the Exchange Directory might look like this:

```
Object-Class,Mode,Delivery-Mechanism,Directory Name
Mailbox,Delete,0,Julie Rice
```

Adding Users to DLs

In addition to deleting user accounts from the Directory, you can also use the Import/Export tool to add users to distribution lists by creating a Distribution List object-class header file. This can be useful if you are migrating and have lists of your current DL membership but don't want to have to manually create all of the DLs in the Exchange Administrator Program. A sample file to add the distribution list Georgia

Managers to a DL already containing Julie Rice and Florida Managers might look like this:

```
Obj-Class,Directory Name,Members
dl,Managers,/ou=Merritt Island/cn=Recipients/cn=JRice%/ou=Merritt
Island/cn=Recipients/cn=Florida Managers%/ou=Merritt
Island/cn=Recipients/cn=Georgia Managers
```

Don't delete any of the existing entries from the Members column in the .CSV file. Also, notice the format for adding users is as follows:

```
%/ou=Site Name/cn=Recipients/cn=Alias
```

`Alias` is the Exchange alias of the recipient you want to add to the DL.

Creating Custom Recipients

The Import/Export tool can also be used to add custom recipients to your Directory. To add a custom recipient named Thomas Rice, create an import file in the Remote-Address object class with required information as follows:

```
Obj-Class,Directory Name,E-mail address
Remote,TRice,SMTP:tomrice@hts.com
```

You can of course populate all of the custom recipient fields using the Import/Export tool by adding those fields to the header.

Installing a New Exchange Server

Directory replication of large directories can take hours and use a lot of bandwidth. To minimize this impact across WAN connections, you should do two things. First, you should consider installing Exchange while the server is located on the same LAN as a large part of your Exchange organization so that replication can occur across the LAN. Second, you should add the new users to the new server while the new server is on the LAN so they can replicate to the rest of the Exchange servers over a good connection rather than adding them while the server is in the final location. You can add users to the new server with the Import/Export tool. (The Migration utility is a better choice for this function if it supports the system from which you are migrating because it will import not just directory data, but user data as well.)

Index

J-K

L

Q-R

S

Implementing Exchange Server

TECHNICAL SOLUTIONS FOR DEPLOYING EXCHANGE SERVER IN THE ENTERPRISE

- Written by Hauger, Leon and Wade III
- 1st Edition
- 400 pages
- $29.99
- ISBN: 1-56205-931-9

Implementing Exchange Server™

Doug Hauger, Marywynne Leon &
William C. Wade III
Excell Data Corporation

New Riders

Trustworthy Advice

With over 300,000 seats of practical Exchange deployments between them, Hauger, Leon, and Wade are some of the foremost practitioners of Exchange design and implementation in the world. Professional trainers, they have also participated in the development of all three Microsoft Exchange Server MCSE exams. They have written this book to share their considerable insight and experience.

Technical and Comprehensive

The first book to satisfy the practical needs of those tasked with deploying Exchange, *Implementing Exchange Server* gives you a hands-on analysis of the most difficult aspects of creating an Exchange infrastructure. Focusing on architecture and connectivity, the authors illustrate how to effectively implement and run a robust, integrated system.

Implementing Exchange Server helps you analyze your current environment and create an Exchange architecture that complements that environment while meeting your business needs. It's the authoritative reference that provides you with uncommon consulting experience.

If you plan to deploy Microsoft Exchange Server, this book will show you how to:

- Develop the best Exchange solution for your company
- Provide reliable connectivity — between Exchange servers, and to the Internet
- Coexist with or migrate from the other popular messaging systems
- Integrate Exchange with your existing network and messaging system
- Optimize, monitor, and administer your Exchange organization
- Develop a Disaster Recovery plan
- Scale your solution — especially for the next version of Exchange

Advanced Information on Windows Technologies

New Riders Books Offer Advice and Experience

LANDMARK
Rethinking Computer Books

The *Landmark* series from New Riders targets the distinct needs of the working computer professional by providing detailed and solution-oriented information on core technologies. We begin by partnering with authors who have unique depth of experience and the ability to speak to the needs of the practicing professional. Each book is then carefully reviewed at all stages to ensure it covers the most essential subjects in substantial depth, with great accuracy, and with ease of use in mind. These books speak to the practitioner – accurate information and trustworthy advice, at the right depth, at an attractive value.

ESSENTIAL REFERENCE
Smart, Like You

The *Essential Reference* series from New Riders provides answers when you know what you want to do but need to know how to do it. Each title skips extraneous material and assumes a strong base level of knowledge. These are indispensable books for the practitioner who wants to find specific features of a technology quickly and efficiently. Avoiding fluff and basic material, these books present solutions in an innovative, clean format – and at a great value.

MCSE CERTIFICATION
Engineered for Test Success

New Riders offers a complete line of test preparation materials to help you achieve your certification. With books like *MCSE Training Guides*, *TestPrep*, and *FastTrack*, and software like the acclaimed *MCSE Complete* and *Top Score*, New Riders offers comprehensive products built by experienced professionals who have passed the exams and instructed hundreds of candidates.

Books for Networking Professionals

Related Titles from New Riders Press

Windows NT
TCP/IP

Windows NT TCP/IP
By Karanjit Siyan
1st Edition
480 pages, $29.99
ISBN: 1-56205-887-8

If you're still looking for good documentation on Microsoft TCP/IP, then look no further—this is your book. *Windows NT TCP/IP* cuts through the complexities and provides the most informative and complete reference book on Windows-based TCP/IP. Concepts essential to TCP/IP administration are explained thoroughly, then related to the practical use of Microsoft TCP/IP in a real-world networking environment. The book begins by covering TCP/IP architecture, advanced installation and configuration issues, then moves on to routing with TCP/IP, DHCP Management, and WINS/DNS Name Resolution.

Windows NT
DNS

Windows NT DNS
By Michael Masterson,
Herman L. Knief, Scott
Vinick, and Eric Roul
1st Edition
340 pages, $29.99
ISBN: 1-56205-943-2

Have you ever opened a Windows NT book looking for detailed information about DNS only to discover that it doesn't even begin to scratch the surface? DNS is probably one of the most complicated subjects for NT administrators, and there are few books on the market that really address it in detail. This book answers your most complex DNS questions, focusing on the implementation of

the Domain Name Service within Windows NT, treating it thoroughly from the viewpoint of an experienced Windows NT professional. Many detailed, real-world examples illustrate further the understanding of the material throughout. The book covers the details of how DNS functions within NT, then explores specific interactions with critical network components. Finally, proven procedures to design and set up DNS are demonstrated. You'll also find coverage of related topics, such as maintenance, security, and troubleshooting.

Windows NT
Registry
A Settings Reference

Windows NT Registry
By Sandra Osborne
1st Edition
564 pages, $29.99
ISBN: 1-56205-941-6

The NT Registry can be a very powerful tool for those capable of using it wisely. Unfortunately, there is very little information regarding the NT Registry, due to Microsoft's insistence that their source code be kept secret. If you're looking to optimize your use of the registry, you're usually forced to search the Web for bits of information. This book is your resource. It covers critical issues and settings used for configuring network protocols, including NWLink, PTP, TCP/IP, and DHCP. This book approaches the material from a unique point of view, discussing the problems related to a particular component, and then discussing settings, which are the actual changes necessary for implementing robust solu

Windows NT Performance

By Mark Edmead and Paul Hinsberg
1st Edition
288 pages, $29.99
ISBN: 1-56205-942-4

Performance monitoring is a little like preventative medicine for the administrator: no one enjoys a checkup, but it's a good thing to do on a regular basis. This book helps you focus on the critical aspects of improving the performance of your NT system, showing you how to monitor the system, implement benchmarking, and tune your network. The book is organized by resource components, which makes it easy to use as a reference tool.

Windows NT Terminal Server

By Ted Harwood
1st Edition
416 pages, $29.99
ISBN: 1-56205-944-0

It's no surprise that most administration headaches revolve around integration with other networks and clients. This book addresses these types of real-world issues on a case-by-case basis, giving tools and advice on solving each problem. The author also offers the real nuts and bolts of thin client administration on multiple systems, covering such relevant issues as installation, configuration, network connection, management, and application distribution.

Windows NT Security

By Richard Puckett
1st Edition Summer 1999
600 pages, $29.99
ISBN: 1-56205-945-9

Swiss cheese. That's what some people say Windows NT security is like. And they may be right, because they only know what the NT documentation says about implementing security. Who has the time to research alternatives; play around with the features, service packs, hot fixes and add-on tools, and figure out what makes NT rock solid? Well, Richard Puckett does. He's been researching Windows NT Security for the University of Virginia for a while now, and he's got pretty good news. He's going to show you how to make NT secure in your environment, and we mean really secure.

Windows NT Network Management

By Anil Desai
1st Edition Spring 1999
400 pages, $34.99
ISBN: 1-56205-946-7

Administering a Windows NT network is kind of like trying to herd cats—an impossible task characterized by constant motion, exhausting labor and lots of hairballs. Author Anil Desai knows all about it—he's a Consulting Engineer for Sprint Paranet, and specializes in Windows NT implementation, integration and management. So we asked him to put together a concise manual of best practices, a book of tools and ideas that other administrators can turn to again and again in managing their own NT networks.

Planning for Windows 2000
By Eric K. Cone
1st Edition Spring 1999
400 pages, $29.99
ISBN: 0-73570-048-6

Windows 2000 is poised to be one of the largest and most important software releases of the next decade, and you are charged with planning, testing, and deploying it in your enterprise. Are you ready? With this book, you will be. Planning for Windows 2000 lets you know what the upgrade hurdles will be, informs you how to clear them, guides you through effective Active Directory design, and presents you with detailed rollout procedures. Eric K. Cone give you the benefit of their extensive experiences as Windows 2000 Rapid Deployment Program members, sharing problems and solutions they've encountered on the job.

MCSE Core NT Exams Essential Reference
By Matthew Shepker
1st Edition
256 pages, $19.99
ISBN: 0-7357-0006-0

You're sitting in the first session of your Networking Essentials class and the instructor starts talking about RAS and you have no idea what that means. You think about raising your hand to ask about RAS, but you reconsider—you'd feel pretty foolish asking a question in front of all these people. You turn to your handy MCSE Core NT Exams Essential Reference and find a quick summary on Remote Access Services. Question answered. It's a couple months later and you're taking your Networking Essentials exam the next day. You're reviewing practice tests and you keep forgetting the maximum lengths for the various commonly used cable types. Once again, you turn to the MCSE Core NT Exams Essential Reference and find a table on cables, including all of the characteristics you need to memorize in order to pass the test.

BackOffice Titles

Implementing Exchange Server
By Doug Hauger, Marywynne Leon, and William C. Wade III
1st Edition
400 pages, $29.99
ISBN: 1-56205-931-9

If you're interested in connectivity and maintenance issues for Exchange Server, then this book is for you. Exchange's power lies in its ability to be connected to multiple email subsystems to create a "universal email backbone." It's not unusual to have several different and complex systems all connected via email gateways, including Lotus Notes or cc:Mail, Microsoft Mail, legacy mainframe systems, and Internet mail. This book covers all of the problems and issues associated with getting an integrated system running smoothly and addresses troubleshooting and diagnosis of email problems with an eye toward prevention and best practices.

Exchange Server Administration

By Janice K. Howd
1st Edition Spring 1999
400 pages, $34.99
ISBN: 0-7357-0081-8

OK, you've got your Exchange Server installed and connected, now what? Email administration is one of the most critical networking jobs, and Exchange can be particularly troublesome in large, heterogenous environments. So Janice Howd, a noted consultant and teacher with over a decade of email administration experience, has put together this advanced, concise handbook for daily, periodic, and emergency administration. With in-depth coverage of topics like managing disk resources, replication, and disaster recovery, this is the one reference book every Exchange administrator needs.

SQL Server System Administration

By Sean Baird, Chris Miller, et al.
1st Edition
352 pages, $29.99
ISBN: 1-56205-955-6

How often does your SQL Server go down during the day when everyone wants to access the data? Do you spend most of your time being a "report monkey" for your co-workers and bosses? *SQL Server System Administration* helps you keep data consistently available to your users. This book omits the introductory information. The authors don't spend time explaining queries and how they work. Instead they focus on the information that you can't get anywhere else, like how to choose the correct replication topology and achieve high availability of information.

Internet Information Server Administration

By Kelli Adam, et. al.
1st Edition Fall 1999
300 pages, $29.99
ISBN: 0-73570-022-2

Are the new Internet technologies in Internet Information Server giving you headaches? Does protecting security on the Web take up all of your time? Then this is the book for you. With hands-on configuration training, advanced study of the new protocols in IIS, and detailed instructions on authenticating users with the new Certificate Server and implementing and managing the new e-commerce features, *Internet Information Server Administration* gives you the real-life solutions you need. This definitive resource also prepares you for the release of Windows 2000 by giving you detailed advice on working with Microsoft Management Console, which was first used by IIS.

SMS Administration

By Wayne Koop and Brian Steck
1st Edition Summer 1999
350 pages, $34.99
ISBN: 0-7357-0082-6

Microsoft's new version of its Systems Management Server (SMS) is starting to turn heads. While complex, it's allowing administrators to lower their total cost of ownership and more efficiently manage clients, applications and support operations. So if your organization is using or implementing SMS, you'll need some expert advice. Wayne Koop and Brian Steck can help you get the most bang for your buck, with insight, expert tips, and real-world examples. Brian and Wayne are consultants specializing in SMS, having worked with Microsoft on one of the most complex SMS rollouts in the world, involving 32 countries, 15 languages, and thousands of clients.

Unix/Linux Titles

Solaris Essential Reference
By John Mulligan
1st Edition Spring 1999
350 pages, $19.99
ISBN: 0-7357-0230-7

Looking for the fastest, easiest way to find the Solaris command you need? Need a few pointers on shell scripting? How about advanced administration tips and sound, practical expertise on security issues? Are you looking for trustworthy information about available third-party software packages that will enhance your operating system? Author John Mulligan—creator of the popular Unofficial Guide to Solaris Web site (sun.icsnet.com)—delivers all that and more in one attractive, easy-to-use reference book. With clear and concise instructions on how to perform important administration and management tasks and key information on powerful commands and advanced topics, *Solaris Essential Reference* is the reference you need when you know what you want to do and you just need to know how.

Linux System Administration
By James T. Dennis
1st Edition Spring 1999
450 pages, $29.99
ISBN: 1-56205-934-3

As an administrator, you probably feel that most of your time and energy is spent in endless firefighting. If your network has become a fragile quilt of temporary patches and workarounds, then this book is for you. For example, have you had trouble sending or receiving your email lately? Are you looking for a way to keep your network running smoothly with enhanced performance? Are your users always hankering for more storage, more services, and more speed? *Linux System Administration* advises you on the many intricacies of maintaining a secure, stable system. In this definitive work, the author addresses all the issues related to system administration, from adding users and managing files permission to Internet services and Web hosting to recovery planning and security. This book fulfills the need for expert advice that will ensure a trouble-free Linux environment.

Linux Security
By John S. Flowers
1st Edition Spring 1999
400 pages, $29.99
ISBN: 0-7357-0035-4

New Riders is proud to offer the first book aimed specifically at Linux security issues. While there are a host of general UNIX security books, we thought it was time to address the practical needs of the Linux network. In this definitive work, author John Flowers takes a balanced approach to system security, from discussing topics like planning a secure environment to firewalls to utilizing security scripts. With comprehensive information on specific system compromises, and advice on how to prevent and repair them, this is one book that every Linux administrator should have on the shelf.

Developing Linux Applications

By Eric Harlow
1st Edition
400 pages, $34.99
ISBN: 0-7357-0214-7

We all know that Linux is one of the most powerful and solid operating systems in existence. And as the success of Linux grows, there is an increasing interest in developing applications with graphical user interfaces that really take advantage of the power of Linux. In this book, software developer Eric Harlow gives you an indispensable development handbook focusing on the GTK+ toolkit. More than an overview on the elements of application or GUI design, this is a hands-on book that delves deeply into the technology. With in-depth material on the various GUI programming tools and loads of examples, this book's unique focus will give you the information you need to design and launch professional-quality applications.

Linux Essential Reference

By David "Hacksaw" Todd
1st Edition Summer 1999
400 pages, $19.99
ISBN: 0-7357-0852-5

This book is all about getting things done as quickly and efficiently as possible by providing a structured organization to the plethora of available Linux information. We can sum it up in one word: VALUE. This book has it all: concise instruction on how to perform key administration tasks; advanced information on configuration; shell scripting; hardware management; systems management; data tasks; automation; and tons of other useful information. All coupled with an unique navigational structure and a great price. This book truly provides groundbreaking information for the growing community of advanced Linux professionals.

Lotus Notes and Domino Titles

Domino System Administration

By Rob Kirkland
1st Edition Summer 1999
500 pages, $34.99
ISBN: 1-56205-948-3

Your boss has just announced that you will be upgrading to the newest version of Notes and Domino when it ships. As a Premium Lotus Business Partner, Lotus has offered a substantial price break to keep your company away from Microsoft's Exchange Server. How are you supposed to get this new system installed, configured, and rolled out to all of your end users? You understand how Lotus Notes works—you've been administering it for years. What you need is a concise, practical explanation about the new features, and how to make some of the advanced stuff really work. You need answers and solutions from someone like you, who has worked with the product for years, and understands what it is you need to know. *Domino System Administration* is the answer—the first book on Domino that attacks the technology at the professional level, with practical, hands-on assistance to get Domino running in your organization.

Lotus Notes and Domino Essential Reference

By Dave Hatter & Tim Bankes
1st Edition Spring 1999
500 pages, $24.99
ISBN: 0-7357-0007-9

You're in a bind because you've been asked to design and program a new database in Notes for an important client that will keep track of and itemize a myriad of inventory and shipping data. The client wants a user-friendly interface, without sacrificing speed or functionality. You are experienced (and could develop this app in your sleep), but feel that you need to take your talents to the next level. You need something to facilitate your creative and technical abilities, something to perfect your programming skills. Your answer is waiting for you: *Lotus Notes and Domino Essential Reference*. It's compact and simply designed. It's loaded with information. All of the objects, classes, functions, and methods are listed. It shows you the object hierarchy and the overlaying relationship between each one. It's perfect for you. Problem solved.

Networking Titles

Cisco Router Configuration and Troubleshooting

By Pablo Espinosa and Mark Tripod
1st Edition
300 pages, $34.99
ISBN: 0-7357-0024-9

Want the real story on making your Cisco routers run like a dream? Why not pick up a copy of *Cisco Router Configuration and Troubleshooting* and see what Pablo Espinosa and Mark Tripod have to say? They're the folks responsible for making some of the largest sites on the Net scream, like Amazon.com, Hotmail, USAToday, Geocities, and Sony. In this book, they provide advanced configuration issues, sprinkled with advice and preferred practices. You won't see a general overview on TCP/IP—we talk about more meaty issues like security, monitoring, traffic management, and more. In the troubleshooting section, the authors provide a unique methodology and lots of sample problems to illustrate. By providing real-world insight and examples instead of rehashing Cisco's documentation, Pablo and Mark give network administrators information they can start using today.

Implementing and Troubleshooting LDAP

By Robert Lamothe

1st Edition Spring 1999
400 pages, $34.99
ISBN: 1-56205-947-5

While there is some limited information available about LDAP, most of it is RFCs, white papers, and books about programming LDAP into your networking applications. That leaves the people who most need information—administrators—out in the cold. What do you do if you need to know how to make LDAP work in your system? You ask Bob Lamothe. Bob is a UNIX administrator with hands-on experience in setting up a corporate-wide directory service using LDAP. Bob's book is NOT a guide to the protocol; rather, it is designed to be an aid to administrators to help them understand the most efficient way to structure, encrypt, authenticate, administer, and troubleshoot LDAP in a mixed network environment. The book shows you how to work with the major implementations of LDAP and get them to coexist.

Implementing Virtual Private Networks

By Tina Bird and Ted Stockwell

1st Edition Spring 1999
300 pages, $29.99
ISBN: 0-73570-047-8

Tired of looking for decent, practical, up-to-date information on virtual private networks? *Implementing Virtual Private Networks*, by noted authorities Dr. Tina Bird and Ted Stockwell, finally gives you what you need—an authoritative guide on the design, implementation, and maintenance of Internet-based access to private networks. This book focuses on real-world solutions, demonstrating how the choice of VPN architecture should align with an organization's business and tech-

nological requirements. Tina and Ted give you the information you need to determine whether a VPN is right for your organization, select the VPN that suits your needs, and design and implement the VPN you have chosen.

Understanding Data Communications, Sixth Edition

By Gilbert Held

6th Edition Summer 1999
500 pages, $34.99
ISBN: 0-7357-0036-2

Updated from the highly successful fifth edition, this book explains how data communications systems and their various hardware and software components work. Not an entry-level book, it approaches the material in a textbook format, addressing the complex issues involved in internetworking today. A great reference book for the experienced networking professional, written by noted networking authority, Gilbert Held.

Other Books By New Riders Press

New Riders | How to Contact Us

Visit Our Web Site

www.newriders.com

On our Web site you'll find information about our other books, authors, tables of contents, indexes, and book errata. You can also place orders for books through our Web site.

Email Us

Contact us at this address:

newriders@mcp.com

- If you have comments or questions about this book
- To report errors that you have found in this book
- If you have a book proposal to submit or are interested in writing for New Riders
- If you would like to have an author kit sent to you
- If you are an expert in a computer topic or technology and are interested in being a technical editor who reviews manuscripts for technical accuracy

slayton@mcp.com

- To find a distributor in your area, please contact our international department at the address above.

slayton@mcp.com

- For instructors from educational institutions who wish to preview New Riders books for classroom use. Email should include your name, title, school, department, address, phone number, office days/hours, text in use, and enrollment in the body of your text along with your request for desk/examination copies and/or additional information.

Write to Us

New Riders Publishing

201 W. 103rd St.

Indianapolis, IN 46290-1097

Call Us

Toll-free (800) 571-5840 + 9 +3567

If outside U.S. (317) 581-3500. Ask for New Riders.

Fax Us

(317) 581-4663

Fold here and tape to mail

- -

New Riders Publishing
201 W. 103rd St.
Indianapolis, IN 46290

We Want to Know What You Think

To better serve you, we would like your opinion on the content and quality of this book. Please complete this card and mail it to us or fax it to 317-581-4663.

Name _____

Address _____

City_____State_____Zip _____

Phone _____

Email Address _____

Occupation _____

Operating System(s) that you use _____

What influenced your purchase of this book?
❏ Recommendation ❏ Cover Design
❏ Table of Contents ❏ Index
❏ Magazine Review ❏ Advertisement
❏ New Rider's Reputation ❏ Author Name

How would you rate the contents of this book?
❏ Excellent ❏ Very Good
❏ Good ❏ Fair
❏ Below Average ❏ Poor

How do you plan to use this book?
❏ Quick reference ❏ Self-training
❏ Classroom ❏ Other

What do you like most about this book?
Check all that apply.
❏ Content ❏ Writing Style
❏ Accuracy ❏ Examples
❏ Listings ❏ Design
❏ Index ❏ Page Count
❏ Price ❏ Illustrations

What do you like least about this book?
Check all that apply.
❏ Content ❏ Writing Style
❏ Accuracy ❏ Examples
❏ Listings ❏ Design
❏ Index ❏ Page Count
❏ Price ❏ Illustrations

What would be a useful follow-up book to this one for you?_____

Where did you purchase this book? _____

Can you name a similar book that you like better than this one, or one that is as good? Why?

_____

_____

How many New Riders books do you own? _____

What are your favorite computer books?_____

_____

What other titles would you like to see us develop? _____

_____

Any comments for us? _____

_____

_____

Exchange System Administration, 0-7357-0081-8

www.newriders.com • Fax 317-581-4663

Colophon

The photograph on the cover of this book was taken by Frank Howd on a visit to Sequoia National Park, the second oldest national park in America. Along with lesser-known landmarks, such as Moro Rock, this park on the southernmost end of the Sierra Nevada mountain range boasts the highest mountain in the contiguous United States, Mount Whitney. Elevation in the Sequoia National Forest, of which the park only is a part, spans from 1,000 to more than 12,000 feet.

Sequoia National Park is, of course, best known for the huge trees (*sequoiadendron giganteum*) that give it its name. Though not as tall as their coastal cousins, the Sierra sequoias make up in girth what they lack in height, extending as much as 40 feet in diameter. The park hosts the General Sherman Tree, which is not only the largest sequoia, but is also officially known as the World's Largest Living Thing.

In the 1800s, lumbering entrepreneurs sought to profit from the Sierra sequoias. Like the Gold Rush pioneers, these entrepreneurs' aim seemed unlikely at best—making the business of splitting up, dynamiting, and transporting over long distances a type of wood whose size made it unmanageable and brittle a profitable venture. Again, like the Gold Rushers, the lumber companies were undeterred by repeated failures. Battling against the odds, one group, the Sanger Lumber Company, began to harvest the sequoias in the 3,000-acre Converse Basin in the Sequoia Forest. Their David-and-Goliath struggle continued for eleven long years, after which they had made little money but had succeeded in decimating the competition—trees that had possibly stood as long as 2,700 years. To commemorate this proud period in our nation's history and to pay tribute to the men who made it happen, a 269-foot sequoia in the Basin was named Boole after the company's general manager. You can personally pay tribute to their struggles by visiting Stump Meadow, which is about 2 miles down Converse Road.

If you do visit the Sequoia Forest—in particular, the Sequoia National Park—be sure to be on your guard for an insidious beast that is enemy to car and man. Weighing in at about the size of your Persian Fluffy, this large, sciurid rodent—known as the marmot—snacks on car wiring and radiator hoses. The occasional troublemaker will go so far as to hop in and take a ride under your hood—traveling all the way to Southern California in some cases. You may be surprised to learn that this pest has an impeccable reputation. A national holiday is even named in honor of one of its species, the *marmota monax*—otherwise known as the lovable, huggable groundhog, represented by the famous Punxutawney Phil. You can even sing an anthem to a marmot ("Oh Murmeltier!") and attend an international triannual meeting devoted to its study.